French Entrée

Brittany

Independent reviews of the best restaurants and hotels in the area

second edition

The French Entrée series of travel guides provides independent reviews and opinions on the best local restaurants and hotels in the regions of France. Unlike many other guides, no charge is made and the reviews are the author's own opinions.

To see our complete range of travel books, menu guides and themed phrase books for independent travellers, visit our website **www.aspectguides.com**

In the French Entrée series:
Bed and Breakfast in France (1-904012-04-3)
Brittany (1-904012-03-5)
Calais, Boulogne and the North of France (1-904012-00-0)
Normandy (1-904012-02-7)

Companion to Food and Drink in France (1-904012-05-1)
French Business Phrase Book (1-904012-10-8)
French Family Phrase Book (1-904012-09-4)
French Young Traveller's Phrase Book (1-904012-11-6)

French Entrée
Brittany

Independent reviews of the best restaurants and hotels in the area

second edition

Peter King

Aspect Guides

First published in 1986

Second edition published by Aspect Guides 2002, an imprint of
Bloomsbury Publishing Plc, 38 Soho Square, London, W1D 3HB

© Peter King 2002

All rights reserved. No part of this publication may be reproduced in any
form or by any means without the permission of the publishers.

British Library Cataloguing-in-Publication Data
A catalogue record for this book is available from the British Library
ISBN 1-904012-03-5

Produced for Aspect Guides by Navigator Guides Ltd, Norfolk
Printed and bound in Italy by Legoprint

Every effort has been made to ensure that the information in this guide is
accurate and up-to-date and the advice is given in good faith. However,
neither the publisher nor the author is responsible for any problems or
disappointments encountered before or during your travels.

Contents

Raisons d'être	1
Using the Book	3
Stars	4
Entrée to the Entrées	5
Tips for Beginners	7
Introduction	10
A Short History of Brittany	10
The Food of Brittany	11
The Megaliths of Prehistory	14
Follow the Customs Paths	16
The Parish Close	16
The Legend of Arthur	17
The Breton Language with Glossary	18
The Best in Brittany	20
Three Cycle Tours in Brittany	24
BRITTANY	**37–232**
Wines and Spirits by John Doxat	233
Glossary of Cooking Terms and Dishes	242

The French Entrée Difference

This book is part of the *French Entrée* series of guide books that provide individual and personal reviews of restaurants and hotels in a particular region of France.

Unlike many of our competitors, we do not make any charge to include establishments. This might seem like financial suicide, but it does ensure that you get a true review of the restaurant and, most importantly, the choice of restaurants and hotels is ours. Many of the best restaurants and hotels are not featured in other guides because the owners are already very busy and don't need to pay to get extra custom. But you'll find them in these guides – because they offer great food.

You can blame Patricia Fenn for having the original idea for this series of guides. And 20 years ago, this was an inspirational idea! Still, Pat and the fellow editors who compile these guides travel thousands of kilometres every year in search of great food and a great atmosphere. We hope you'll find the guide useful, or simply enjoy reading the travels around France.

www.aspectguides.com

Raisons d'être

The first *French Entrée – Guide to Brittany* appeared in 1986. It was an instant success and subsequent reprints appeared in 1987, 1989, 1991 and 1995.

Seven years have now passed since that last appearance – but then Brittany's most famous attraction, its megalithic stones, have been there for 6,000 years and they still tower over the landscape of Northern France, superciliously indifferent to the passage of a mere half decade.

Modern man's contributions, however, do not last as long as those of our prehistoric ancestors. Hotels and restaurants are particularly vulnerable to change and the *French Entrée* series is, after all, a 'Sleep and Eat' guide. So the time has come to update this book.

The format remains the same – as it must. Pat Fenn's formula has been a winner for nearly 20 years and the *French Entrée* books are the first choice for many a traveller. It is worthwhile though to review some of the approaches that have resulted in such success.

The chain hotels are not included in this guide. In the first place, they are heavily publicized so that anyone can find them and, in the second place, they are (deliberately) almost all the same as the others in their family so descriptions are superfluous.

Negative reviews of hotels or restaurants are not included. There is an argument that says people need to be warned against severely over-priced or below-standard establishments but, on the other hand, the reader does not want to spend time reading a review telling them where not to go. A few exceptions to this will be found: (1) where a particularly splendid hotel is also a landmark, you may want to visit it as you would a museum or you may want to stay there (despite the price) to celebrate some special occasion; and (2) a place with a fine reputation may have allowed its standards to slip.

The emphasis of the book is on smaller hotels and restaurants, preferably those which are family-run. This generally means that the place has character and it also ensures a continuity of personalized service and attention, often carried on through generations. The principal criterion continues to be high value for a modest price.

Hotels in Brittany are much cheaper than in Britain. There has been a big increase in the number of bed-and-breakfast establishments and as many as possible have been included in this guide. They are listed as 'Cd'H' (*chambre d'hôte*) and their only disadvantage is that most have only two or three rooms. This means a close acquaintance with the hosts but may also mean disappointment in booking. For a wider range of *chambres d'hôtes* in Brittany and throughout the rest of France, see our companion book *Bed and Breakfast in France* (ISBN 1-904012-04-3).

The food in France continues to be a major reason for going there and Brittany rates highly among the *départements* in this respect. Like all other Western countries however, France has adopted the microwave, the deep freeze and the infra-red heater among other devices. Debates over meat persist and will undoubtedly still do so for reasons which may be primarily bureaucratic but inevitably devolve on the traveller. Insecticides and pesticides will be increasingly used and will shoulder more blame for depleted taste.

Brittany is one of the few *départements* in France where these criticisms are minimized. Seasonal vegetables and fruits are widely sold and served and the long coastline ensures that what many consider the best seafood in Europe is here. There are a great many local specialities in Brittany and you can spend several weeks of holiday and not get around to all of them.

Brittany is *pays de campagne* – countryside – more so perhaps than any other part of France. There are few large cities and several of these are large industrial ports of little interest to the visitor. A glance at a map though will show many hundreds of small towns and villages and, in the coastal areas, these are all close together. This is the real Brittany, with country markets, small shops, old churches, great beaches and history – lots of history.

Such a large number of towns and villages has meant that only a small percentage were included in previous editions of *French Entrée – Guide to Brittany*. The aim of this edition has been to offer the reader a much more extensive coverage. The number of entries has been increased and, to keep the size of the volume reasonable, the length of some entries has been reduced.

Using the book

Prices

Prices are in euros. When we started updating this edition, most of the establishments had not yet decided on a tariff in euros. In these cases, we have converted the French franc prices into euros. However, we also found that some establishments used the change to euros to round-up their prices. (This type of price increase does, however, seem to be true across many different types of service!)

Telephone

The (0) in brackets at the beginning of a telephone number should be used when dialling in France, but when making calls from outside the area, e.g. from UK, dial 0033 then the nine digits omitting the 0.

The five digit number given in the address, eg. 62000, is the post code, which should be used in all correspondence.

Grading

L, M or S in the margin stand for 'L' = Luxury, 'S' = Simple and 'M' for those in between.

☆ The establishment fulfils exceptionally well at least one of the author's criteria of comfort, welcome and cuisine.

Acronyms and symbols

🛏 stands for hotel

✗ for restaurant

(Cd'H) for Chambre d'hôte

In combination with the grading as above, i.e. 🛏 S, ✗ L, etc.

(Cd'A) stands for Côtes d'Armor

(Î-et-V) for Îlle-et-Vilaine

o.o.s. = 'out of season'

s.t.c. = service and taxes are included

USING THE BOOK

Stars ☆

These are to point you in the right direction – to the bullseyes. Pick of the bunch, they are chosen because they fulfil superbly well at least one – and preferably all – of the overriding criteria: welcome, good food, comfort and situation. Other entries may be there simply because there is none better in that particular town; the stars are there because they have been tried and tested and proved to be winners.

Entrée to the Entrées

Hotels and restaurants are graded into three categories: **L** for Luxury, **M** for Medium and **S** for Simple, but always the prime criterion for recommendation is value for money. Service with a smile scores top marks. Few chain hotels are included because (a) they are not difficult to locate without any help from me and (b) I happen to prefer a degree of individuality and owner-management to even the most efficient plastic uniformity.

L – Luxury

To spend a night in an **L** hotel you should expect to spend around 80–112€ for the room and find it equipped with every necessity. Bathrooms will be luxurious, often offering a Jacuzzi and certainly a bath as well as a shower. Look for the ones that have a Michelin star attached to their restaurant – anything in this category should take their food seriously, and not just charge a lot for superficial gloss. Often there will be cheaper, less luxurious rooms, and these are well worth investigating if you like the trappings – the comfortable salons, the good restaurant, the swimming pool, the smooth service – without wanting to spend too much on the room. Remember though that the extras will push up the bill – breakfast, drinks at the bar, wine with dinner. If it's a special occasion it's worth going for the hotel's best, and even at top prices – around 160€ – you will be doing a far better deal than in the UK where beds, not rooms, are charged for.

    L restaurants are another matter and every visitor to France should try and budget to sample them. Lunch menus offer particularly good value, with a talented chef cutting costs to rock bottom in order to fill his restaurant. There are several listed where a four-course meal need only cost around 23€. When you get to the double Michelin stars you are talking about 53€ for dinner, but even then there will often be a lunch menu at about 30€.

M – Medium

The **M** category covers the majority of hotels, safe and not too expensive. The cost should be between 32€ and 64€, and my selection is nearly always owner-managed, bringing in the personal touch which we all appreciate above gloss. Rooms will be well-equipped, usually with telephone, TV, good hanging space and with any luck some efficient lighting (but this is France). They will have en suite bathrooms with bath or shower, and you should have a choice of twin or double beds and the use of a garage.

M restaurants range from the typical French bourgeois style, with draped curtains, well-upholstered chairs, patronne likewise, and a clientele of local worthies, businessmen during the week and families for the sacred Sunday lunch gathering, to the small but tasteful new venture of a young couple anxious to get established. In the first group you will probably eat traditional French dishes, prepared by a patron/chef who knows what his regulars like and is not over-keen to experiment; in the latter there may be a new Michelin star chef striving for recognition, who may well enjoy extending the range of established cuisine with new ingredients and ideas from other countries. There is excellent reliable value to be found in this category, where a meal should cost between 12.5€ and 29€.

S – Standard

It is the **S** category that causes me most pleasure and most pain. Pleasure because we all like a bargain and there is great satisfaction in discovering one which is probably not listed in other guides, and pain because obviously short cuts are a temptation. With **S** hotels I have to be particularly careful – one bad meal you can forget, a night with bedbugs you can't. There is a limit to just how simple you can get, so nowadays most people would expect en suite 'facilities', probably a shower not a bath for a price between 24€ and 40€. There are some winners in this category, relying more on the owners' welcome and good will than on the frills, and these are the ones that the faithful Brits return to year after year.

S restaurants can imply a simple bucolic meal served at scrubbed tables in a farmhouse, one dish in a brasserie, a crêperie, a salad bar, or a basic town restaurant often attached to a hotel, where the patron cooks, and his wife and family serve to a devoted bunch of regulars, who rely on his plat du jour. These last are the ones to make for with an appetite but not if you require finesse.

Tips for Beginners

Maps and Guides

Good maps are essential. I suggest you use the excellent Michelin maps for the area: 230 covers all Brittany; 58, 59 63 will deal with smaller areas. The red Michelin, apart from all its other virtues, has useful town maps.

Booking

Sunday lunch is the Meal of the Week, when several generations settle down together to enjoy an orgy of eating, drinking, conversation and baby-worship that can well last till teatime. You should certainly book then and on fête days. Make tactical plans and lie low, or it could be a crêpe and a bed in the car. French public holidays are as follows:

New Year's Day	France's National Day, 14 July
Easter Sunday and Monday	The Assumption, 15 August
Labour Day, 1 May	All Saints' Day, 1 November
VE Day, 8 May	Armistice Day, 11 November
Ascension Day	Christmas Day
Whit Sunday and Monday	

If you wish to book ahead and do not speak French, try to find someone who does to make a preliminary telephone call. If necessary, write in English and let them sort it out, but make sure when you get the letter of confirmation that you understand what you've booked. Many hotels nowadays will ask for a deposit. My method is to send them an English cheque; they then either subtract the equivalent from the bill or return the cheque. Make good use of the local tourist bureaux, clearly indicated in the centre of every town, where you will find English spoken. Let them do the booking for you if you have problems. This is the place to pick up maps and brochures.

Closing Times

The markets, like the rest of the town, snap shut abruptly for lunch. I regularly get caught out by not shopping early enough; if it's going to be a picnic lunch, the decision has to be made in good time. From

12 noon to 14.30 and sometimes 15.00, not a cat stirs. At the other end of the day it's a joy to find shops open until 19.00. Mondays tend to be almost as dead as Sundays and it's likely to prove a grave disappointment to allocate that as a shopping day.

It does not pay to be casual about the weekly closure (*fermeture hebdomadaire*) of the restaurants. It is an excellent idea to ensure that not every restaurant in the same town is closed at the same time, but do check before you venture. Thwarted tastebuds are guaranteed if you make a special journey only to find the smug little notice on the door 'fermé'. Sunday p.m. and Monday are the most common and often it will involve a good deal of perseverance to find a possibility that is open for business at such times.

The acronym *closed: o.o.s.* means closed out of season (usually from October to Easter).

Changing Money

Everyone has their pet method, from going round all the banks to get a tiny advantage, to playing it the easy and very expensive way of getting the hotel to do it. It depends on how much is involved and how keen a dealer you are as to how much trouble is worth it. I change mine on the boat, where I have always found the rate to be very fair. If you get caught outside banking hours, the bureaux de change stay open late.

Telephoning

To telephone any of the numbers within Brittany shown in this book from England you should dial the international code 00, then the country code 33, then 2 followed by the number. If you are phoning within France you should insert 0 before the 2, and this the format I have used in the book, on the assumption that most of the reservations will be made when you are in France.

Bring Home

The list of Best Buys doesn't change much. Obviously wine, but not the more expensive varieties, which are, surprisingly, cheaper in England. Be a lager lout and take as much as you can carry. Coffee is much cheaper; jams, plain chocolate, stock cubes are worth considering, as are some compatible electrical goods, ironmongery, kitchen gadgets, and glassware. Best of all are impulse buys in the local markets.

Breakfast

A sore point. The best will serve buttery croissants, hot fresh bread, home-made preserves, a slab of fresh butter, lots of strong coffee and hot milk, with fresh orange juice if you're lucky. The worst — and at a price of around 8€ this is an outrage — will be stale toasted bread, a foil-wrapped butter pat, plastic jam, a cup of weak coffee and cold sterilized milk. Synthetic orange juice can add another 1.5€ to the bill. If you land in an hotel like this, get out of bed and go to the café next door.

Tipping

Lots of readers, used to the outstretched British hand, worry about this. Needlessly — bills are often stamped 's.t.c.' (service, taxes, compris) and it means what it says — all service and taxes included. The only exception perhaps is to leave the small change in the saucer at a bar.

Garages and Parking

Considerably older and wiser since I started travelling so often, I now have sympathy with readers who insist on a garage. I can only advise removing any valued belongings, however tiresome that may be, and taking out adequate insurance.

Reader Comments

I am, as always, grateful for your help — none of these books would have been possible without readers' help. If you have any comments or suggestions, please write to me:

Peter King, c/o Aspect Guides, Bloomsbury Publishing Plc, 38 Soho Square, London, W1D 3HB

email: comments@aspectguides.com

Please let me know your comments, favourable or otherwise, and stating if you object to being quoted. Alternatively, visit our new website (www.aspectguides.com) and submit your comments online. I do try and answer each letter personally but please be patient!

INTRODUCTION

Few parts of Europe can offer such a wide variety of attractions as Brittany. Its proximity to England and the fact that it is one of the least expensive *départements* in France — all of these combine to make it the most popular destination for British tourists.

The coastline — which is long and varied — is a constant delight of tiny ports, coves, harbours, rocky cliffs, headlands, estuaries and wonderful walks.

Churches, castles, abbeys and the calvaries that are a special feature of Brittany bring the medieval past to life, while from the misty fringes of prehistory, the 5,000 megalithic monuments perplex and fascinate.

Some of the finest beaches in Europe are here, and sailing, surfing and other nautical sports revel in the Atlantic winds and ocean. The extensive network of waterways stretches from coast to coast through rivers and canals.

Inland are the legendary forests where the Knights of the Round Table sought the Holy Grail, where King Arthur, Lancelot and Merlin the Magician still lend their ghostly presence.

Seafood in Brittany is unsurpassed in both quality and variety. Artichokes, strawberries, *crêpes*, and lamb from the salt-marshes are other Breton specialities.

Brittany has something for everybody and every age. It is a holiday destination without equal.

A Short History of Brittany

The megalithic monuments that cover Brittany date from as far back as 5,000 BC and are the earliest known remains of Breton society, though traces of Mesolithic hunters and farmers go back to 10,000 BC.

The Roman conquest of Brittany in 57 BC began what might be described as the current civilized era. Celtic influences arose shortly after, with monks and missionaries preaching Christianity and building churches. Many of these became saints and their names can be found today scattered throughout the peninsula though they were not recognized by the Church of Rome.

By AD 500, the occupation by the Roman legions had ended and Northern France had lapsed into barbarism. At this time, settlers began crossing the Channel from the British Isles and they gave it the name of Brittany, 'Little Britain'.

The armies of Charlemagne conquered Brittany in AD 799 but conflicts among the many dukes, battling for supremacy, kept the region divided and when the Normans came, they found the conquest of Brittany an easy victory.

Brittany's location with its many fine harbours made it a base for ships setting out on the trade routes around the world and from 1200 to 1500, powerful mercantile families such as Rohan, Montfort and Clisson struggled for control.

England became involved, also seeking use of the same ports, and was in turn wooed by would-be French allies. When the Dukes of Montfort gained a position of significant power during the 14th and 15th centuries, the region saw considerable economic and cultural growth.

Anne, Duchess of Brittany, is the best-known of all Breton rulers and though it was officially ceded to France, Brittany formed an independent parliament. This fierce autonomy resisted all efforts at national control and it was not until the Edict of Nantes in 1598 that the rebellious attitude was contained.

Uprisings against taxation, against Republicanism, against the Church and in favour of the newly formed trade unions kept that independent spirit alive and it remains strong today.

Many Breton ports were destroyed in World War II, particularly St-Nazaire, Lorient and Brest – all of which were Nazi U-boat bases for attacks against Allied Atlantic shipping.

Breton nationalist groups, such as the Breton Liberation Front and the Breton Revolutionary Army, still have strong voices and occasionally use violent means to draw attention to their cause. Politically, the peninsula remains divided between Left and Right.

The Food of Brittany

Unlike many other *départements* of France, Brittany is not a gastronomic region. Plain food, well prepared is what you will find here. Nevertheless, some foods which are considered delicacies in England are commonplace and inexpensive in Brittany.

Food from the sea

Seafood dominates, as it must in a *département* with such a coastline. Lobsters are one of the most commonly encountered types of seafood, which means they are much cheaper in Brittany than anywhere else in France or in England. *Écrevisses* are crayfish, like small lobsters. Langoustines are spiny lobsters. The three kinds of crab are: *tourteau*, which is the crab we are familiar with; *araignée*, the spider crab; and *étrille*, a tiny, less tasty variety.

Clams, mussels, cockles, winkles, scallops and ormers (tiny shellfish) are all plentiful. The best scallops come from Brest, Quiberon Bay and St-Brieuc. Brittany is famous for its oysters, and the best come from the Auray and Belon rivers. You will be offered two kinds: *les plates*, flat oysters, which most people prefer; and *les creuses*, a cross-breed of Portuguese and Japanese oysters.

Quiberon is famous for its sardines and the Etel River for tuna. Salmon from the Aulne and the Scorff rivers excel and you will find trout from the mountain rivers. Smoked eels and small eels called *civelles* are found in the Nantes region.

The ocean around Brittany yields sole, turbot, brill, plaice, mackerel and herrings, while the rivers produce pike, carp and shad. *Cotriade* is a Breton version of *bouillabaisse*, and *matelote d'anguille* is an eel stew.

Food from the land

Pig farming is still an important business and the Morlaix area is renowned for its ham and sausages. The Nantes area is known for turkeys and ducklings, Rennes for its chickens and the Broceliande and Vilaine for geese.

The Île d'Ouessant off the west coast of Finistère has sheep grazing on pastures regularly covered over by the sea (as at Mont St-Michel). The meat from these sheep is called *pré-salé* and has a very distinctive taste. You can find it in other parts of France too but its origin is in Brittany – in the form of leg of lamb with haricot beans and called *gigot à la bretonne*.

Roscoff is famous for its cauliflowers and artichokes, while onions, turnips and peas grow in such profusion that they are exported. Plougastel-Daoulas is known for its strawberries, *petits gris* are the melons of Rennes, and Fouesnant, in the south, grows outstanding cherries.

Crêpes

Bretons eat them at any of the courses in a meal and they appear at breakfast, lunch, dinner and supper. Their variety is endless and throughout Brittany, *crêperies* are more common than McDonalds.

Crêpes come basically in two kinds – *crêpes de sarrasin* and *crêpes de froment*. *Crêpes de sarrasin* are made from buckwheat flour (*blé*

THE FOOD OF BRITTANY

noir) and have evolved from the *galette*, the symbolic cake eaten on Twelfth Night. These are usually eaten with a savoury filling such as cheese, eggs, ham, mushrooms, onions or sausage. *Crêpes de froment* are made from wheat flour and are a dessert *crêpe*, filled with cooked fruit, honey, jam, chocolate or ice cream. *Galette fourée* is like a cakey, soft fruit pie.

Every village has *crêperies* and in many, you can watch them being prepared in front of your eyes.

Pastries
Brittany is celebrated for its pastries and most are very rich. Lots of sugar and butter are used. Popular pastries are *kouign amann*, a butter cake, and *gâteau brestois*, with lemons, almonds and Curaçao liqueur. *Far breton* is a flan made with prunes or raisins and *galettes de Pont Aven* are similar to shortbread biscuits.

Cheese
It is strange that Brittany has a very weak representation as far as cheese production is concerned. Few, if any, other *départements* produce so little cheese despite the fact that there is a large number of dairies.

Drink
It is not reasonable to expect a climate like that of Brittany to produce wine. The Loire–Atlantique in the south-east corner does produce a Muscadet and a Gros Plant but they have to be drunk young. Most of the Muscadet you will drink in Brittany will be from the Loire Valley and it is a perfect accompaniment to seafood.

Most Bretons drink cider, as both Normandy and Brittany produce a lot of apples. *Bouche* means flat and that is how most Bretons like it.

One unusual drink that you will not encounter anywhere else is *Chouchen*. It was the favourite drink of the ancient Celts and they called it 'the nectar of the Gods'. It is a type of mead made from fermented honey and when passed around at a celebration, it was believed to induce a sacred state of drunkenness in the gods and a state of immortality in humans. It may be drunk today as a digestif or an aperitif but don't expect Celtic results.

Beer is a popular drink and French beers have always had a good reputation. The brands brewed in Brittany draw their names from Celtic legend and the best of these are Coreff from Morlaix, Lancelot beer made from barley and Tenn Du, a buckwheat beer.

The Megaliths of Prehistory

Brittany has over 5,000 prehistoric stones. They are among the most famous monuments in Europe and have astonished visitors to Brittany for centuries.

The stones are not arranged in such a precise manner as Stonehenge, just across the Channel in England, but Brittany has far more of them and they are remarkable for their diversity as well as their number.

First, you need to know what the names of the various stones and arrangements mean. *Menhirs* are long stones between 2 metres and 20 metres in height, weighing from 2 tons to 200 tons and planted upright in the ground. (In the Breton language, *men* means stone and *hir* means long.) *Dolmens* are stone burial chambers (*dol* means table) and while some are freestanding, others are entered through narrow passages. *Tumulus* means mound and these are usually burial mounds, often built over dolmens.

Stones can be seen singly, in pairs and in groups, some of which resemble circles while others are squares, rectangles and horseshoe shapes. 'Alignments' are rows of stones, sometimes single, sometimes double and even more, and some of these stretch for quite a distance.

Who built them, when and why?

Celtic tribes built them from 5,000 BC to 1,500 BC. These people's lives consisted of farming and tending sheep and cattle. This was the Neolithic period – a drastic departure from the early Paleolithic period when hunting was the main occupation.

'Why?' is a much more difficult question and the answer at present is 'we don't know'. More and more scientific equipment is being employed to determine the purpose behind these huge stones but it still remains unknown. Many theories have been put forth though:

- they were processional roads for ancient religious ceremonies
- they were originally roofed-in and served as shelters from the elements
- they are part of serpent temples
- they were used for gymnastic displays and tournaments
- they symbolized armies drawn up in battle formation
- they have astrological significance

THE MEGALITHS OF PREHISTORY

- they were race tracks
- they replicate the pattern of underground passages and chambers.

These suggestions remain after we have discarded others such as their being petrified Roman legionnaires and landing markers for intergalactic spaceships.

Places of assembly was a theory that had popular support until calculations at Carnac showed seven 'buildings' each of 15,240 square metres, all in one location. This postulates gatherings of 100,000 people and such a population is not believable. Astronomical observatories is another suggestion that has always had a lot of adherents but astronomers today dismiss the idea. The people of those times had no knowledge of the true nature of the sun, moon and stars, did not know of their movements and had no reason to track them.

Some *tumuli* might have been used as burial mounds and traces of carbon have been found which could have resulted from burning the bodies so that their spirits could transport more easily. But the charcoal could also have been used for cooking purposes and this does not explain other stone formations.

Such megaliths are not confined to Brittany even though it has the most. Similar constructions are found in England, Scotland, Ireland and Wales and on the islands of the Hebrides and the Orkneys. What is the connection between the peoples who erected these, separated as they were by vast, inhospitable stretches of water? Did the same people travel throughout these regions, using their knowledge to put up these structures?

Carnac is at the heart of a territory rich in these prehistoric monuments and you should start there. The Musée de Prehistoire will help considerably before you set out to view the stones. The map shows the Carnac area in detail but you will encounter megaliths all over Brittany.

The best places to see prehistoric stones
Carnac
Guerche-de-Bretagne, Roche-aux-Fées
Langon, Les Demoiselles
Locmariaquer, Table des Marchands

Follow The Customs Paths

Brittany has a very long and varied coastline. It has even longer stretches of 'Customs Paths'.

Smuggling and the looting of wrecks occupied the lives of thousands of men and women in earlier and more lawless times. These activities also provided the livelihood of many large communities and the most strenuous efforts of army detachments to arrest them were ineffective. Local police were no deterrent as they were usually in league with the smugglers and the wreckers.

With the army and the police force unable to capture the perpetrators, shielded as the latter always were by their fellow villagers, it was the unenviable task of *Les Douaniers*, the Customs Men, to attempt to apprehend the culprits.

The 'Customs Paths' were the coastal footpaths running along cliff tops, past dunes, around capes and headlands that *Les Douaniers* used as routes for their interceptions. Almost all of these remain, and are perfect for a walk – often with fantastic views.

The Parish Close

In the period from the 15th century to the 17th century, a unique kind of religious architecture appeared in Brittany and particularly in Finistère. It was known as the *'enclos paroissial'*, which is usually – if unhelpfully – translated as 'parish close'.

In those days, the social life was centred on the parish church and, as an expression of religious fervour, a collection of buildings was erected around the church and it would consist typically of: a gateway, a calvary, a cemetery, an ossuary and a fountain. These would be carved from granite while wood would be used for the interior decoration and some of the statues.

The gateway often consisted of monumental gates that symbolized the transition from earthly to heavenly life. A calvary is a scene from Christ's life and contained figures in 15th-, 16th- and 17th-century costumes. An ossuary was a storehouse for the bones of the dead.

Of these, the calvary is the most typically Breton and may be considered as having its origin in the prehistoric standing stones which were decorated with Christian symbols and had a cross mounted on top.

Towns and villages listed in this guide that have particularly impressive parish closes are listed below, along with their outstanding features.

Commana – the church and its south porch and the 17th-century retable.
Guimiliau – the most elaborate of all the calvaries with over 200 stone characters.
Lampaul-Guimiliau – the baptistery, the retables and the beam in the nave with scenes from the Passion.
Roche Maurice – the ossuary dates from 1640.
Sizun – the ceremonial arch and the ossuary. (The museum here must be seen too.)
St-Thégonnec – the calvary and the pulpit.

The Legend of Arthur

King Arthur, the Knights of the Round Table and Merlin the Magician are considered such an integral part of British folklore that it is startling to realize that the same characters and the same legends are just as prominent in Brittany.

'How did English characters get to France?' we ask and at the same time, the French are asking why the English are making claims on their characters.

There is no satisfactory answer to these questions and the easiest solution is to allow both nations to enjoy their folk heroes. Besides the main figures, there are: Morgan le Faye, wicked half-sister of Arthur; Viviane who loved Merlin; Guinevere; Lancelot; his son, Galahad; and a large supporting cast.

As this is a book on Brittany, it will concentrate on the French view and most of the activity is in the legendary forest of Broceliande. Le Forêt de Paimpont, west of Rennes, is popularly believed to be Broceliande.

The castle of Comper is a focal spot of Arthurian interest and there, the Centre de l'Imaginaire Arthurien (open April to September) has exhibits, waxworks, movies and an extensive bookshop.

The Fontaine de Barenton, which in Arthur's day had the power to unleash tremendous storms, is another location from folklore and at the village of Tréhorenteuc, you can see the Church of the Holy Grail. South of the village, a road leads to Le Val Sans Retour and is said to be the valley where Morgan le Faye trapped knights accused of infidelity.

THE LEGEND OF ARTHUR

These and other sites dot the forest and you will see parking areas with 'Arthur' signs which will direct you along walking paths towards those sites. Paimpont is the hub of this area which looks real enough today but with a few memories of childhood reading and a liberal sprinkling of imagination can re-create the lost glories of Camelot and the Island of Avalon where Arthur went to die (or as one more belief maintains, to sleep until summoned to save his country).

The Breton Language

Breton is a Celtic language and belongs to the Indo-European family. Celtic is divided into two groups – the Gaelic and the Brythonic.

In the fifth century, immigrants from Wales, Cornwall and Devon crossed the water and settled in Armorica – which later became Brittany – and spoke the Breton language.

After the French Revolution, attempts were made to stamp out this language. Children who spoke it were forced to wear a wooden shoe around their neck and it required state intervention to prevent this minority language from disappearing.

Today, there are about 750,000 Breton speakers. A nursery school was opened in Finistère in 1978, free and open to all, for the purpose of teaching Breton alongside French and the idea has spread so that there are now 31 such schools with over 2,000 pupils. The system is based on total immersion and the Breton language is taught from the first year in nursery schools all the way through to the final year.

Breton glossary

Below are some of the Breton words you may encounter. Many of them occur in placenames and this list will help you interpret many of the names you will see signposted.

aber	estuary	*bihan*	small
ar	the	*bre*	hill
argoat	wooded area	*breizh*	Brittany
armor	coastline	*bro*	country
aval	apple		
aven	river	*castel*	castle
		chaland	flat-bottomed boat
bae	bay	*chupen*	embroidered waistcoat
bed	world	*coat*	wood
beg	point	*coz*	old

THE BRETON LANGUAGE

deiz	day	*marc'h*	horse
demat	hello	*men*	stone
dol	table	*menez*	mountain
douar	earth	*meur*	large
dour	water	*mor*	sea
du	black	*mortas*	bog oak
enez	island	*nann*	no
		nant	valley
far	pudding		
fest	festival	*palet*	quoits
feunteum	spring	*pariz*	parish
		penn	summit
gall	French	*pleu*	parish
giz	folk dress	*ploe*	parish
glaz	green	*plo*	parish
goat, goet	wood	*porz*	port
goemonnier	seaweed gatherer	*poull*	pond
gui, guic	borough		
gwenn	white	*roc'h*	rock
		ros	mound, hill
heol	sun	*ruz*	red
hir	long		
		sistr	cider
iliz	church	*steir*	river
izel	low		
		tann	oak
kant	hundred	*ti*	house
ker	village	*tre, tref*	hamlet
kenavo	goodbye	*trez*	sand
koad	forest	*tro*	valley
koan	dinner	*trugarez*	thank you
krampouezh	crêpe		
		uhel	high
lan	church	*vag*	boat
loc	monastery	*ya*	yes

The Best in Brittany

No trip to Brittany lasts as long as we would like. Most people's time is limited and it helps to have an opinion of the sights and places not to be missed.

'The Best in Brittany' is a purely personal viewpoint on the outstanding entries in each of the following categories:

- Chambres d'Hôtes
- Festivals
- Foods
- Hotels
- Hotel-restaurants
- Restaurants
- Sights

The best *chambres d'hôtes* in Brittany

Chambre d'Hôtes	Town/Village	*Département*
Manoir de Kervezec	Carantec	Finistère
Kerfornedic	Commana	Finistère
Ty Horses	Guidel	Morbihan
Manoir de Kervent	Douarnenez	Finistère
La Carrière	Josselin	Morbihan
Château du Blois Glaume	Poligne	Île-et-Vilaine
Kerdevan	Larmor-Baden	Morbihan
Château de Bonabry	Hillion	Côtes d'Armor
Le Val aux Houx	Guégon	Morbihan
La Maison du Latz	Le Latz	Morbihan
Manoir de Kergrec'h	Plougrescant	Côtes d'Armor
Manoir de Kérguéreon	Lannion	Côtes d'Armor

The best festivals in Brittany

These run during the high season: May to September.

Town	Département	Festival	Date
Tréguier	Côtes d'Armor	*Pardon de St-Yves*	3rd Sun in May
Lamballe	Côtes d'Armor	Folklore Festival	Jul 1-10

THE BEST IN BRITTANY

Town	Département	Festival	Date
Quimper	Finistère	*Festival de Cornouaille*	Last week in Jul
Locronan	Finistère	*Pardon de la Tromenie*	2nd Sun in Jul
Ste-Anne d'Auray	Morbihan	Pardon	Last weekend in Aug
Plomodiern	Finistère	Folklore Festival	1st 2 weeks in Aug
Guingamp	Côtes d'Armor	Breton Dance Festival	Last 2 weeks in Aug
Carnac	Morbihan	*Grande Fête des Menhirs*	3rd Sun in Aug
Perros-Guirec	Côtes d'Armor	*Pardon de Notre Dame*	Aug 15
		Fête des Hortensias	Aug 16

The best foods in Brittany

What — and where — to enjoy the best foods of the area.

Oysters	Cancale, Carantec
Lobsters	Camaret-sur-Mer
Crêpes	Gourin
Scallops	St-Brieuc
Sardines	Douarnenez
Mussels	Le Vivier-sur-Mer
Clams	Plouharnel
Andouille	Guémené-sur-Scorf
Pré-salé lamb	Lampaule
Conger eels	Île-de-Sein
Cod	Brest, Guingamp

The best hotels in Brittany

Chosen for comfort, welcome, location and price. Not necessarily in order.

Hotel	Town/Village	*Département*
Le Vieux Manoir	Dinard	Îlle-et-Vilaine
Manoir de la Rance	Pleurtuit	Îlle-et-Vilaine

THE BEST IN BRITTANY

Hotel	Town/Village	*Département*
Le Manoir de Rigourdaine	Plouer-sur-Rance	Côtes d'Armor
Men Du	Raguénès-Plage	Finistère
La Korrigane	St-Servan	Morbihan
Hôtel du Château	Vitré	Île-et-Vilaine
Château du Val d'Arguenon	St-Cast-le Guildo	Côtes d'Armor
Le Logis de Jerzual	Dinan	Côtes d'Armor
Hôtel Ty Mad	Douarnenez	Finistère

The best hotel-restaurants

Chosen for comfort, welcome, location, service and food. In alphabetical order.

Hotel-restaurant	Town/Village	*Département*
Auberge St-Thégonnec	St-Thégonnec	Finistère
Château de la Motte Beaumanoir	Pleugueneuc	Île-et-Vilaine
Chez Crouzil	Plancoët	Côtes d'Armor
Hostellerie Les Ajoncs d'Or	Plouharnel	Morbihan
Ker Moor	St-Quay-Portrieux	Côtes d'Armor
Le Minaret	Bénodet	Finistère
Manoir de Kerhuel	Ploneur-Lanvern	Finistère
Manoir de Moëllien	Locronan	Finistère
Manoir de Vaumadec	Pleven	Côtes d'Armor
Moulin de Rosmadec	Pont Aven	Finistère
Ti al Lannec	Trébeurden	Côtes d'Armor

The best restaurants in Brittany

Chosen for tasty food, imaginative cooking, fresh ingredients, price, value and attentive service.

Restaurant	Town/Village	*Département*
Chez Crouzil	Plancoët	Côtes d'Armor
Chez Jacky	Riec-sur-Bélon	Finistère
L'Azimut	La Trinité-sur-Mer	Morbihan
L'Écrivain	Combourg	Île-et-Vilaine
La Closerie de Kerdrain	Auray	Morbihan

THE BEST IN BRITTANY

Restaurant	Town/Village	*Département*
La Duchesse Anne	St-Malo	Île-et-Vilaine
La Grève	St-Suliac	Île-et-Vilaine
La Ville Blanche	Lannion	Côtes d'Armor
Le St-Placide	St-Servan	Île-et-Vilaine
Le Temps de Vivre	Roscoff	Finistère
Maison de Bricourt	Cancale	Île-et-Vilaine
Petit Auberge	Fougères	Île-et-Vilaine
Relais St-Aubin	Erquy	Côtes d'Armor

The best sights in Brittany

The prehistoric stones around Carnac in Morbihan.

The walled city of St-Malo in Île-et-Vilaine.

The fishing village of Camaret-sur-Mer in Finistère.

The medieval castles of Vitré, Josselin and Combourg.

The pink granite coast from Perros-Guirec west through Ploumanac'h to Trégastel.

The Emerald Coast from St-Malo west to Val André.

THREE CYCLE TOURS IN BRITTANY
(Two easy routes and one which is a little more challenging.)

These tour routes are designed for cyclists who prefer to take their time, enjoy the countryside and sample the delights of the hotels recommended in this guide. The routes assume the reader will want to explore each daily destination and experience the culinary delights that Brittany has to offer, so the daily distance is designed to enable you to cycle in the morning and go sightseeing in the afternoon. These tours are not intended for cyclists who prefer to carry their bedding and a tent with them, risking the weather and living al fresco. There are plenty of books catering for these hardy souls. It is cheaper to camp, of course, but the additional burden on both rider and cycle is not to everyone's taste or ability.

Each route is designed to enable you to leave your car in the UK and travel across the Channel without it, using the ferry service to Roscoff or St-Malo. Two of the routes are round trips. They start and finish in either Roscoff or St-Malo. The third option is slightly more adventurous, starting in Roscoff and returning via St-Malo. Because Brittany Ferries do not operate services to Roscoff and St-Malo from the same port in the UK, you will need to arrange some way of getting back to Plymouth from Portsmouth, if that is where you started. It is possible by rail, but you might find it more appropriate to leave the car at home altogether and rely upon the railway for all UK-based transport.

Most bikes can be adapted to carry a rear pannier rack and a handlebar bag. It is surprising how much you can pack into a simple, old-fashioned saddlebag. It is also possible to get a front pannier rack fitted to most machines, but this can be more expensive and most people should not need front bags for the sort of touring recommended here. Besides, if you are a novice, front bags impact upon the steering and you need to minimize the weight you are carrying. Much has been written on the selection of cycles for touring and it is not our purpose to repeat this advice here. However, in general, any mountain bike, all-terrain bike (ATB) or hybrid machine will do for these routes, provided it fits and you are comfortable with it. Proper touring bikes, though desirable, are not necessary for this type of holiday. We have seen all sorts including a Moulton folder used very effectively for this purpose.

Remember, however, that, to a certain extent, your daily distance is likely to be dictated by the weight of your bike and its suitability for the purpose. Obviously an experienced cyclist on a good touring bike will be able to cover a greater distance more easily than someone on a heavy ATB, but the latter is fine, provided the rider plans a suitable daily mileage. These cycle routes therefore assume a daily distance of between 40 and 64 kilometres, which will be within the capability of even novice riders. The more experienced can extend the route to cover greater distances each day.

Whatever bike you use, it is important that you have it serviced before leaving the UK and that you are familiar with it. Remember also to take a puncture kit, pump, spare inner tubes, spare spokes and tools to carry out simple repairs. Find room for a chain tool as well – if your chain develops a faulty link in the middle of nowhere, this tool could be a life-saver. Lights may be necessary if you intend to travel on an overnight ferry, though none of these routes should require you to pedal between hotels after dark. We have found lightweight LED lights to be suitable for loading on and off ferries.

In every case we have cycled these routes and checked their feasibility. Wherever possible, we have used the hotels recommended in this guide that can cater in some measure for cyclists, though it is possible that changes have occurred to accommodation since our visit. Perhaps the most important additional information that does not normally appear in the *French Entrée* series is advice on where the hotel will store your bikes overnight, because if you are dependent upon them they need to be secure. We remember turning up at a highly respected hotel in Normandy and being told that the bikes would reside in the front garden overnight. We chained them up, of course, but for extra security removed the saddles, placing a used champagne cork in the open tube of each to stop rain from getting into the frames. It was amusing to watch a couple of old ladies the following morning regarding our bikes with horror and wondering, no doubt, how on earth we managed to ride them!

We have found it appropriate to book hotels in advance by phone, confirmed by letter quoting a credit card number. If you are dependent upon cycles, you may not have the energy to cycle another 32 km if your preferred choice is fully booked on arrival, so be safe and book in advance.

Route 1 – A Circuit around St-Malo

MAP: IGN Serie Verte (1:100000) No 16 (Rennes – Granville)

An easy circuit starting and finishing in St-Malo, partly following the River Rance. About 209 km which can be completed in a few days but has the potential to be extended. The Rance towpath is not passable all the way to Rennes and back, but is usable in places, providing a good and interesting alternative to the highway.

Hotel Options in St-Malo

The best is **Les Charmettes** (tel: 02 99 56 07 31; see page 198). This is the perfect choice for cyclists and can be reached by a pleasant ride along the promenade from St-Malo centre. Some good-value rooms overlook the seafront. Although no proper restaurant is provided (or needed), the proprietor runs a small *crêperie* in what amounts to the front garden overlooking the beach, where one can relax in the evening and buy a range of simple food and drink. Cycles are locked away in the laundry room overnight.

Day 1 – St-Malo to Combourg (48 km)

Cycling off an overnight ferry into a busy port can be a frightening experience, but in St-Malo, there are cycle tracks alongside many of the roads into and out of the port. You can use these to reach the station, but from there it is difficult to avoid using the dual carriageway for a short distance.

There is a marked cycle route to Rennes from St-Malo, which provides a good route out, but it is not easy to find from the centre. If you find the station in St-Malo it is possible to reach this route by following the busy D301 ring road. At the junction, follow the signposts to St-Méloir des Ondes, then branch off this road to Château Malo. Avoid using the extremely busy D301 dual carriageway, except where it is unavoidable in the centre; once on this road it can be difficult to get off it and the traffic is heavy at times.

An alternative is to follow the coastal D201 east to Cancale, perhaps for breakfast off an overnight boat, but this will add about 20 per cent to the journey distance.

From Château Malo, follow the D74 to St-Père and the D275 to St-Guinoux. Then across the marshes, following signs to Plerguer and the D75 to Le Tronchet. From Le Tronchet, follow various side roads to Bonnemain, where you should arrive by lunchtime. From there it is an easy 7 km to Combourg.

In Combourg the choice is between the *Hôtel du Château* (tel: 02 99 73 00 38) and the *Hôtel du Lac* (tel: 02 99 73 05 65; see page 66). Both have excellent reputations, well deserved. Both cater well for cyclists. Neither is cheap. Both are worth it. We have used both and found the rooms in the Hôtel du Château superb, if somewhat expensive. A simpler room in the Hôtel du Lac with a meal served in the terrace dining room overlooking the lake is a romantic experience that you will not forget. Menus at around 15€ and 18€. Good-quality breakfasts, served buffet style.

Day 2 – Combourg to Betton (42 km)

From Combourg, follow the D82 south to Dingé, then the D83 south to Montreuil-sur-Îlle. Continue along the D221, then branch right on an unnumbered road to St-Médard. From here take the D106 to St-Aubin d'Aubigné to Chasné, then the D97 south to St-Sulpice la Forêt and Betton.

This route takes you through country lanes, touching the Canal d'Îlle et Rance at St-Médard-sur-Îlle. There is a nice forest section towards the end.

A good choice of hotel in Betton is the popular *Hôtel de la Levée* (tel: 02 99 55 81 18). Excellent value for both the rooms and food. The staff are friendly and helpful. Cycles are housed in a garage under cover behind the hotel.

Day 3 – Betton to Hédé (40 km)

An undulating, though fairly short ride north to Hédé, using the towpath of the Canal du Rance when possible. Locals have advised us that the towpath is not navigable by cycle between Hédé and Chevaigné, but from there it can be followed up to St-Germain-sur-Îlle, although it is difficult in places. Take side roads from St-Germain on the west side of the river as far as Montreuil-sur-Îlle. Then follow the D221 through Guipel to Hédé.

An excellent choice of hotel at Hédé is *Le Vieux Moulin* (tel: 02 99 45 45 70), located just below the ramparts on the N137 to Tinténiac. Despite its location, a quiet and well-appointed hotel, with excellent rooms and some of the best-value food on offer in the area. Bikes are stored securely in a garage at the back. The 20€ menu is particularly good. A small footpath at the back of the hotel leads up through the ramparts to the town and there is plenty to see in the remains of the old water mill alongside the hotel.

Day 4 – Hédé to Dinan (35 km)

A downhill run from Le Vieux Moulin at Hédé takes you past the cheaper option for food (Le Genty Homme) to Tinténiac. Here the *Hôtel des Voyagers* offers a slightly cheaper option for cyclists on a budget, though it is somewhat nearer to Dinan. It would be possible to reach Tinténiac without difficulty from Betton, thus making the run back to St-Malo feasible in two days, but you would have to miss out on Dinan.

Continue on the N137 to St-Domineuc, then take the D11 to Evran. From Evran to Dinan the rest of the journey can be done on the Rance towpath and this particular section is well worth doing – it avoids the traffic, is flat as a pancake, quiet and peaceful. And it takes you through some interesting places.

To find the towpath at Evran, take the side road leading to La Lande du Tournay and you will see a path off to the right leading down to the river. The towpath is rideable all the way from here to Dinan and there are plenty of places to stop and eat. This route also takes you through the picturesque village of Léhon, just before arriving in Dinan. The towpath takes you directly into the old port at Dinan, where it makes sense to choose a hotel. Do not be tempted to select a hotel in the main town, which requires a significant climb/push up the hill to the area within the ramparts.

A possibility in the old port is *Le Papillon*, a small hotel with a bar, run by a couple from Guernsey. There are plenty of restaurant options, including several nearby along the quayside and, of course, others further up in the town.

Day 5 – Dinan to St-Malo (40 km)

An easy and pleasant ride along the Rance towpath to La Vicomte-sur-Rance, where it is possible to cross the river at a swing bridge. From here, there is a choice of routes on the East bank of the Rance. Alternatively, it is possible to select side roads on the West bank, via Plouer Langrolay-sur-Rance, crossing at Port St-Hubert or La

Richardais. The latter offers an easier entry into St-Malo via St-Servan sur Mer, but whatever you do, avoid the N137 dual carriageway at St-Jouan des Guérêts – it is not easy to get off and very busy.

If you select to return on the East bank of the Rance, remember to go via Château Malo, where you can pick up a clearly marked cycle route to St-Malo centre.

Route Alternatives

If you make a detour from Hédé, or Evran westwards via Yvignac, using side roads, it is possible to reach Jugon Les Lacs, where there is a clean, economic Logis, *La Grande Fontaine*, which offers good-value accommodation and excellent menus.

From Jugon Les Lacs, it is only half a day's ride northwards to the coast where other options are available, such as the *Vieux Moulin* (tel: 02 96 27 71 62) at St-Jacut. At Plancoët, where the exceptional but expensive *Hôtel l'Écrin* (tel: 02 96 84 10 24; see page 136) is situated, you will also find the better-value *Hôtel Normandie*.

Route 2 – Roscoff to Pointe du Raz and Back
MAP: IGN Serie Verte (1:100000) No 13 (Brest – Quimper)

A more challenging circuit from Roscoff south over the Mont d'Arrée to the Pointe du Raz and back. Total distance about 420 km, over 8 days. Although the daily distances suggested here are not excessive, the route involves strenuous hills and is quite hard, especially if the bike is heavily loaded. A two-day stopover in Plogoff is suggested. Some cyclists may prefer to vary the route, with a stopover in Douarnenez.

Hotel Options in Roscoff

There are several useful hotels in Roscoff. We have used Daniel Person's excellent hotel-restaurant *Les Arcades*, which is on the waterfront. Nearer to the port, around the back streets, you will find the *Hôtel Armen Le Triton*, which caters well for bikes in a large garage at the rear of the property. This hotel has no restaurant – not a handicap in Roscoff, where there are many places to eat. A decent-sized breakfast is provided and the staff are very helpful.

The Plymouth–Roscoff night service often arrives quite early, so go prepared for a chilly start the next morning if travelling overnight. St-Pol de Léon is only half an hour by bike at 7 am, but don't expect any cafés to be open much before 8 am.

Day 1– Roscoff to Landernau (51 km)

From Roscoff, south on the D58 to St-Pol de Léon and then follow the D788 towards Landivisiau. Use any of the side roads and pick a route to bypass Landivisiau and join D712 at Pont Christ or La Roche Maurice. Then follow signs to Landernau. A straightforward, interesting run that is suitable for a first day. But expect to arrive late morning from an overnight sailing, especially if you get kicked off the boat at 6.30 am.

We have used the *Clos du Pontic* hotel (tel: 02 98 21 50 91; see page 104) in Landernau. They put our bikes into a shed that is locked at night, though this involved negotiating several flights of steps. The accommodation and food were good, though bordering on nouvelle cuisine. The wine list appeared to be quite expensive. Although we found the *Clos du Pontic* a suitable stop, if you are working on a budget it might prove to be too expensive.

The hotel is located on a substantial hill, so a warm-up might be wise before starting out the following day.

Day 2 – Landernau to Port Launay (50 km)

This section is hilly, involving a climb over the Mont d'Arrée to Quimerc'h, which seems to start the moment you leave the hotel. Turn left out of the hotel and follow the road to St-Urbain, then downhill to Dauolas, before taking the D770 south to Hôpital-Camfrout to avoid the busy N road. Just south of here, take a left turn and follow the unnumbered road around the estuary to Pointe de Gluzian, to avoid using the dual carriageway. This route will get you to Le Faou by late morning. Then continue on the D770 east to Quimerc'h and Pont de Buis. The climb out of Le Faou is long, and it is not obvious from the map that this is the case, though it mounts to the eastern edge of the Mont d'Arrée. The highest point on this road is about 120 metres above sea level and there can be a significant difference in temperature between the bottom and the top. There follows an easy run down the hill into Port Launay.

In Port Launay we used the *Au Bon Accueil* (tel: 02 98 86 15 77; see page 162). Cycles were placed in a secure conservatory out the back. The accommodation and food were adequate and the staff helpful.

An alternative on this route would be to stay at Le Faou, but if you do this, then the distance on Day 3 would be significantly longer. The option is to have a relative easy day on either day 2 or day 3.

Day 3 – Port Launay to Plogonnec (24 km)

Two routes are possible. The shortest involves a serious hill climb from Châteaulin to Cast. An alternative would be to follow the D770 to Moulin du Lay and then turn left for Plogonnec. If weather and your energy permit, it would be feasible to go beyond Plogonnec and on to Douarnanez.

From Port Launay, continue south to Châteaulin, then climb steeply out of the town, following signs to Locronan and Cast on the D7. When we attempted this section, we experienced appalling weather conditions, driving winds, heavy rain and low temperatures. This was not pleasant and 24 km seemed quite far enough. But you are bound to get better weather and find it a pleasure. From Locronan, there is an easy, short ride on the D63 to Plogonnec.

The short distance option is to stop at Plogonnec. There is only one hotel here, the *Relais du Nevet*. Unfortunately, when we tried this route the restaurant was closed, so we had to make do with a good *crêperie* on the other side of the village. The message is to check this in advance by phone. The Relais du Nevet provides an excellent breakfast.

Day 4 – Plogonnec to Plogoff (48 km)

From Plogonnec, follow the D39 towards Douarnenez. From here, follow the D7 marked Poullan sur Mer and Beuzic Cap Sizun. Just beyond Beuzic, turn south towards Quatre Vents. This is a moderate route, which delivers you on the southern coast near Estrebien. From here it is an easy ride through Primelin to Plogoff.

We stayed in the *Hôtel Kermoor* (tel: 02 98 70 62 06) at Plogoff, partly because we are familiar with it and partly because we planned a two-night stay here, to give us time to explore the area. This hotel has been progressively refurbished and has gone upmarket somewhat and is now a Logis. The restaurant is well known and appreciated. It is possible to get better value here by going half-board.

It is worth staying at Plogoff for more than one night, to give you an opportunity to explore the area around the Pointe du Raz.

Day 5 – Plogoff to Morgat (74 km)

If you consult the map, several options are apparent for the return journey from Plogoff, but they either require using the same route that you used to get there, or the distances are not sensible. We used a route back to Crozon-Morgat, but it represents a longer run than we would normally recommend. Remember if you plan to do this, that wind and rain could make this journey seem a lot harder. Some people may prefer to split the journey in Douarnenez or find an alternative return route, for example via Landrevarzec to Châteaulin or Port Launay.

From Plogoff, make your way to Douarnenez via Cledun/Cap Sizun and the D7, then continue on the D7 towards Plonévez-Porzay, then the D47 to Ploumodiern. Using the map, select a route that follows the coast avoiding Menez Hom, which is a serious, but avoidable, climb. For example, pick up the D63 south of Plomodiern which routes via St-Nic. This road then goes on to join the D887 near Telgruc sur Mer and on to Crozon and Morgat.

We stayed in Morgat at the *Hôtel Julia* (tel: 02 98 81 90 31), which is reasonable value, though they do not appear to have anywhere secure to store cycles. Ours were placed outside round the back.

Day 6 – Morgat to Le Faou (47 km)

This run does not seem far on the map, but it will be far enough if you cycled over 64 km the day before. Make a detour via the D60 to explore Landevennec. There are not many route options between Crozon and Le Faou, since the only convenient crossing of the Aulne is on the D791. From the bridge a choice of direct (D791) or indirect (D47) routes to Le Faou are available.

A good choice of hotel in Le Faou is the *Hôtel de la Place*. Centrally located and large, but with excellent, helpful staff and good food on the menu. Our cycles were placed safely at the back of the hotel. The hotel bar also sells an excellent Belgian Trappist beer.

Day 7 – Le Faou to St-Thégonnec (35 km)

It is difficult to avoid the D130 from Le Faou to Sizun, because all the roads seem to be going in the wrong direction. It has the advantage of being direct, but the route is undulating. From Sizun, a choice of less busy roads makes it possible to reach St-Thégonnec by midday from a reasonably early start in Le Faou.

Of course, the main reason for stopping at St-Thégonnec is to experience the *Auberge St-Thégonnec* (tel: 02 98 79 61 18; see page 213) where superb-quality accommodation is available at a reasonable price. The menu, though of course superb, may be somewhat expensive for cyclists who are looking for volume and carbohydrates at a reasonable cost. However, there is an excellent Relais Routier over the road, which provides the sort of fare with which most cyclists are more familiar!

The *Auberge St-Thégonnec* were extremely helpful about the bikes and garaged them for us. They had clearly thought of this in advance.

Day 8 – St-Thégonnec to Roscoff (43 km)

A straightforward run, following the D31 through Guiclan to Penzé and the D769 to St-Pol de Léon.

Route 3 – Roscoff to St-Malo

MAP: IGN Serie Verte (1:100000) Nos 13, 14 and 16

A coastal tour across the top of Brittany, incorporating just over 321 km of undulating roads and offering spectacular, varied scenery.

(For hotel options in Roscoff and St-Malo, see Routes 1 and 2.)

An excellent route, which can be done in either direction, but it is important to plan transport in the UK between the port of departure and the port of arrival. Variations on the basic route described will enable you to explore more of the coastline, but will inevitably add mileage.

Day 1 – Roscoff to Plougasnou (48 km)

South to St-Pol de Léon on the D769 and then use the D58 to cross the Penze at Pont de la Corde. From here, follow the D173 and D73 along the coast to the Rade de Morlaix. The only way to cross the River is to continue on the south bank right into Morlaix and cross there. Then follow the D76 northwestwards out of Molaix to Plouézoch. You then have a choice of using the D46 directly to Plougasnou or the coastal route via Diben if time and energy permit.

Good-value accommodation is available at the **Hôtel de France** in Plougasnou and it offers an excellent range of food. Our cycles were locked under cover out the back. We also thought the breakfast was exceptional.

Day 2 – Plougasnou to Trébeurden (48 km)

Southeast out of Plougasnou on D78 to Lanmeur, then follow the side road through Pont Menou to Pléstin-les-Grèves, avoiding the D786 up to this point. Note that there is a steep descent into and out of Pont Menou. In Pléstin-les-Grèves join the D786 and enjoy the spectacular view as you follow it down to the bay at Le Grand Rocher. To avoid the climb out at St-Michel en Grève, turn east and follow the D30 to Ploumilliau, then the D38 towards Lannion. Steeply out of Lannion on the D65 to Trébeurden.

There are several hotel options in and around Trébeurden. We used the **Ker an Nod** (tel: 02 96 23 50 21; see page 219), which is near the beach.

Day 3 – Trébeurden to Port Blanc (43 km)

Follow the D788 north out of Trébeurden towards Trégastel Plage and Perros-Guirec. Then continue on the coastal D6 to Louannec. Branch left onto a side road and pick up the D74 into Port Blanc.

A good reason for staying at Port Blanc is to take in the exceptional coastal scenery in this remote, beautiful part of Brittany. The only option here is the **Grand Hôtel**, situated on the seafront. This is a fairly large Logis, offering a wide range of facilities.

Day 4 – Port Blanc to St-Quay Portrieux (53 km)

Exploring the coast between Port Blanc and Paimpol would absorb several days, but to cross the peninsular and make progress towards St-Malo, start by following the D74 south to Penvénan and La Roche Derrien. Continue on the D6 to Pontrieux, Pommerit-Jaudy, Trévérec and Lanvollon. Then follow the D9 to St-Quay Portrieux.

We found St-Quay Portrieux to be a bit like an upmarket version of Clacton. However it was well situated about halfway between Port Blanc and Le Val André. We used the **Hôtel Gerbot d'Avoine**, which is a Logis though somewhat expensive. Our cycles were stored in a locked garage over the road.

Day 5 – St-Quay Portrieux to Le Val André (50 km)

It is difficult to avoid using the busy D786 between St-Quay Portrieux and St-Brieuc, though some minor roads exist that could be exploited. The problem in St-Brieuc with a cycle is to cross the deep gorge of the estuary around which the town is built. We discovered that a *piste cycliste* or cycle track runs alongside the major N road and, by using it, we avoided the necessity of dropping down into the gorge and having to climb back the other side. The track begins at a roundabout near Plerin and the bridge is at Légué. It is not well signposted. Failing this, you will need to follow the D786 down into the town before crossing the gorge.

Follow the D712 from St-Brieuc to Yffrinic – again this is not well marked. The troubles of crossing St-Brieuc all become worthwhile when you follow the D80 north out of Yffrinic to Hillion and the D34 through Morieux and Planguenoual to Pléneuf–Val André. Don't be tempted to stay on the D786 to St-Alban; the side roads are much better for cyclists.

In Val André, a treat awaits for you if you are fond of seafood. The recently refurbished *Hôtel de la Mer* (tel: 02 96 72 20 44) is a short stroll from the beach and all you could want. Rooms are well appointed and good value; the menus are excellent and seafood is a speciality.

Day 6 – Val André to Cap Fréhel (40 km)

This is an easy run, allowing time to explore the many sandy bays and coves along this part of the coast. From Pléneuf–Val André, follow the unnumbered coast road to Erquy. Then stay on the D34 all the way to Cap Fréhel.

In Cap Fréhel make time to explore the Château de la Lutte, built on a promontory of land jutting out into the sea. This is where they filmed Kirk Douglas in the 1960s classic *The Vikings*. It is about 8 km there and back from the hotel.

Our recommendation at Cap Fréhel is the rambling old converted farmhouse, the *Relais de Fréhel* (tel: 02 96 41 43 02). The rooms are excellent and well appointed and they will look after you on the food front as well. The menus were generally good value when we stayed there. Cycles were placed out of harm's way and securely locked up.

Day 7 – Cap Fréhel to St-Jacut sur Mer (32 km) or St-Malo (55 km)

It is only a short ride along the coast via the D16 and D786 to the sleepy little town of St-Jacut sur Mer. A detour via St-Cast-Le-Guildo is well worth considering, for this old seaside town has many charms worth exploring.

In St-Jacut the well-established *Vieux Moulin* (tel: 02 96 27 71 62) offers probably the best choice of both accommodation and restaurant, though you should check that the restaurant is open. There are other options for food, such as La Presque Isle, not far from the beach, but they are not catering for the same market

Alternatively, it would be feasible to cycle all the way into St-Malo from Cap Fréhel, a total distance of around 55 km.

Michael and Janet Howes

ARGENTRÉ-DU-PLESSIS

35370 (Î-et-V)
10 km SE of Vitré

Too many of Île-et-Vilaine's finest castles (and there are over a thousand of them) are not open to the public but here is one. It took about 400 years for the Du Plessis d'Argentré family to build it and you can tour it today and get a close idea of just how a family lived in those days when they were lucky enough to be born into the aristocracy. The tour is well arranged so that you can see the progress of building the castle through the centuries. It is open every day through the year, 2 pm to 6 pm.

Two smaller castles are close by – Le Pinel and La Fauconnerie, both having their constructional origin in the 15th century.

Le Cheval Blanc ⊨ ✕ S

1 rue d'Anjou
tel: 02 99 96 61 30
fax: same
closed: first two weeks Aug, Sun eve

Comfortable, cosy and popular, M. Couasnon runs a tight operation here and the ten rooms are very good value at 35€ plus 5€ for breakfast. Meals are simple but also good value at 11–20€.

ARGOL

29560 (Finistère)
20 km SE of Brest

This whole region is known as the Parc Régional d'Armorique and covers the long peninsula that sticks out into the Atlantic. You will certainly want to go out to the westernmost tip to see Camaret and, on the way, you can go through Argol which is right in the middle of the peninsula.

A popular attraction here is the Cider Museum at the Ferme de Kermarzin. The cider-making operations have been going on through three generations here and show the earlier ways of making this delicious brew and the modern method. With videos, displays and tours, you will find the visit very rewarding.

'Boire la pomme . . . et aussi le houblon' is a phrase you will hear or see. 'Drink the apple – and also the hop', for the hop, an important ingredient for the brewing of beer, is grown here too. In addition, aperitifs and digestifs are made. These include *chouchen*, the famous drink of the ancient Celts.

Children enjoy the farm because of the rabbits, chickens, ducks, guinea fowl, horses and other animals that roam around and there is a *crêperie* featuring the *Crêpes Bretonnes*.

The Church of St-Pierre and St-Paul was built in 1576 and has some notable murals and every summer, Argol puts on a *Son et Lumière* relating the legend of Ys. It runs from mid-July to mid-August.

ARRADON

56610 (Morbihan)
7 km SW of Vannes
market: Tues, Fri

Arradon is on the Gulf of Morbihan, which has bays, coves and islands dotted everywhere. At the Pointe d'Arradon is a tiny harbour, with beaches and sweeping views around the huge bay.

Logis Parc er Greo ⊨ ✗ M
9 rue Marie Guen
tel: 02 97 44 73 03
fax: 02 97 44 80 48
closed: first six weeks in the year; third week in Nov

You will get a sincere welcome from M. and Mme. Bermond to this three-storey house with a large swimming pool. It is well decorated with paintings, model boats, antique furniture and looks out on to small inlet on the Gulf of Morbihan.

The 12 rooms have a bath or shower and TV and are 48–80€ for two people, breakfast 7€. All are nicely decorated and very comfortable. Demi-pension is available at 40–64€ per person, three days minimum.

No meals are served at lunchtime but an evening meal is available by reservation. Menus are 20€ or special seafood menus at 32–48€.

Les Vénètes 🛏 ✘ M
La Pointe
tel: 02 97 44 85 85
fax: 02 97 44 78 60
restaurant closed: Sat lunch and Tues

The 11 rooms here are all well furnished and have TV and bath. They range in size from small to large and in price from 52€ to 84€, with breakfast costing 7€. All have some view of the sea and the management is helpful. Demi-pension is required in season; it is 45€ per person. Meals are modest in quality and priced at 21–36€ and the seafood choices are probably the best.

ARZON

56640 (Morbihan)
32 km SW of Vannes

On the Gulf of Morbihan, the village of Arzon sits out at the western tip of the peninsula Presqu'île de Rhuys. Protected from the worst of the Atlantic weather by the Quiberon Peninsula, Rhuys enjoys a mild climate and you will see Mediterranean plants in profusion.

The Tumulus de Thumiac is about 3 km from Arzon, a prehistoric earth mound with a good view of the gulf and the bay. The story goes that it was from this vantage point that Caesar watched the sea battle against the Vénètes which completed the Roman occupation of Armorica.

The 17th-century mill of Pen-Castel is just outside Arzon. Two kilometres away, the magnificent building that looks like an ocean liner is the Hôtel Miramar. It has over 100 rooms that go up to 288€ and is a health spa with a thalassotherapy institute. Its restaurant, Le Ruban Bleu (now you know why it looks like a liner), is dietetic and meals are 40€.

Glann Ar-Mor 🛏 ✘ S
27 rue des Fontaines
tel: 02 97 53 88 30
hotel open: all year
restaurant closed: from 15 Nov for winter

ARZON

On a more modest level, the Breton-named Glann Ar-Mor has only eight rooms but they are a mere 48€ and 6€ for breakfast. These are good prices for a place only a hop and a skip from an ocean beach. The restaurant is so-so.

Crouesty 🛏 M
> rue du Crouesty
> **tel:** 02 97 53 87 91
> **fax:** 02 97 53 66 76
> **closed:** mid-Nov to 1-Feb

At the port of Crouesty, a short distance from Arzon, is this modest hotel with 26 rooms, a less expensive alternative to the jazzy Miramar. All the rooms have a bath or shower and TV and are 61–72€ for two people plus 6.5€ for breakfast.

AUDIERNE

29770 (Finistère)
35 km W of Quimper

A busy fishing port, specializing in lobster and crayfish. You can visit the pools where the lobsters are stocked. Opposite them is a thatched cottage that is now a museum with objects from the 17th and 18th centuries. A long sandy beach is backed by sand dunes and from the pier, boats take you on the hour-long ride out to the Île-de-Sein.

Le Goyen 🛏 ✕ M
> place Jean Simon
> **tel:** 02 98 70 08 88
> **fax:** 02 98 70 18 77
> **closed:** Easter holidays, 25 Dec
> **restaurant closed:** Mon o.o.s.
> **no credit cards**

The 24 elegant rooms are all fully equipped and with a bath, at 52–120€ in season. The guest sitting-room has TV. The restaurant charges 24–72€ but there are plenty of dishes at the lower end of the range. The emphasis is on fish and shellfish.

L'Horizon ⊨ ✗ S-M
40 rue J.J. Rousseau
tel: 02 98 70 09 91
fax: 02 98 70 01 49
hotel closed: 15 Dec to 31 Jan
restaurant: open every day, tel: 02 98 70 04 51

A popular and pleasant hotel-restaurant with 50 rooms at 43–55€, sauna and tennis. The restaurant serves ample meals with a range of choices at 14–48€.

AURAY

56400 (Morbihan)
18 km E of Vannes
market: Mon

Auray is divided into two parts by the River Auray. During the high season, the most popular pastime is to take the Vedette Verte boat-ride into the Gulf of Morbihan.

The tiny port of St-Goustan has cobblestoned streets and grey stone buildings, their grimness happily alleviated by brightly coloured flowers.

Across the bridge, a path goes up through the trees to the promenade du Loc with its market square, fine views, shops and the Church of St-Gilda with a fine reredos behind the altar.

☆ La Closerie de Kerdrain ✗ M
20 rue Louis Billet
tel: 02 97 56 61 27
fax: 02 97 24 15 79
closed: Mon and Wed am; last two weeks Nov

Outstandingly good food for a reasonable price in this 16th-century manor house. Langoustines and mullet with artichokes have long been one of the favourite dishes and so has the fricasséed lobster.

Desserts include some interesting touches such as ginger to bring out the intense fruit flavours. A meal will cost 19€ to 48€ but it will be a memorable experience from the experienced and talented hands of Fernand Corfmat.

AURAY

Restaurant l'Églantine ❌ S
place St Sauveur
tel: 02 97 56 46 55
closed: Wed o.o.s.
no credit cards

This is the place for traditional, reliable Breton cuisine. Fish with sauerkraut is often listed as a variant and the roast sea bass with rosemary is a favourite. Menus are 12€, 17€, 22€ and 28€.

BAUD

56150 (Morbihan)
28 km NE of Lorient

Baud stands at a junction of the N24 autoroute which goes east-west and several major roads going roughly north-south. It is by the Evel River, a tributary of the Blavet.

Its main claim to fame is the statue known as the Venus de Quinipily, which Flaubert said was 'both barbarous and refined'. The statue is believed to have been sculpted during Gallic-Roman times. However, when Christianity arrived, locals attributed miracles to the statue, which was then called 'the Virgin of the Couarde'.

At the opposite end of the cultural spectrum is the Cartopole in Baud. That means 'Conservatoire Régional de la Carte Postale', which you will translate – from having sent so many home – as a postcard museum. Before you laugh (as I did at first), see this as a panorama of Breton life through the past century. It is a surprisingly good exhibition and the 20,000 postcards amuse, interest and inform you to a remarkable degree. It is open June to September, every day, 9.30 am–12.30 pm and 2 pm–7 pm; the rest of the year it is open Wednesday, Thursday, Saturday and Sunday, 10 am–12.30 pm and 2 pm–5.30 pm. You can ask for the tour in English.

Baud puts on a music festival in mid-June. If you want to, take in the big fireworks display on Bastille Day (Quatorze Juillet), but beware that when a Sunday intervenes, they are then set off the night before.

Auberge du Cheval Blanc 🛏 ✕ S
16 Rue de Pontivy
tel: 02 97 51 00 85
hotel closed: Jan

A popular little hotel due partly to its location by so many major highways and partly to its comfort and prices. The ten rooms all have TV and are 32–40€ or 34€ for demi-pension. English is spoken.

L'Apollinaire ✕ S-M
Le Pont de Baud
tel: 02 97 51 03 66
closed: two weeks in Sept, Wed o.o.s.

A brasserie well frequented by the locals and also by drivers passing by. Nothing really fancy but solid, reliable food with a surprise or two when an edible speciality becomes available. You can enjoy a three-course meal for 16€ – even including a glass of wine.

BEG MEIL

29170 (Finistère)
20 km W of Concarneau

Rocky shores and great beaches, an old lighthouse and lots of walks by the cliffs.

Bretagne 🛏 ✕ M
14 rue Glenan
tel: 02 98 94 98 04
fax: 02 98 94 90 58
closed: 1 Oct to 1 Apr

There are other hotels in Beg Meil but they all have drawbacks and, overall, the Bretagne emerges as the most reliable. The 30 rooms are comfortable and equipped with a bath or shower and TV. They are 48–58€ plus 5.5€ for breakfast. The meals are 16–32€ and are reliable too.

BELLE-ÎLE-EN-MER

56360 (Morbihan)
market: Tues and Fri

A 45-minute boat ride from Quiberon will take you to Belle-Île-en-Mer, the largest of all the islands lying off the coast of Brittany although it is only 20 kilometres long and 5 to 9 kilometres wide. It is a plateau riddled with tiny rivers and green valleys. It has excellent sandy beaches, natural harbours and towering cliffs. Le Palais is the 'capital' – of an island of 4,500 inhabitants!

Claude Monet came here and painted many of the local sights while Sarah Bernhardt came for relaxation. There are three other villages: Locmaria, Bangor and Le Sauzon. The nicest is Le Sauzon, a tiny port, very picturesque with its white washed cottages with coloured shutters. There, you will find the following.

Hôtel Les Pougnots (Cd'H) M
rue du Chemin Neuf
tel: 02 97 31 61 03
open: all year except Christmas
no credit cards

You need to be agile here for the Hôtel Les Pougnots has several stairways and it is located high up in the village. The five bedrooms are simple, almost austere, but comfortable. All have a shower and are 72–88€, breakfast included. No restaurant but plenty nearby.

Hôtel Village La Désirade M
tel: 02 97 31 70 70
fax: 02 97 31 89 63
closed: end Sept to 1 Apr

La Désirade consists of five small houses, stark white with brown roofs, circled around a heated swimming pool. Each house has four bedrooms, an unusual arrangement but very suitable for large families or groups of friends. These price out at 63–95€ per two people and breakfast is a buffet by the pool at 12€. An evening meal can be had by arrangement.

This is a convenient place to stay to visit the Vauban fortifications and a golf course is nearby. The hotel is just 2 km from Bangor.

Roz Avel ✗ S
tel: 02 97 31 61 48
closed: early Jan to early Feb; early Nov to 20 Dec; Wed (but not in school holidays)

You will find it behind the church and it may be busy because it is one of the most popular eating spots on the island. All the produce is fresh and you can eat very well for about 16€.

Café de la Cale ✗ S
tel: 02 97 31 65 74
closed: for two weeks before Christmas; early Jan to early Feb; late Feb to early Apr

Mostly seafood, all fresh and very well prepared. You can eat well for just 16€.

BELLE-ÎLE-EN-TERRE

22810 (Cd'A)
18 km S of Guingamp

Just off the N12 motorway is this quiet and attractive village, with a population of only a thousand and named for its location as an island between two rivers, the Guic and the Leguer.

Le Relais de l'Argoat ⌐ ✗ M
9 rue du Guic
tel: 02 96 43 00 34
fax: 02 96 43 00 76
closed: Sun eve and Mon

The Relais has been appearing in this guide since it was a simple inn with country cooking. Under M. Robert's skilled direction, it has gained renown steadily since then and it is still a recommended place to stay and to eat.

The eight rooms at 32–48€ have not gone up in price much and a couple of the bedrooms are large with magnificent furniture. The food is the big attraction without doubt and at 20–48€ including wine is a bargain. Seafood is prominent on the menu and you will often find duck and quail. The welcome is always warm and sincere.

BÉNODET

29950 (Finistère)
16 km S of Quimper

Not surprisingly, Bénodet is one of the most popular places in all Brittany with British visitors especially. It is at the mouth of River Odet and yachts come across the Channel and battle for berthing spots with French yachts.

The atmosphere is completely Breton, and lace – made in the local factories – is on sale in the street markets.

☆ Le Minaret ⌨ ✕ M
Corniche de l'Estuaire
tel: 02 98 57 03 13
fax: 02 98 66 23 72
closed: 15 Oct to 1 Apr
restaurant closed: Tues in Apr and May

It's well-named – it really looks like a minaret, a gleaming white square tower above a long, three-storey building with 20 rooms and a fine restaurant.

The story goes that an Arab sheik's life was saved by a Bénodet doctor and the minaret was erected in memory. It is hard finding verification of the tale but the minaret is there sure enough and it seems that a good reason must have existed for putting it up.

From the top of the minaret, the views of the estuary of the river are spectacular, with busy sail-boat traffic in both directions, sea, gardens and a lighthouse. Inside, the atmosphere continues to be Middle Eastern and the Pasha bedroom is decorated in full Moroccan style with wide windows opening on to the view.

Room prices might be expected to be high but Mme. Kervran keeps the range from a modest 40€ to an equally modest 72€, with breakfast an additional 7€. Demi-pension is mandatory during high season.

Earlier editions of *French Entrée – Guide to Brittany* have reported that the food was not up to standard but this has now been remedied. Menus are modestly priced too and are 15–32€.

Domaine de Kereven 🛏 ❌ S-M
route de Quimper Clohars-Fouesnant
tel: 02 98 57 02 46
fax: 02 98 66 22 61
closed: end Sept to Easter
no credit cards

The massive building of the Domaine and its adjoining old farmhouses are surrounded by farmlands and fields and are eloquently typical of the charm and tradition of the Breton countryside. To add to that, beaches and sea are right at hand too and, for some history, you could visit the châteaux of Cheffontaines and Bodinio.

The hospitality of Mme. Berrou has been commented on by many and the family atmosphere is the kind that Brittany does so well.

The 16 rooms are small and simply but well furnished. Each has its own bath or shower and is 48–64€. Breakfast is an additional 6.5€ and though there is no restaurant (as there are so many good ones very close by), you can have demi-pension at 50–56€ per person.

Armoric Hôtel 🛏 ❌ M-L
3 rue de Penfoul
tel: 02 98 57 04 03
fax: 02 98 57 21 28
open: all year

Bente and Erwin Clement (who speak English and other languages) welcome you warmly to their fine hotel where large, romantic rooms have a personalized charm and, more practically, large and beautifully equipped bathrooms. There are 30 rooms with a wide range of options from 64€ to 152€ and one sumptuous apartment at the top end of that range. The breakfast buffet is 9€ and demi-pension is 63–116€. The trees shade the large pool and there is a bar and terrace.

In the dining room, excellent meals use regional products according to the season and, of course, seafood and shellfish are dominant. Meals are 23–39€.

Superb beaches of fine sand are nearby and sailing and diving instruction are available, while a golf course is only a 3-kilometre drive away.

BÉNODET

La Ferme du Letty ✗ M
le Letty Izella
tel: 02 98 57 01 27
fax: 02 98 57 25 29
closed: mid-Nov to 1 Mar, Tues and Wed in season

Lobster and pork are two of the basic ingredients here, and Chef Jean-Marie Guilbault's adventurous cooking uses locally produced ingredients. Jean-Marie Guilbault was voted one of the handful to be included in the 'Jeunes Restaurateurs de 2000.' Menus at 24€, 31€, 58€ and 87€ are enthusiastically applauded by locals and visitors alike in this charming old farmhouse restaurant.

Restaurant du Centre ✗ S-M
56 avenue de la Plage
tel: 02 98 57 00 38
fax: 02 98 66 22 92
closed: 1 Nov to 1 Apr

Mme. Bourbigot's reliable cooking and excellent value have made this into a very popular place for eating downtown. The seafood platter is superb and all the catches of the day are on the menus too, at 13–30€.

BIGNAN

56500 (Morbihan)
30 km N of Vannes

Just 2 km south of the busy N24 autoroute, Bignan is where you will head for when you go to visit the Château Kerguehennec. Before you go in, you will want to wander around the park and see the great variety of trees and the sculptures. The château is open all day, every day. It is also the Centre of Contemporary Art so, particularly in season, there is usually an art show.

Auberge de la Chouannière ✗ M
6 rue Général Cadoudal
tel: 02 97 60 00 96
fax: 02 97 44 24 58
closed: Sun pm, Mon, Wed pm, two weeks in Oct

You will receive a hearty welcome at this pink-decorated country-style *auberge*. Knowledgeable diners come from far and wide to enjoy exceptionally good food, well-prepared and served with a smile. The home-made terrine of duck is a long-time favourite and so is the pigeon breast which is served in different ways. Some imagination is shown in cooking lobster in chartreuse (first time I have encountered that). The bottles in the wine cellar are carefully chosen. Lunches around 20€ and dinners at 28–48€.

BILLIERS

56190 (Morbihan)
27 km SE of Vannes

A tiny Breton village with stone houses, period manor houses, flower gardens and terraces. It has fewer than a thousand people but all are proud of its beauty. Located on the wild and rocky headland of Pointe de Pen Lan with only the sea beyond there is an outstanding hotel-restaurant.

Domaine de Rochevilaine ⊨ ✗ M-L
Pointe de Pen Lan
tel: 02 97 41 61 61
fax: 02 97 41 44 85
open: all year

The 40 cosy bedrooms and suites look out from under the heavy slate roofs at the sea and so does the dining room. The prices of the rooms vary immensely with view and size – from 90€ to 384€ – and while it is true luxury at the top end of the scale, the standard is still high at the other end. An indoor pool, a fitness centre, saunas, Jacuzzis are in a Phoenician-inspired style.

The restaurant is renowned and Chef Patrice Caillault is a rising star of the kitchen. His *langoustines en brochette* with rosemary is outstanding and the *galette de homard* is almost in the same class. Menus are 40–77€ and demi-pension is 84–192€.

BINIC

22520 (Cd'A)
14 km N of St-Brieuc

A busy marina, a pleasant seaside resort and the port where the boats take you out to the Île de Brehan, Binic (on the River Ic) was once a major port for the cod fishing boats that went out to the Newfoundland banks for six months at a time. (If you're wondering why the fish didn't go bad in that time, they dried it.) But by the end of the 19th century that kind of fishing was no longer competitive and Binic's importance declined.

There are two fine beaches to the north and a popular place to stay that is still reasonable.

Benhuyc ⌨ ✗ S-M
1 quai Jean Bart
tel: 02 96 73 39 00
fax: 02 96 73 77 04
closed: 15 Dec to 1 Feb

A very comfortable hotel with 26 rooms, pleasingly furnished and priced at 56–64€ for two people, breakfast 6.5€. Demi-pension is 47–56€ and naturally the food emphasis is seafood. Lunch is 13€ and dinner 16–32€ including wine.

BRASPARTS

29190 (Finistère)
35 km S of Morlaix

A fine parish close is here with the base of the calvary showing St-Michel doing battle with the dragon. On the other side of the church, which, though it dates from much earlier, was largely rebuilt in the 18th century, the pinnacled porch has statues of the 12 apostles.

Tuchennou (Cd'H) S
tel: 02 98 81 43 02
open: only Jul and Aug
no credit cards

In a tranquil spot surrounded by woods and valleys, you will find this old farmhouse that belonged to Marie Pierre Jacquemet's mother. The main rooms are in the house itself but the two bedrooms, each with its own bathroom and kitchen, are in a separate building. The rooms have white walls with old Breton furnishings and are 32€ including breakfast.

BRÉLIDY

22140 (Cd'A)
13 km N of Guingamp

It is located in one of the most unspoiled parts of the Breton countryside amid woods and narrow country lanes and is a perfect place to encounter an enjoyable château.

Château Hôtel de Brélidy ⊨ ✕ M
tel: 02 96 95 69 38
fax: 02 96 95 18 03
closed: 20 Oct to Easter

The granite walls give a feeling of comfort and security. The 14 bedrooms run from 80–128€ for two people but many prefer the cheaper rooms. All have a bath and some have TV. Breakfast is an additional 10€.

Fish dishes are offered in one of two attractive dining rooms and other items such as duck are always on the menus at 24–32€.

There is a large lounge and a billiard room, and M. and Mme. Yoncourt-Pemezec are welcoming hosts.

BRIGNOGAN-PLAGES

29890 (Finistère)
25 km N of Landerneau

This quiet village on the northern coast of Finistère has been discovered by families as a great holiday location but it has not yet been spoilt.

The sandy beach runs around a horseshoe-shaped bay and the huge granite rocks have weathered into weird shapes that the imaginative have named Elephant, Toad, Camel and so on. The dunes are popular for walking and dozens of tiny islands can be seen offshore.

To the west of Brignogan, you can see the large Menhir Men Marz, the Miracle Stone.

Castel Regis 🛏 ✗ M
    plage du Garo
    tel: 02 98 83 40 22
    fax: 02 98 83 44 71
    closed: 22 Sept to Mar
    restaurant closed: Wed

On a promontory with great views of the sea, the 22 rooms here are 48–104€, many of them rustic bungalows among the trees. All are modern and very comfortable. A heated swimming pool, saunas and a tennis court complete the amenities and the restaurant serves good Breton fare using local ingredients. Menus start at 16€.

Ar Reder Mor 🛏 ✗ S
    35 avenue Général de Gaulle
    tel: 02 98 83 40 09
    fax: 02 98 83 56 11
    open: all year
    restaurant closed: Mon and Wed lunch except Jun–Sept

The 25 rooms are pleasant and nicely furnished while being modestly priced at 29–52€ plus 6.5€ for breakfast. The dining room has a rural look with exposed stone walls and antique furnishings. Meals are Breton dishes and 15–30€, while demi-pension is 34–44€.

BROONS

22250 (Cd'A)
23 km SW of Dinan

Le Relais du Connetable 🛏 ✗ S
    15 place Duguesclin
    tel: 02 96 84 62 18

fax: 02 96 84 62 18
closed: Sept and Sat o.o.s.

A very pleasant little restaurant cooking traditional food in traditional style. The terrace is delightful for eating out in the summer. There is a plat du jour every day and a choice of three menus from 15–28€. Although the restaurant dominates, 10 rooms are available, all with a shower and satellite TV.

CALORGUEN

22100 (Cd'A)
7 km S of Dinan

La Tarais 🛏 **S**
  tel: 02 96 83 50 59
  no credit cards

This old farmhouse in a tiny Breton village has been completely redecorated by a Dutch couple, Deborah and Bernard Kerkhof (who speak English) and the four bedrooms are extremely good value for money, at 36–44€ including breakfast. There is a separate dining room and also a sitting room. Several restaurants are nearby. It is open all year but meals are served only from the beginning of July to the end of September.

CAMARET-SUR-MER

29570 (Finistère)
36 km W of Le Faou

A popular resort, Camaret is out on a peninsula and surrounded by beaches. The fishing fleets dock here and bring lobster and crayfish to the markets and restaurants so you can be assured of really fresh seafood.

The town was fortified in the 17th century by Sebastien Vauban, King Louis XIV's brilliant military architect, and, in the Tour Vauban in Camaret, you can go through the local history museum and see how effective the defences were. As an Anglo-Dutch fleet attempted to invade the coast through Camaret, they were repelled by a force containing a large number of home defence volunteers from the local villages. During this engagement, a cannonball from an English warship sliced the top off the belfry of the Chapelle de Notre Dame de Rocamadour and it has not been repaired so as to remind us all of the ultimate victory.

Camaret Bay was also the site of another naval event, for it was here that the American nautical engineer, Robert Fulton, demonstrated his invention – an oar-powered submarine that could stay under water for six hours. He called it the 'Nautilus' and experiments by the French Navy some years later influenced the Breton writer, Jules Verne, born and educated in Nantes, to write his classic *Twenty Thousand Leagues Under the Sea*.

An alignment of prehistoric stones is at Lagatjar, just south of the town and impressive views of natural rock formations are at Pointe de Penhir.

Hôtel de France ⊨ ✕ M
  19 quai Toudouze
  tel: 02 98 27 93 06
  fax: 02 98 27 88 14
  closed: mid-Nov to Apr

The port views are great from this modern hotel where the 21 rooms are bright, well-appointed and reasonable at 40–80€ for two people, breakfast 7€.

Seafood specialities in the restaurant include calamari and lobster. The turbot in thyme sauce is a fish favourite and menus are 32–64€.

Vauban ⊨ S
  4 quai du Styvel
  tel: 02 98 27 91 36
  fax: 02 98 27 96 34
  closed: Dec, Jan

A less expensive alternative to the Hôtel de France. The 16 quite adequate rooms are 28–44€, with breakfast 5.5€.

Hôtel du Styvel ✕ S-M
  2 quai du Styvel
  tel: 02 98 27 92 74

fax: 02 98 27 88 37
closed: 1 Jan to 1 Feb

The pleasant terrace is the place to eat in summer although the food is so good that any time will do. The *ragoût* of lobster, Breton-style, is the most popular dish but lots of other seafood will catch your eye also. M. Tephany has a winning way with all of them and the price range of 12–37€ makes this restaurant attractive to every wallet, large or small.

CAMPÉNÉAC

56800 (Morbihan)
9 km E of Ploërmel

Campénéac is a good location to stay for exploring the woods-and-lake region known as the Forêt de Paimpont with all its history and legend.

You may think that an abbey is an unusual place to find a boutique but at the Abbaye la Joie Notre Dame, you will find one of the best in the region. Biscuits, cakes and chocolates of all kinds including regional specialities are on sale and they are open every day but on Sunday in the afternoon only.

Le Cobh in Ploërmel (see page 144) is excellent value, with prices appealing to a range of customers.

CANCALE

35260 (Î-et-V)
15 km E of St.-Malo
market: Sun

The fishing boats bring seafood into the row of seafront restaurants where visitors are always sure of a fresh and satisfying meal. The cliffs are famous for their walks.

Cancale was famous for its oysters until a mysterious disease afflicted them in the 1960s, but now they have come back and are as popular as ever.

At nearby Le Vivier-sur-Mer, the *Fête des Moules* is celebrated every July.

CANCALE

☆ Maison de Bricourt ✕ L
rue Duguesclin
tel: 02 99 89 64 76
fax: 02 99 89 88 47
closed: mid-Dec to mid-March

Its two rosettes and three toques are well earned and this remains one of the best seafood restaurants in Brittany. Some visitors come here just to see a *Malouinière*, one of the most beautiful of the old mansions built by the corsairs who, although pirates, still remained loyal to the crown of St-Malo.

Lunch is 40€ and dinner will run from 64–88€ so it's a restaurant for a special occasion. They have a way of lightly spicing lobster that is unique and the *St-Pierre* cooked in the style of the Indies is superb.

Hôtel Richeux ⌑ ✕ L
tel: 02 99 89 25 25
fax: 02 99 89 88 47
restaurant closed: Mon and Tues lunch

6 km from Cancale along the D76 heading for Mont St-Michel, you will find this roomy old house which has been bought by Olivier Roellinger and his wife, Jeanne. He was formerly chef at the Maison de Bricourt (see above) when it was known as the Restaurant de Bricourt. They have converted it into a magnificent *auberge* and the views look out across the bay at Mont St-Michel, one of Europe's most photographed sights.

Its 17 rooms and two suites are bright and airy and all with a bath, TV and minibar. The bad news is the price of 104–256€, but the standard is high throughout. The cheaper rooms are very good value and at the high end of the price range, the only word is 'luxurious'. The meals are of a high standard too, as you would expect from a two-star chef. They are largely seafood and the fruit and vegetables come from the hotel's own gardens. Menus from 18€ up but *à la carte* is available too.

Hôtel des Rimains ⌑ M
1 rue Duguesclin
tel: 02 99 89 64 76
fax: 02 99 89 88 47
closed: mid-Dec to mid-Mar

Six bedrooms, small but cheerful, well decorated and equipped with a bath, TV and minibar. From its clifftop position, the hotel has a view of the Bay of Mont St-Michel.

The gardens are beautiful and well used and breakfast is usually served here. The rooms are 104–136€ plus 14€ for breakfast. There is no restaurant but the hotel is owned by M. and Mme. Roellinger, mentioned above, and you can stroll the short distance from the hotel to their restaurant.

Le Cancalais ⊨ ✕ S-M
12 quai Gambetta
tel: 02 99 89 61 93
fax: 02 99 89 89 24
closed: Dec, Jan; Sun eve and Mon o.o.s.

A modest but highly reliable hotel-restaurant that has won local awards. The 10 rooms have a bath or shower and TV and are 44–72€. There is a pleasant salon. The restaurant has a covered terrace with a view of the port and the food is mostly from the sea. Menus are priced at 15–34€.

La Pointe de Grouin ✕ S-M
tel: 02 99 89 68 95
fax: 02 99 89 79 01
open: all year
closed: Wed

Two of the best seafood restaurants are at this address in Cancale (one with views). The grilled lobster is superb, though the langoustines and the *St-Pierre* in hollandaise sauce are excellent too. Menus are 16–48€ which accommodates all requirements.

CAP FRÉHEL

22240 (Î-et-V)
23 km W of Dinard

Mont St-Michel, one of the most spectacular sights in Western Europe, is not too far away in neighbouring Normandy. It is therefore not covered in this book but you won't want to miss seeing Cap Fréhel – which is. The Cap's dramatic coastal scenery of cliffs, hidden coves, moors and dunes all come together here with a castle, a menhir and a lighthouse added for good measure.

Fort de la Latte is a popular spot for visitors and stands at the foot of a steep hill, down at the water's edge. It is open every day 10 am–12.30 pm and 2.30 pm–6.30 pm from Easter to the end of September, but Sunday afternoons only from 1 October to Easter. Near it is the menhir known as Le Doigt de Gargantua (Gargantua's Finger). It has been dated at about 6,000 BC. Burial mounds, knives and axes of bronze have been unearthed by archaeologists digging in the vicinity.

The people in this area declared in favour of the republic during the French Revolution and a few decades later, many locals died in the Napoleonic Wars. Action was renewed in World War II when the Germans built powerful defences along this coastal section. Ruins of some of the pillboxes remain and can be seen on the west coast of the cape.

La Réserve Ornithological du Cap Fréhel is on the northern tip of the cape where amateurs and experts alike can study petrels, penguins, cormorants, gulls and puffins. The lighthouse is just a short distance west of the bird sanctuary.

All of these sights can be taken in by one walk of about 8 km. You may want to plan such a walk, or even part of it, and have lunch. There are several choices and you can stay overnight if you wish.

Le Relais de Fréhel (Cd'H) S

    route du Cap
    Plévenon
    tel: 02 96 41 43 02
    fax: 02 96 41 30 09
    closed: Nov to Easter
    no credit cards

An old farmhouse with simple but good food. Nothing elaborate but satisfying favourites such as chicken escalopes in cream sauce, trout with almonds and mussels marinara. You can eat very satisfactorily for 16€.

Rooms are available, small but adequate and some have a bath. They are priced at 39–44€.

CARANTEC

29660 (Finistère)
15 km N of Morlaix

A small port town, Carantec sits almost alone out at the tip of a small peninsula on the northern coast. The name means 'love' in the Breton language and one very good reason to visit Carantec is to take the tour of the Château de Taureau. This is a spectacular castle-fortress on a small island in the Bay of Morlaix. If you are there in July or August, wait till the tide is out and you can take the walkway to Île Callot where guided tours of the castle are available.

If you are not there during peak season, you may still wish to go to enjoy the spectacular beaches and at least see the exterior of the château. Then, there's always the Casino ...

An alternative to using the walkway is the inexpensive bus service which goes several times a day from the railway station in Morlaix.

Manoir de Kervezec (Cd'H) S
tel: 02 98 67 00 26
open: all year
no credit cards

A grey stone manor house looking out to sea that attracts a wide clientele who come back year after year from all parts of the world.

This exemplary bed and breakfast has six large and very comfortable rooms, three doubles and three twins, at 48–56€. All rooms have a private bath. A fine breakfast is included with hot *crêpes* and home-made jams. The sitting room is a popular gathering place and it is very cosy and filled with antiques and souvenirs of Mme. Anne Bohic.

CARHAIX

29270 (Finistère)
45 km SW of Guingamp

This is about as inland as you can get in Brittany and this central location means that Carhaix is inevitably the hub of major roads. It was once a Roman fortress but today it makes a good base for exploring the Montagnes Noires, the Argoat and the Parc Régional d'Armorique. Pity it is not better equipped with places to stay.

Manoir de Prevasy (Cd'H) S
tel: 02 98 93 24 36
no credit cards

Just two kilometres south of town is this fine bed and breakfast in a beautifully restored Breton mansion house of the 16th century. Rooms are 45€ including breakfast.

CARNAC

56340 (Morbihan)
37 km S of Lorient
market: Wed and Sun

It's a close tie whether Stonehenge in England or Carnac is the most famous prehistoric site in Europe. Stonehenge is more spectacular because of the circular formation of the stones – this implies purpose even if we are still guessing as to what that purpose is.

Carnac, though, is more remarkable because of the vast number of stones – probably 5,000. Experts and amateurs have come, and still come, from all over the world to marvel and to measure, to study and to speculate, to wonder and to write books. If you intend to tour the sites of the stones, it is a good idea to visit the reception area at Kermario first. It is open every day in season and 9 am to 10 pm o.o.s.. The Archeoscope at the Alignments of Menec is also helpful.

On the third Sunday in August, Carnac holds its Grande Fête des Menhirs and on the second Sunday in September, the colourful cattle festival of St-Cornély (Cornelius), the patron saint of Carnac. His church in the village, with its fine carved wooden ceilings, is worth a visit. Carnac's other half contains excellent beaches.

Auberge le Ratelier (Cd'H) S
4 chemin du Douet
tel: 02 97 52 05 04
fax: 02 97 52 76 11
closed: two weeks in Jan

A recent addition to the hotel scene in Carnac and a very welcome one. It is right in the heart of busy Carnac and clearly dates way back as it was once an old farmhouse. It has been very cleverly converted and the ten rooms are small and simple but comfortable, very reasonably priced at 40–47€, with breakfast additional at 5.5€. The kitchen does an unusually fine job and specializes in the use of seasonal foods. Menus are 16–36€.

Le Bateau Ivre ⊨ ✕ M
70 boulevard de la Plage
tel: 02 97 52 19 55
fax: 02 97 52 84 94
hotel closed: Jan
restaurant closed: o.o.s.

If you want to be in the beach part of Carnac, here is a good place to be. Even if you want to explore the megalith area, it is convenient and here you get views of the ocean as well. It is at the eastern end of the beach and away from the other beach hotels. The rooms are extremely comfortable and many have private balconies with sea views. The walled garden has a heated swimming pool. Rooms are 56–95€ and the restaurant is quite smart, with menus from 28–48€.

CAUREL

22530 (Cd'A)
7 km NW of Mur-de-Bretagne

A convenient location between Gouarec and Mur-de-Bretagne and on the north shore of the pretty Lac de Guerlédan where lots of water sports are available and there are boat trips around the lake. The beach is especially lively in summer.

Beau Rivage ⊨ ✕ S
Lac de Guerlédan
tel: 02 96 28 52 15
fax: 02 96 26 01 16
closed: last two weeks Oct, most of Feb, Sun eve, Mon eve and Tues
no credit cards

M. Le Roux has a welcoming hotel-restaurant with only eight rooms, very popular at 44–52€ plus 6.5€ for breakfast. Its setting on the edge of the lake is very calm and peaceful and the restaurant is popular too, with menus at 15–48€ or demi-pension at 44–56€.

Le Relais du Lac 🛏 ✕ S
Le Bourg
tel: 02 96 67 11 00
fax: 02 96 67 11 09
open: all year
no credit cards

A slightly cheaper alternative to the Beau Rivage, le Relais is an old posting inn, right in the old village of Caurel. It has seven rooms but they are only 36–42€. Menus are 9€ up, English is spoken and demi-pension is 34–40€.

CESSON-SÉVIGNÉ
35510 (Î-et-V)
6 km E of Rennes
market: Sat am

A pleasant village, convenient as an alternative to the busier Rennes nearby.

Floréal 🛏 ✕ S-M
ZA La Rigourdière
tel: 02 99 83 82 82
fax: 02 99 83 89 62
open: all year
restaurant closed: Sun

The 48 rooms are a good size and well equipped with a bath or shower and TV. They are well priced too at 44–53€ with 6.5€ for breakfast. The restaurant is popular with the locals and serves an interesting selection of well-cooked meals at 12–22€ including wine. Demi-pension is 32–48€.

CHÂTEAUBOURG

35220 (Î-et-V)
19 km E of Rennes

The octagonal church spire can be seen from afar and is Châteaubourg's most distinguishing landmark. The area north of the village is dotted with dense forests.

Ar Milin 🛏 ✕ M
30 rue de Paris
tel: 02 99 00 30 91
fax: 02 99 00 37 56
closed: before Christmas to after New Year
restaurant closed: Sun Oct–Feb

An old mill converted into a good hotel and a popular restaurant. The 30 rooms are priced at 53–92€, with breakfast at 5.5€. It has a pleasant situation in a pretty park on the edge of the Vilaine River. In the restaurant, you'll find many Breton pork specialities that attract a faithful clientele from the neighbourhood. Two ranges of menus, one from 18–24€ and the other from 24–32€.

Castel J'Huly ✕
'La Goulgatière'
tel: 02 99 00 75 13
fax: 02 99 00 78 92
closed: Sun, Wed eve

Consists of both a restaurant and brasserie in the traditional style, serving good reliable Breton fare. Menus range from 12€ to 26€ giving an extensive choice of dishes in the two rooms.

CHÂTEAUGIRON

35410 (Î-et-V)
15 km SE of Rennes
market: Thurs

A pleasant little town, steeply sloping around its impressive castle. In the Middle Ages, Châteaugiron was one of the most important towns in Brittany, its lords having the right to serve as Grand Chamberlains to the Duke. Many of the houses date from that period, lining narrow streets, gabled, beamed, delightfully crooked. The castle was much besieged, destroyed and re-built, with every century from the 13th to the 18th leaving its mark. The enormous keep, which contains the tourist office and houses exhibitions, is the best-preserved part. The wood-and-wattle style of many of the buildings (including the hotel Cheval Blanc, below) was used in the 17th century when the sail-making industry was keeping Châteaugiron thriving.

Cheval Blanc 🛏 ✕ M
7–9 rue de la Madeleine
tel: 02 99 37 40 27
fax: 02 99 37 59 68
closed: first two weeks Jan, 26–31 Dec, Sun eve, Mon lunch

Right on the main street and it has been here a long time. M. Cottebrune is a zealous hotelier and speaks English. Many prefer staying here to the bigger city of Rennes nearby.

The 12 rooms are only 45€ each, with breakfast at 5.5€, and some have a private bathroom. Meals are 13–26€ and quite good, though for a more elegant meal, many prefer to eat just across the street at L'Aubergade.

L'Aubergade ✕ M-L
2 rue Gourdel
tel: 02 99 37 41 35
closed: Sun eve, Mon and Tues

One of the most popular eating places in the region and one where the residents of Rennes come when they want a good meal so reservations are essential. Jean-Claude Barre has been the patron-chef for a long time and he believes in local products, cooked in Breton style and never seems to run out of ideas for new dishes.

His seafood *crêpes* are rightly popular and he does great things with langoustines. *St-Pierre* with coriander is another original approach but don't think that he is fish-fixated. He has phases when he prepares various dishes using duck and his cream of almond soufflé is an outstanding dessert.

The rustic décor with heavy beams provides a pleasant atmosphere and the service is good. Meals start at 22€ and you can eat very well in the lower range but some of the more elegant meals can run up the price.

CHÂTEAULIN

29150 (Finistère)
30 km N of Quimper
market: Thurs

It is very picturesque and not as touristy as you might expect. Houses line the quay on both sides and numerous bridges cross the Aulne River. It provides lots of good walks and you will see plenty of fishermen. However, salmon are not as abundant as they were when the city coat-of-arms was designed and showed a leaping salmon.

The Chapel of Notre Dame is a beautiful Breton chapel on the river bank and has a 15th-century calvary which incorporates a scene from the Last Judgement, unusual in Breton carving.

Le Chrismas ⊨ ✕ S
33 Grand' Rue
tel: 02 98 86 01 24
fax: 02 98 86 37 09
closed: school holidays, Christmas, Sat eve and Sun

A French hotel of the old style – and English-speaking Mlle. Feillant is the fourth generation here so little has changed, meaning that this is still a very popular place to stay. The 19 rooms are 32–56€ plus 6€ for breakfast or 40–48€ for demi-pension. Menus are 12–29€ and seafood is predominant.

CHEMIN DE L'ÉTOUPE

22980 (Cd'A)
South from Plancoët to Plélan-le-Petit then the D91

Malik ⊨ M
tel: 02 96 27 62 71
open: all year
no credit cards

CHEMIN DE L'ÉTOUPE

In this ancient countryside, where 5,000-year-old stone artifices abound, it is unusual to find an ultra-modern hotel. Martine and Hubert Viannay's 'Malik' is built entirely of wood around a Japanese-style garden. The huge bay windows provide cheerful lighting while antique furniture maintains a nice balance.

The bedrooms are small but charming. One is a suite with a private sitting room and the other is a suite with two bedrooms. Both have a shower and WC and are 45€ for two people. English is spoken and Dinan is only ten minutes away.

CHERRUEIX

35120 (Î-et-V)
7 km N of Dol-de-Bretagne

On the bay of Mont St-Michel, this is a favoured stop to visit the famous abbey. 'The Marine Train' is the only one of its kind in the world and at low tide takes passengers on a 3-km trip around the bay. You'll learn about mussel farming, history, legend, flora and fauna and about the fish tanks that have been in use since the 11th century. The train departs from the Gare St-Michel, April to October, and takes just under two hours. This is 8€ well spent.

La Hamelinais (Cd'H) S
tel: 02 99 48 95 26
open: all year
no credit cards

This carefully renovated stone farmhouse is the hub of a dairy farm, just 3 km in from the coast. The five rooms can accommodate two to four people and each has its own shower. Two of the rooms have their own mezzanine. All are priced at 43€ for two people.

A simple farm meal is available on request at 15€, not including the wine.

COMBOURG

35270 (Î-et-V)
24 km SW of Dinan
market: Mon

The castle is one of the 'must-sees' out of all the 4,000 castles in Brittany. Châteaubriand, France's most famous Romantic writer, spent some of his childhood here and the descriptions of it in his famous *Memoirs* help to explain his disturbed adolescence and his depressive adulthood. 'Prison cells and dungeons, a labyrinth of galleries ... walled-up underground tunnels ... silence ... darkness' is how he saw it.

Construction was begun in the 11th century by a bishop of Dol and continued through to the 15th century. It is definitely a military fortification and does not have much 'family home' atmosphere. You must visit it and make your own judgement, for it is in splendid condition both inside and out. Open for tours July and August, 11 am –12.30 pm and 1.30 pm–5.30 pm every day except Tuesday; April, May, June and September 2 pm–5.30 pm and October 2 pm–4.30 pm.

Hôtel du Lac ⊨ ✗ S

2 place Châteaubriand
tel: 02 99 73 05 65
fax: 02 99 73 23 34
closed: Feb

The rooms are very comfortable and furnished in modern style looking out on to the lake. They are 44–52€.

The dining room is pleasing and menus are 14–24€. Oysters are usually featured in one form or another and local salmon dishes are prominent.

☆ L'Écrivain ✗ S

place de l'Église
tel: 02 99 73 01 61
closed: Sun, Wed eve, Thurs
no credit cards

There would be trouble if I omitted this charming little restaurant opposite the church. Everyone loves it. The cooking is enthusiastic and the dishes refined and highly enjoyable. Menus are start at a very modest 12€ and are excellent value.

COMBRIT

29121 (Finistère)
16 km S of Quimper

A tiny port on a tip of land sticking out at the mouth of the Odet River and across the water from Bénodet.

Hôtel-Restaurant Sainte-Marine 🛏 ✗ S
19 rue du Bac
tel: 02 98 56 34 79
fax: 02 98 51 94 09
closed: Wed o.o.s.

The flavour here is very nautical and the great views of the river are enjoyed by local yachtsmen, writers and movie makers.

The rooms are 48€ (with a shower) and 50€ (with a bath). The restaurant serves dishes such as marinated scallops with seaweed and fresh cod. Menus are 16€, 24€ and 32€. Demi-pension is obligatory in season at 40€.

COMMANA

29450 (Finistère)
25 km SW of Morlaix

This quiet, hilltop village has a renowned *enclos paroissial*. The steeple of the church was built in 1592 and is one of the highest in Brittany. Inside the church are statues, a retable showing Ste-Anne and some very ornate decoration. From the village, you can see the Roc Trévezél and from there, you have the opportunity to take the Chemin des Crêtes, very popular with walking groups.

Kerfornedic (Cd'H) S
2 km from Commana on the D30 to St-Cadou
tel: 02 98 78 06 26
closed: 20–Dec to 15–Jan
no credit cards

An incredibly old (and old-looking) farmhouse with wavy roofs but inside, charming and welcoming with low beamed ceilings, whitewashed walls and antique furniture. Two bedrooms with shower and WC are 45€, breakfast included.

Hikes and walks, a lake with bathing and windsurfing are close by as well as a local history museum. M. and Mme. Le Signor are attentive hosts and well informed about the district.

CONCARNEAU

29900 (Finistère)
24 km SE of Quimper
market: Mon, Fri

The second-biggest fishing port in all of France, Concarneau is a perfect representation of Breton maritime life. The Musée de la Pêche on rue Vauban is an unusually fine museum that will tell you everything you should know about boats and fishing. Entrance to the museum also includes access to real trawlers and, if you are really interested, you can watch the incoming boats unload their catches on the docks on quai Carnot between midnight and 6 am, Sunday to Wednesday.

On Mondays to Thursdays from 7 am to 9 am, you can take in the fish auction at the same location. Also, the Conserveries Courtin on rue du Moros will let you see the preparation and canning of soups, bisques and tuna.

The walled island, the Ville Close, is in the centre of the city and is fascinating to walk around. The building of the ramparts was begun in the 14th century and continued over the next 300 years. On the last Sunday in August, don't miss the Filets Bleus Festival (the Festival of the Blue Nets). It features the traditional Breton clothing with high starched lace bonnets and embroidered jackets and dresses. It began in 1902, organized as a charity to help fishermen and their families during the sardine crisis.

Concarneau has a number of good restaurants but you will not want to miss the Crêperie des Ramparts – in a region that has more *crêperies* than a magnum has bubbles, this one is outstanding. Concarneau is not as well blessed with hotels though so you need to go out to the beaches.

CONCARNEAU

L'Océan ⊨ ✗ M
plage des Sables Blancs
tel: 02 98 50 53 50
fax: 02 98 50 88 81
closed: Sun pm, Mon

Fairly new and still a little impersonal, but has a magnificent view and a heated swimming pool. Its 73 rooms are pleasingly decorated in pastel colours, not large but 17 of them are suites for families. The price is modest at 80–96€. All have a bath or shower and TV. Demi-pension is 64–68€ and meals are 16–40€.

LE CONQUET

29217 (Finistère)
24 km W of Brest

The Brest peninsula is a wild and secret place. Atlantic gales sweep in over tempestuous tides and stirring stories are relayed of shipwrecks and smugglers. Few hotels and restaurants find it appealing. It is therefore all the more welcome to find a little haven in Le Conquet, a quiet family resort, with wonderful sandy beaches. It has a nautical centre for sailing, windsurfing and scuba-diving, you can hire dune buggies and bicycles, go fishing, and take excursions to the remote offshore islands of Ouessant and Molène.

Le Relais du Vieux Port ⊨ ✗ S
1 quai du Drellac'h
tel: 02 98 89 15 91
open: all year
no credit cards

It has been here a long time. Now, after extensive reconstruction, it is a fine combination of modern hotel and comfortable guesthouse.

The five rooms have an excellent view of the estuary and are priced at 32€, 40€ and 52€ for two people. The cheaper rooms are cramped to put it frankly, but even the higher end of the range is reasonable. Breakfast is an additional 5€ and the restaurant serves cheap but satisfying meals.

CROZON

29160 (Finistère)
27 km W of Le Faou

The Parc Régional d'Armorique is also a peninsula that sticks out into the Atlantic so it has creeks, rocks, cliffs, wild seas and wilder waves all along its winding coast. Crozon is in the middle and the only town of any size.

Hostellerie de la Mer ✕ S-M
tel: 02 98 27 61 90
fax: 02 98 27 65 89
closed: Jan

Seafood is naturally the choice here – and you have lots of choices. The fruits de mer is a magnificent spread, the lobsters and the langoustines are great and the *coquilles St-Jacques* come right out of the Rade de Brest, on the north side of Crozon. M. Glemont caters to a range of tastes and appetites with menus at 17–44€.

DAMGAN

56750 (Morbihan)
26 km SE of Vannes
market: Sat

Peninsulas, promontories, bays, creeks, rivers and the sea abound here and the beaches are of exceptional quality.

Hôtel de la Plage ⊨ ✕ S-M
38 boulevard de l'Océan
tel: 02 97 41 10 07
fax: 02 97 41 12 82
closed: All Saints, mid-Nov to mid-Dec, Jan

The 18 rooms are very comfortable and are 45–60€, plus 5.5€ for breakfast. There are tennis courts and though there is not a full restaurant, the salad bar and the ice-cream bar are good for snacks. The conference rooms can be a minor irritation but otherwise, this is a good, inexpensive place.

DAMGAN

L'Albatros 🛏 ✗ S-M
1 boulevard de l'Océan
tel: 02 97 41 16 85
fax: 02 97 41 21 34
closed: 7 Oct to 1 Apr

Modern but attractive and right on the fine beach. The 28 rooms are well furnished and the range of prices from 34–61€ offers varying amenities. Two dining rooms are on the beach side and always busy, meals being similarly wideranging from 10–32€. Demi-pension is 36–50€.

DINAN

22100 (Cd'A)
21 km S of St-Malo
market: Thur, Sat

The Bayeux Tapestry shows William the Conqueror attacking Dinan when it was just a hilltop fortress. Today, you can walk the ramparts with their four gateways and ten towers and enjoy great views of the port and the Rance River. These belong to castles built and remodelled from the 11th to the 14th centuries. The church of St-Sauveur is one of the most famous monuments in Brittany.

The old town is full of historic buildings and they are close and easily visited. The Place du Guesclin and the Place du Champ are good places to start. The Château de Dinan looks like part of the ramparts and it contains a museum which is open during the summer months from 10 am to 6.30 pm. The Tour de l'Horloge, dating from the 15th century, can be climbed and you can wander through the cobbled streets and see old homes, hotels, convents and churches galore.

The Jardin Anglais, 'English Garden', was once a cemetery and going towards the port, full of pleasure boats, takes you through the Jerzual Gate, built in the 15th century.

In the place St-Sauveur, the Flea Market brings buyers from all around every third Wednesday from June to September. There is plenty of time to browse as it runs all day from 7 am to 7 pm.

The Fête des Ramparts is held the third week in August with all kinds of parades, song and dance and merrymaking.

☆ Le Logis de Jerzual (Cd'H) M
25 rue du Petit Fort
tel: 02 96 85 46 54
open: all year
no credit cards

The medieval rue du Petit Fort climbs up to the higher part of Dinan from the old port and nearly halfway up is the 15th-century building that is Le Logis de Jerzual. Further work was done on it during the 18th century. It has antiques throughout and the terraced gardens have views over the port.

Four nicely furnished rooms range from 45€ to 61€. Breakfast is included and an extra person can be accommodated. One room has a bath, one has a shower and both have WC. The other two have private showers but share a WC. If you really want to get into the medieval mood, ask for the room with the four-poster bed.

English is spoken and there is a pleasant sitting room. Although no meals other than breakfast are served, the short walk back down the rue du Petit Fort brings you to the port where the restaurants are lined up.

Hôtel d'Avaugour 🛏 M
1 place du Champ-Clos
tel: 02 96 39 07 49
fax: 02 96 85 43 04
closed: Dec to Mar

A popular favourite for more than 20 years. Mme. Quintin is a welcoming hostess at this grey stone building that looks out over the ramparts of the town. The 27 bedrooms are small but most have now been redecorated with brightly coloured fabrics and all are comfortable. Rooms for two are 112–128€, all have a bath and TV and the ample buffet breakfast is 8.5€.

The public rooms of the hotel are very pleasant and the garden spreads over what used to be the gun emplacement on the ramparts. From here there is a fine view of the Château de la Duchesse Anne. The restaurant is no longer operational since the Quintins opened La Poudrière in a tower of the ramparts in the garden.

DINAN

La Caravelle ✕ M
   14 place Duclos
   tel: 02 96 39 00 11

Chef Jean-Claude Marmion will tell you that he was born in a kitchen (he means it) and he learned cooking from his grandmother. He makes use of those basics and constantly modifies and improves them. He uses herbs rather than spices and the accent of all dishes is light while retaining a strong Breton flavour. You can have lobster or langoustines in various ways. Menus are 22–88€.

Restaurant Saigon ✕ S
   12 rue Ste-Clair
   tel: 02 96 85 21 18
   closed: Mon lunch
   no credit cards

For a fast and simple, inexpensive meal, this is the place to go. A good range of Oriental food and you can have a very satisfying meal for under 12€.

Chez Flouchon ✕ S
   24 rue du Zerzual
   tel: 02 96 87 91 57
   open: for lunch Mon to Sat

A cheerful atmosphere in this provincial French restaurant where the speciality is fondue. Beer or cider fondue are 12€ and there is another speciality that varies. A typical example for 9€ is a big salad, a *galette du jour*, a dessert *crêpe* and a glass of cider.

DINARD

35800 (Î-et-V)
22 km N of Dinan
market: Tues, Sat

Here's a switch! If you are in Dinard at the beginning of October, you will be able to attend the British Film Festival. Should you not want to attend, you can at least marvel over the British films that someone thinks appeal to the French taste.

DINARD

The reason for this anomaly is the popularity of Dinard with British tourists and, in fact, many people say that in all Brittany, Dinard looks the most British. Over the past decades, this has transformed a peaceful little fishing village into a major resort where the Plage de l'Écluse is the hub. The beaches are gorgeous, lots of indoor and outdoor pools, magnificent villas and modest accommodation and eating places maintain the popularity.

The Casino is located at 4 boulevard Président Wilson on the Plage d'Écluse. Roulette and blackjack are the most popular games and, as a break from winning money, you can eat at La Brasserie, the Casino's in-house restaurant which serves very good food at under 15€.

La Roche Corneille ⊨ ✕
4 rue Georges Clémenceau
tel: 02 99 46 14 47
fax: 02 99 46 40 80
open: all year

This is a small château even though it is in the middle of town. It has been recently renovated and the staff are very attentive to your needs. The 28 rooms all have a bath and TV and are 48–100€.

Special attention is being given to the cuisine and the menus are 16–28€ and very good value. The menu changes every week.

☆ Le Vieux Manoir ⊨ M
21 rue Gardiner
tel: 02 99 46 14 69
fax: 02 99 46 87 87
closed: 15 Oct to Mar

A large, classy house with a beautiful tree-shaded garden and a big covered terrace. It is quiet and peaceful and the large bedrooms are 48–68€ and good value. It is only five minutes' walk from the Plage de St-Enogat or the l'Écluse or the port and it is well signposted from the town.

La Plage ⊨ ✕ M
3 boulevard Féart
tel: 02 99 46 14 87
closed: end Sept to Mar

Modest accommodation, but pleasant and cheerful and not far from the beach. Rooms are 68€ and are all fully equipped. Its restaurant, Le Trezen, is well above average. Meals are upwards of 16€, but demi- pension is a good deal at 48–61€.

DOL DE BRETAGNE
35120 (Î-et-V)
26 km NE of Dinan
market: Sat

Founded by a Welshman named Samson in the 6th century who travelled widely as a missionary before coming to Brittany. After he cured the local lord's wife of leprosy, he became renowned. The cathedral named after him is granite. It was burned down in 1203 but rebuilt and has 13th-century stained glass windows and 14th-century choir stalls.

The Musée Historique is open 2 pm to 6 pm, Easter to September and shows you the history of the town. On the D795, just south of the town is the Menhir de Champ-Dolent, a huge pink granite stone. The Musée de la Paysannerie is open 9.30 am to 7 pm every day from May to September and depicts rural life in Brittany in crafts and tools of farming.

Here is a great opportunity to see the medieval art of falconry. Les Aigles de Bretagne in the Château de Landal is about 12 km southeast of the town. Eagles, vultures, owls and buzzards have second billing and times are 2 pm to 4 pm from April to October.

L'Aunay-Begasse (Cd'H) S-M
tel: 02 99 48 16 93
open: all year
no credit cards

You will find this delightful old farmhouse, which has been converted into a fine guesthouse by driving southwest out of Dol de Bretagne towards Baguer-Morvan where it is only 6 km from the coast. The three rooms are 37€ and all are comfortable and with a suitably rustic atmosphere with its big oak beds and beamed ceilings.

La Bresche Arthur 🛏 ✗ S-M
36 boulevard Deminiac
tel: 02 99 48 01 44
fax: 02 99 48 16 32
closed: 23 Dec to end Jan
restaurant closed: Sun eve and Mon

The 24 rooms are 37–48€ (plus 6.5€ for breakfast) and all were modernized a few years ago. The restaurant has always had a good reputation as being the best in town and it opens out on to the garden. Meals are 14–32€ including wine and seafood is well represented but country fare such as rabbit and quail feature too.

DOUARNENEZ

29100 (Finistère)
22 km NW of Quimper
market: Mon and Fri

One of the busiest fishing ports in France. The inlet from the river cuts right into the town, leaving the main harbour of Rosmeur on the east side of the peninsula. Fish auctions are held early in the morning when the boats come in and unload their catches and are an amusing way to spend a little time. Cruise boats leave from here too and go through the inlets and the grottoes of the bay, offering fine views of the cliffs.

There are several beaches and from one of them, the one nearest Rosmeur, you can walk along the Sentier des Plomarc'h.

The Boat Museum is on the Place de l'Enfer and is open every day from June to September, o.o.s. by appointment only. Opposite is Menguy-Maguet, which, baldly described, is a shop selling boat accessories. It's so extraordinary though that passers-by think it's a museum. Old and new parts for boats, many genuine, gleaming brass and shiny bronze, a feast for the eyes.

Out in the bay, so legend has it, is the submerged city of Ys.

☆ Hôtel Ty Mad 🛏 S
plage St-Jean
tel: 02 98 74 00 53
fax: 02 98 74 15 16
closed: end Sept to last week in Mar

DOUARNENEZ

An excellent and reasonable small hotel that has had many famous people living here when it was a home. The painter Max Jacob is probably the best known. The 23 rooms are 40–53€ and breakfast is 7€. This is served in a large cheerful room which opens on to a terrace.

The private beach is a real plus and there is the 17th-century chapel of St-Jean close by.

Manoir de Kervent (Cd'H) S
    tel: 02 98 92 04 90
    open: all year
    no credit cards

This delightful ivy-covered house surrounded by gardens and standing in the middle of wooded farmland is a fine bed and breakfast and Mme. Lefloch is a very helpful and well-informed hostess. There are two rooms and one family sized suite, all with shower and furnished with antiques. The price of 40€ is for two people and the suite, for four people, is 77€. Breakfast is included.

Look for the signs for Pouldavid on the D765 out of Douarnenez heading for Pont-Croix. The Manoir de Kervent is located about four kilometres south of Douarnenez at Point Croix so you will probably be visiting nearby Point du Raz, jutting out into the Atlantic Ocean.

Lanevry (Cd'H) S
    tel: 02 98 92 19 12
    open: all year
    no credit cards

Douarnenez has plenty of various types of accommodation but for a short stay, you won't find a better place than Henri Gonidec's bed and breakfast in an old farmhouse overlooking the bay.

It has two double rooms, one on each floor and both have a modern bathroom. One room has a canopied bed and both are immaculate. Both rooms are a bargain at 40€ for two people including breakfast. M. Gonidec works on his large farm as well as making you comfortable!

Chez Fanch ✘ S-M
    49 rue Anatole France
    tel: 02 98 92 31 77
    fax: 02 98 92 41 60
    closed: mid-Dec to Jan, Fri pm o.o.s.

Super seafood cooked and served by M. and Mme. Boudigou. Many of the dishes are Breton versions of old favourites, for example the *coquilles fruits de mer* and the *ragoût de lotte*. The price range appeals to appetites of all levels – 12–36€.

ELVEN

56250 (Morbihan)
14 km NE of Vannes
market: Fri

Useful as an overnight stop from the N166.

Hostellerie du Lion d'Or ⊨ ✕ S
  5 place Le Franc
  tel: 02 97 53 33 52
  fax: 02 97 53 55 08
  e-mail: liondoresthotel@post.club-internet.fr
  closed: Sun eve, Mon, 23 Sept to 10 Oct; Mar

The ten comfortable rooms at 40–45€ are neat and well kept by M. Belin who also does the cooking. Menus start at 8€ for lunch and 15€ for dinner and the food is wholesome and satisfying.

EPINIAC

35120 (Î-et-V)
5 km S of Dol-de-Bretagne

Des Ormes ⊨ ✕ M
  Domaine des Ormes
  tel: 02 99 73 53 00
  fax: 02 99 73 53 55
  email: www.desormes.com
  closed: 30-Nov to 1-Mar

The trim white buildings contain 45 rooms, all very thoroughly equipped and pleasantly furnished and ranging from 71–92€ plus 7€ for breakfast. A tennis court and swimming pool are among the extras and English is spoken. The demi-pension arrangement is worth considering here, as the cooking is of high standard. This is 62–68€.

ERDEVEN

56410 (Morbihan)
10 km NW of Carnac
market: Thur

Auberge du Sous Bois ⊨ ✕ S-M
    route de Pont Lorois
    tel: 02 97 55 66 10
    fax: 02 97 55 68 82
    closed: Oct to Easter, Mon o.o.s.

A granite building, painted sparkling white and with massive roofs. It looks very much at home in the pine forest and the Piot family keep it that way. The 21 rooms are very smart and fully equipped including TV. They are very good value at 29–61€ depending on size. The restaurant serves reliable grills, salads and meals are around 16€. Demi-pension is 40–58€.

Voyageurs ⊨ ✕ S
    14 rue de l'Océan
    tel: 02 97 55 64 47
    fax: 02 97 55 64 24
    closed: 1 Oct to 1 Apr

A modest but very recommendable hotel-restaurant with 20 rooms looking out over the orchards. The prices have remained remarkably stable for several years thanks to the Gouzerh family, so rooms are still 29–48€. The restaurant serves fresh fish and shellfish and serves them appetizingly. Meals are from 10–24€ and demi-pension is 37–48€.

ERGUÉ-GABÉRIC

29500 (Finistère)
9 km E of Quimper

La Ville au Vert is its nickname because it is surrounded by forests and woods. The River Odet runs through here and traces of an early occupation remain for this area was settled during the Bronze Age. Be sure to see the Chapel of Kerdevot, dating from the 15th century and with one of the finest retables in France. It was built on the spot where the Virgin Mary appeared and stopped a plague epidemic that threatened Ergué-Gabéric. The Church of St-Guinal is worth a visit, as are two other chapels, those of St-Guénolé and St-André.

Hôtel Restaurant Odet 🛏 ✗ S
tel: 02 98 59 53 81
fax: 02 98 59 58 83
restaurant closed: Fri, Sat and Sun eve o.o.s.

A small, quiet and very reliable hotel with rooms at 31–36€. Demi-pension varies with the time of the year from 18–39€. There are fine views from the bar and breakfast room. In the dining room, seafood is king. The Medallions of Monkfish and the Scallops Cassolette au Riesling are to be recommended. The lunch menu is 8€ and in the evening menus are 11€, 14€, 20€ and 28€.

Le Relais de Loch Laë ✗ S-M
Route de Quimper-Coray
tel: 02 98 59 50 67
fax: 02 98 59 62 15
open: all year
closed: Mon

There are 400 seats here and they have no trouble filling them, says M. Kergoulay. The menus from 11–44€ cater to all sizes of appetite. The *croustillant de blé noir aux St-Jacques* is popular and the *plateau de fruits de mer* has always been a bestseller.

ERQUY

22430 (Cd'A)
40 km NW of Dinan, on the D786
market: Sat

Sheltered from the gusty northern winds, Erquy is a pleasant resort which has not been spoiled by overbuilding. The fishing fleet brings in shellfish, particularly scallops and you can usually see classes in canoeing and windsurfing. There are several very fine beaches.

ERQUY

☆ Relais St-Aubin ✕ M
3 km from Erquy on the D68 heading for La Bouillie
tel: 02 96 72 13 22
closed: Mon, Tues

The 17th-century priory on the site has been converted into an antique shop and restaurant. The cooking is good and reliable, and prices are reasonable. An earnest effort to satisfy is the keynote in the Relais. An open fire grills fish, beef, lamb, chicken and langoustines. *Plateaux* of seafood and lobster may be ordered ahead and meals are 13–27€.

ÉTEL

56410 (Morbihan)
16 km SE of Lorient
market: Tues

The River Étel is more like a large bay as it empties into the Atlantic and at its mouth sits Étel, a fishing port mainly active in the tuna trade off Africa. Upriver from it, the best view of the extensive oyster beds can be obtained at Pointe du Verdon. The Chapelle de St-Cado is in Romanesque style on a shaded square about five kilometres upriver.

Trianon ⛉ ✕ S-M
rue du Général Leclerc
tel: 02 97 55 32 41
fax: 02 97 55 44 71
restaurant closed: Sun eve and Mon lunch o.o.s.

The 22 rooms are comfortable and 48–76€ for two people, breakfast at 8€. The food is Breton with a seafood accent and meals are 15–31€. Demi-pension is available at 58–61€.

LE FAOU

29680 (Finistère)
20 km SE of Brest
market: Sat

A busy market town with a high street lined with 16th-century houses, with slate-covered façades and heavy granite chimney stacks. The 16th-century church on the river bank is attractively decorated. Two recommendable places are on the square.

Relais de la Place 🛏 ✗ M
    7 place aux Foires
    tel: 02 98 81 91 19
    fax: 02 98 81 92 58
    closed: 23 Sept to 8 Oct

A pleasant three-storey place to stay with 34 rooms, priced at 40–44€ plus 5.5€ for breakfast. Rooms in the back are quieter as the front is on a busy square. Demi-pension is 39–40€ and M. Le Floch is a reliable hotelier.

The restaurant is popular with locals and always full. A wide range of fish and shellfish is always on offer and menus run from 14€ to 40€.

Vieille Renommée 🛏 ✗ M
    11 place aux Foires
    tel: 02 98 81 90 31
    fax: 02 98 81 92 93
    closed: Sun eve and Mon lunch o.o.s., 8–28 Dec

The 38 rooms are spacious and well furnished, all with a bath or shower. Prices are 44–56€. In the restaurant, budget meals are the order of the day and you can eat extremely well for 13–32€.

LE FAOUET

56320 (Morbihan)
37 km N of Lorient

The village is on a plateau and popular as a base for touring the picturesque region which has numerous chapels and abbeys, all well above the average. Among the interesting chapels is St-Fiacre, 2 km south of Le Faouet, in Gothic style and with a superb gable belfry. The painted wood screens are so finely carved that they look like lace.

To the northeast about three kilometres is the Chapel Ste-Barbe on a rocky height looking over the river valley. Much of it dates from the 15th century and, if you are there at the end of June, you will see the *pardon* (procession) to the chapel. Then to the east, the 16th-century Chapel St-Nicholas stands in the woods and has carved wooden statues and wood panels. The Abbey of Langonnet is a few kilometres further and dates from the 12th century. Near it, the village of Kernascleden has a 15th-century Gothic church with a high steeple and statues of the 12 apostles.

La Croix d'Or 🛏 ✗ S
9 place Ballinger
tel: 02 97 23 07 33
fax: 02 97 23 06 52
closed: 15 Dec to 15 Jan, Sun eve, Mon

A convenient place in a convenient village. The 11 rooms are more than adequate at 48€ with 5.5€ for breakfast. Demi-pension at 37€ is a good deal and the meals are 14–29€, considered by many to be exceptional quality for the money – particularly as that includes wine.

LA FORÊT-FOUESNANT

29940 (Finistère)
16 km SE of Quimper
market: Tues

It used to be a little-visited hamlet, at the mouth of one of the creeks which are left dry when the tide flows out. Now, it is a busy village since a vast yacht harbour was built and its Church of Our Lady of the Low Sea of the Bay gets a lot of visitors. It has an ancient calvary, a tall slim steeple and and bells cast in 1614. Several unusual statues are inside the church, most of them carved from wood.

Orchards and woods surround the village even though the beach at Kerleven is less than 2 km away.

Manoir du Stang 🛏 ✗ M-L
tel & fax: 02 98 56 97 37
closed: mid-Sept to mid-May
restaurant open: Jul and Aug only
no credit cards

This 16th-century manor house sitting in extensive grounds of beautiful parkland takes your breath away. The 'Stang' in the name means a lake and there are several. Flowers of all kinds abound around the house and you can play tennis.

The interesting point about this place is that it was the first of the old châteaux to be converted into a hotel – that was more than 60 years ago. It's hard to believe today as the building has been kept up so well and anyway, when it has already lasted from the 16th century, it can easily shrug off another handful of years.

The 24 rooms are all delightful and almost all different, furnished with antiques and varying in size to fairly large to very large, hence the wide price range of 72–152€ plus 7€ for breakfast. Demi-pension is 74–104€. No lunch is served but dinner is 28–31€.

FOUESNANT

29170 (Finistère)
17 km SE of Quimper
market: 3rd Fri

Apple and cherry orchards surround Fouesnant and it is claimed that the local cider is the most powerful in Brittany. The *Fête des Pommiers* is the cider makers' festival day and is held on the third Sunday in July. It has competition though from a Beer Festival which is held every summer.

The *Pardon de Ste-Anne* also takes place in summer and goes to the church at the north end of the village. This is a good opportunity to see a fine display of ancient Breton costumes.

Auberge du Bon Cidre 🛏 ✗ S
rue de Cornouaille
tel: 02 98 56 00 16
fax: 02 9851 60 15
closed: early Nov to mid-Feb, Sun eve, Mon o.o.s.

This smart grey stone three-storey hotel is well-named for the principal product of the area. The 32 rooms are very good value at 32–52€ plus 6€ for breakfast while demi-pension is 39–48€. Mme. Gleonec makes sure that the restaurant is popular too where meals are 13–25€.

FOUGÈRES

35300 (Î-et-V)
79 km SE of St-Malo
market: Sat

Its massive 12th-century château is in a valley, rather than on the usual hilltop and the Nançon River fills its great moat. Fougères is now a town of 25,000 people with busy industries of electronics and robotics, but it has always been an important one and its castle always a vital link in the castles comprising Brittany's 'citadel frontier'.

The castle is the focal point though and you can walk the ramparts and climb the tall Melusine Tower for a fine view of the town. This is one of 13 towers still remaining and the whole castle covers quite a large area.

To see the town in its entirety, consider the 'Orient Express'. No, this is not a pipe dream but a trolley that takes you from the castle gates on a 45-minute tour. It runs from 10 am till 7 pm but only in the summer months.

The Emmanuel de la Villeon Museum, on the Rue Nationale, is one of the best in the *département*. On view here are oils, watercolours, pastels and drawings by one of the greatest of the impressionist painters.

The places to stay in town are not very enticing and the best bets are out on the edge.

☆ Petit Auberge ✕ S
route de Laval
tel & fax: 02 99 95 27 03
closed: Sun pm, Mon, Tues pm

It's a few kilometres out of town but worth it for one of the best *auberges* in the district. It's always full of locals which is a good sign. They serve good, hearty Breton food with a lunch menu at 12€ and a dinner menu at 16€. A good choice of *à la carte* dishes is available up to 40€ and, in the evenings, wine is included in both prices.

Château du Bois Guy ⊨ ✕ M
tel: 02 99 97 25 76
fax: 02 99 97 27 27

e-mail: château.bois.guy@wanadoo.fr
hotel & restaurant closed: mid-Oct to mid-Apr
restaurant closed: Sat lunch, Sun pm, Mon

A very impressive old stone château that has recently become a choice place to stay and to eat. The 12 rooms are very well appointed and all have a bath or shower and TV. They range from 45–88€ depending on how large and how fancy are your needs. Breakfast is an additional 8€. The kitchen has received considerable attention and it serves excellent meals with a fine selection of Breton and other dishes. Demi-pension is 52–64€. English is spoken. It is located just to the north of Fougères near Parigne.

FRÉHEL

22240 (Cd'A)
35 km W of St-Malo

Some of the most spectacular views along the Emerald Coast are here and even the Channel Islands are often visible.

La Voile d'Or 🛏 ✕ M
tel: 02 96 41 42 49
fax: 02 96 41 55 45
closed: mid-Nov to 1-Mar

La Voile d'Or is not in Fréhel, but down the coast to the west near the popular seaside resort of Sables-d'Or Les Pins. The restaurant overlooks a beautiful lagoon fed by the sea and that same sea supplies the shellfish and seafood served up here by Michel Hellio. Menus are 24€, 32€ and 48€, while the 26 rooms, mostly with a view of the lagoon, are 48–80€ and are comfortable and spacious.

Le Victorine ✕ S
place de la Mairie
tel: 02 96 41 55 55
closed: Tues; last two weeks Nov; first three days Jan

Popular in the area for its fine, fresh seafood. Meals at 20–55€.

LA GACILLY

56200 (Morbihan)
16 km N of Redon
market: Sat

It is pleasingly situated on the slopes of the Aff River, a tributary of the Oust. The old houses have been taken over by craftsmen in recent years and you can watch them making articles out of leather, wood, metals, willow, glass.

Hôtel de France ⊨ ✗ S
15 rue du Montauban
tel: 02 99 08 11 15
fax: 02 99 08 25 88
closed: 23 Dec to 7 Jan

A simple, old-fashioned hotel right on the main street. The rooms are simple too but only 20€ in the main hotel and up to 40€ in the newer annex. Meals are simple and good value at 12–29€.

GOUAREC

22570 (Cd'A)
12 km W of Mur-de-Bretagne
market: 2nd Sat

The town is unremarkable but is handily located by the N164 and the intersection of the Nantes–Brest Canal.

Hôtel du Blavet ⊨ ✗ S
tel: 02 96 24 90 03
fax: 02 96 24 84 85
closed: one week in Sept, over Christmas, two weeks in Feb
restaurant closed: Sun pm, Mon
no credit cards

A nice view over the Blavet River and four-poster bedroom with a bath is only 56€ and other rooms are down to 26€. Views from the dining room too and traditional dishes at 15–48€.

GOUESNACH

29950 (Finistère)
6 km N of Bénodet

Only a few minutes away from some fine beaches. You can rent kayaks and canoes. The first week in April sees a big swap meet cum flea market. The Château de Boutiguery is nearby but is not yet open to the public.

Aux Rives de l'Odet 🛏 ✘ S
10 place de l'Odet
tel: 02 98 54 61 09
closed: over Christmas
restaurant closed: Fri pm, Sat, Sun pm
no credit cards

A simple place, inexpensive and unpretentious. Rooms are 27–48€ and the meals are excellent value, different every day and under 24€.

LA GOUESNIÈRE

35350 (Î-et-V)
12 km SW of St-Malo

It is at the junction of the D4 and the D76 and conveniently located for visits to St-Malo and the coast.

Hôtel Tirel 🛏 ✘ M
tel: 02 99 89 10 46
fax: 02 99 89 12 62
closed: from mid-Dec to mid-Jan
restaurant closed: Sun eve o.o.s.

Opposite the station is the Hôtel de la Gare but it has been known for years by the name of its owners, the Tirels. The hotel is modern and it is very comfortable and well equipped. There is an indoor pool, a sauna and a tennis court and the 60 rooms range from 48–68€. The large dining room tries for a classy look with wood panelling, brick and marble and velvet. The food is what counts though and lobster continues to be the speciality. Menus are 23€ but you can also order à la carte.

GOURIN

56110 (Morbihan)
55 km N of Lorient
market: Mon

The capital of the Black Mountains, the capital of Breton emigration – and the capital of *crêpes*. In mid-July, a two-day celebration is held in the grounds of the Château de Tronjolly. You can eat dozens of kinds of *crêpes* and enjoy Breton songs, dances and music.

GROUIN, POINTE DU

35260 (Î-et-V)
5 km N of Cancale

It's a small promontory sticking out into the bay of Mont St-Michel. Offshore is the bird sanctuary on the Île des Landes while the sheltered bays of Port-Mer and Port-Pican and the tiny cove of Port-Briac are very photogenic.

Hôtel Pointe du Grouin 🛏 ✕ M
tel: 02 99 89 60 55
fax: 02 99 89 92 22
closed: 1 Oct to 1 Apr
restaurant closed: Tues, Thurs lunch

A popular place with a regular clientele. Its location gives fine views from all the windows. The 16 rooms, not large but nicely furnished, are 64–84€. Excellent seafood is served in the restaurant which is very smart. Meals start at 20€.

GUÉGON

56120 (Morbihan)
3 km SE of Josselin

Le Val aux Houx (Cd'H) S
tel: 02 97 22 24 32
open: all year
no credit cards

This attractive old manor house by a narrow stream has just opened after being thoroughly and beautifully renovated as a bed and breakfast by Melle. Moussu who is young, enthusiastic and also speaks English.

The four large bedrooms each have a bathroom with a shower and all are simply but well furnished. The price is 48€ for two people and an extra bed is available at 13€. Breakfast is included and is served on a terrace above the stream.

The swimming pool is an uncommon luxury in such a place and although no lunch or dinner is served, plenty of restaurants are nearby and tennis courts, fishing and riding are available. The medieval town of Josselin is just across the Oust River from Guégon.

GUÉMENÉ-SUR-SCORFF

56160 (Morbihan)
21 km W of Pontivy

Bretagne ⊟ ✕ S
rue J. Pérès
tel: 02 97 51 20 08
closed: Christmas and New Year

A very comfortable and reasonable old place with 19 rooms, all with a bath or shower and TV. They are priced at 32–48€, plus 5.5€ for breakfast or you can take demi-pension at 32–40€. The restaurant serves a modest range of foods including Breton specials at up to 32€ with wine included.

GUERLESQUIN

29650 (Finistère)
15 km SE of Morlaix

An ancient Breton village located in the forested countryside of the Parc Régional d'Armorique. The large village square is fronted by old granite houses where the 17th-century courthouse stands, a big square building with a turret on one corner.

GUERLESQUIN

Monts d'Arrée 🛏 ✕ S
14 rue du Docteur Quéré
tel: 02 98 72 80 44
fax: 02 98 72 81 50
closed: Sun eve
no credit cards

The simple rooms are quiet and comfortable and most have a bathroom. They are priced at a very modest 24–40€ but the real attraction here is the restaurant which is renowned in the neighbourhood. The two dining rooms are always busy and the chef uses only good-quality local ingredients. Oysters and crab feature regularly and a three-course meal is 12€, while a more sumptuous repast is 24€.

GUIDEL

56520 (Morbihan)
12 km NW of Lorient
market: Sun

Ty Horses (Cd'H) S
route de Locmaria
tel: 02 97 65 97 37
open: all year
no credit cards

This lovely old country house is now a welcoming and inexpensive bed and breakfast. The four bedrooms are quiet and cosy, each is decorated differently and they cost a mere 40–45€ for two people, plus an extra 12€ for a third person, breakfast included. No other meals are served but there are a lot of eating places nearby.

Gardens on one side and fields on the other provide a true country atmosphere and the beach is only ten minutes away. M. and Mme. Harmon speak English. Guidel is easy to find, it is located by the signposted sliproad from the N165 autoroute.

GUILLIERS

56490 (Morbihan)
13 km N of Ploërmel
market: Tues

A small village in the Argoat interior.

Au Relais du Porhoët ⊨ ✗ S
11 place de l'Église
tel: 02 97 74 40 17
fax: 02 97 74 45 65
closed: first week of Oct, three weeks in Jan
restaurant closed: Sun pm, Mon

A solid-looking granite building with a rustic interior. Oak beams and a big brick fireplace add to the charm inside and the 15 rooms are all nicely decorated and some have brass beds. Most have bathrooms and range from 31–42€.

The restaurant is much more upper crust with fresh local produce and tasty meals at 24€ cooked by the chef-owner. Demi-pension is worth considering at 36–39€.

GUILVINEC

29730 (Finistère)
10 km SW of Pont l'Abbé

A thriving little fishing port where one of the popular pastimes is watching the boats unload their catches when they come in during the afternoon. Near the port are some fine beaches.

Centre ⊨ ✗ S
rue Général de Gaulle
tel: 02 98 58 10 44
fax: 02 98 58 31 05
closed: Sun eve, Mon, Jan

A delightful small hotel with 17 rooms, all very attractive and priced at 40–64€. The cooking is dedicated and the ingredients all fresh, mainly seafood, of course. Meals start at 15€.

GUIMAËC

29620 (Finistère)
12 km E of Roscoff

Le CapLan et Co ✗ S
Lieu-dit Poul Rodou
tel: 02 98 67 58 98
closed: Sept, Oct

This is a strong contender for the most unusual entry in this guide. Café-bookshops are not that common in France but if they were, this one would be at the top of the list. Owners Lan and Caprini were in the publishing business and when they got out of it, they opened this delightfully casual and cosy place where you are surrounded by piles of books — there are books everywhere. There are some real bargain buys and all the prices are reasonable.

The café part of the operation provides another surprise, as the food is very tasty and inexpensive. The dishes have a Greek accent and at 8.5€ including wine, you have money left over to buy books.

It's on the Plougasnou road out of Guimaëc. While you're in town, the cider mill offers tours and tasting.

GUIMILIAU

29400 (Finistère)
15 km SW of Morlaix

A tiny village, most of which is taken up with one of the finest *enclos paroissial* in Brittany. The parish close is a fascinating local speciality and the calvary here was built in 1588. The granite figures of the Holy Family, the Disciples, the legendary Katell-Gollet, damned for eternity by her immoral way of life, and a lady in court dress believed to represent Mary, Queen of Scots, look almost alive and are a supreme example of this art form.

Intense rivalry has always persisted between Guimiliau and the neighbouring village of St-Thégonnec, mostly originating from their claims to the best *enclos*.

Not much in the way of restaurants here but the Épicerie-Café-Bar is a good place to sit and watch the village population go about its daily tasks.

GUINGAMP

22200 (C.d'A)
30 km W of St-Brieuc
market: Sat

Guingamp is an old town of cobbled streets and stone-built houses on the banks of the River Trieux and a brief look around is rewarding.

The belltower and spire of the church overlook a fountain with carved dolphins and nymphs. The Basilica of Notre-Dame-de-Bon-Secours has a 'Black Virgin'. On the first Sunday in July, you can see the famous *Pardon de Notre-Dame-de-Bon-Secours* and in mid-August, the festival of Breton dance. The bombarde and the biniou are two of these dances. Biniou means bagpipes, another interesting Celtic connection. The danse de loup involves a lot of stamping without music, a reminder of the days when the dance was for the purpose of scaring away the wolves that were stalking the flocks of sheep.

The town is also popular as a hub for trips in various directions. The wooded areas are specially delightful – to the east are the woods of Malaunay, to the south are Bois Meur, Coat Liou and d'Avagour and from there the Trieux River meanders through the deepest Argoat, with its rocky gorges, lakes, churches and chapels, calvaries and megalithic monuments.

Relais du Roy ⊨ ✕ M

42 place du Centre
tel: 02 96 43 76 62
fax: 02 96 44 08 01
closed: Sun, Mon lunch, two weeks in Jan

A 17th-century house on the market square with several ancient features. Jacques Mallegol has been here a long time and the six rooms are stylishly furnished and have a bath or shower and TV. They are 72–120€, 9€ for breakfast or, if you prefer, demi-pension at 72€.

The restaurant is more active than the hotel, particularly with its central location. Fresh ingredients are used and, from the Argoat region, you will find on the menu items such as trout. Crab dishes are popular too and the *ris de veau* seems to be a favourite with the locals.

Menus are 20–40€ though you could also choose more elaborate meals up to 56€ with wine included.

HENNEBONT

56700 (Morbihan)
10 km NE of Lorient
market: Tues

It is known as the City of Breton Art. Along the estuary of the Étel River runs the Oyster Route which is well signposted. The château is impressive and massive but only 19th century.

Le Château de Locguénolé ⊨ ✗ L
route de Port Louis
tel: 02 97 76 29 04
fax: 02 97 76 82 35
closed: Jan
restaurant closed: Mon to Thur lunch only

The prices are high – better get that warning out at the beginning. But it is something to see even if you don't eat or sleep there – a graceful early 19th-century château, built of native Breton granite, with white shutters and an immense lawn that stretches all the way down to a bay on the Blavet River. The name of the château comes from St-Guénolé who stepped across this arm of the sea to escape the Devil.

Despite the price, this is a very popular place for bicycle groups and the genial owner, M. de la Sablière, will supply you with steeds should you not have your own. Other facilities include an outdoor heated pool, a sauna, a hammam (bath) and table tennis.

The 18 rooms range from 112 to 248€, are mostly well appointed and large, and many friends have told me that they genuinely preferred the cheaper rooms as they are 'cosier'. The four suites with demi-pension are from 216–368€ (well, I did say 'high').

The restaurant has one Michelin star and the succulent pigeon is delicious. So is the ravioli stuffed with spider crab and large sea crab. Chef Philippe Peudenier goes from strength to strength and his tart of mixed berries is a superb dessert. Meals are 48–64€.

Les Chaumières de Kerniaven 🛏 ✗ M
route de Port Louis
tel & fax: 02 97 76 82 35
closed: beginning Dec to end Feb

A *chaumière* is a thatched cottage and two of these, which are part of the Château de Locguénolé, form this small country hotel. It is located a short way south of Hennebont. The château itself is rated extremely highly as a hotel (see above). The *chaumières* are therefore a less expensive alternative and you can enjoy all the advantages of the château including a large swimming pool, sauna and tennis as well as being able to wander around the very extensive grounds and gardens.

Rooms for two are about 96€, those on the first floor are large and many have fireplaces. Other rooms are a little smaller but all are beautifully decorated and furnished. The cuisine is almost up to the standard of the château but priced more modestly, 126€ for demi-pension and 168€ for full pension per person, three days minimum.

Alyette de la Sablière will make you just as welcome here as in the château.

HILLION

22120 (Cd'A)
10 km E of St-Brieuc

Hillion sits on the east coast of a small bay which is a protected nature reserve so there are fields, woods, cliffs teeming with wildlife and an enormous beach.

Château de Bonabry (Cd'H) M
tel: 02 96 32 21 06
fax: same number but after 8.30 pm
closed: 1 Oct to 1 Apr
no credit cards

It has more the look of an old Brittany manor house rather than a château and this makes it appear very inviting. The outside has changed little in the past centuries, the chapel and the pigeon loft are the same too. Inside though, it has been elegantly restored by the Vicomte and Vicomtesse Louis du Fou de Kerdaniel, thus making it a very superior bed and breakfast.

Two suites both have a large salon/sitting room and a bedroom with a bath or shower, and TV available on request. Both are sumptuously appointed and decorated and are 80€ and 96€ respectively, breakfast included.

The host and hostess speak English and the family ambience is evident from the paintings, the trophies and other personal possessions as well as the numerous antiques.

HUELGOAT

29690 (Finistère)
24 km S of Morlaix

This is a pleasant inland resort by a quiet lake. The town is busy and cheerful with fishing and walks by the lake but cross the bridge over the outflow from the lake and you have an entirely different panorama.

Rocks piled everywhere, narrow footpaths, rushing streams and what some claim to be the prettiest forest in Brittany. This is King Arthur country and you are faced with signposts giving you a multiple choice of visiting the Virgin's Kitchen or the Devil's Grotto. You can make your walk as short or as long as you wish as you wander through leafy glades among conifers, oaks and beeches.

Huelgoat's name is '*An Uhelgoat*' in the Breton language and it is an excellent base for exploring the forest of Argoat. This is where King Arthur's treasure is buried (the best of luck if you want to try) but even if you don't find it, the unusual rock formations, the menhirs and the dolmens are worth seeing. You can also see the abandoned silver and lead mines that were worked from the 15th century. Hiking trails go all through this area and one easy and rewarding walk starts in the Place Aristide Briand in Huelgoat and goes past the lake. From there it is clearly marked.

The Moulin du Chaos, on the Argent River about a kilometre out of town to the east, has exhibits on the flora and fauna, the archaeology, and the geology of the Argoat. It is open every day except Monday in July and August from 1.30 pm to 6.30 pm. The Grotte du Diable is on the hiking trails and here the river goes underground. You can climb down a steep ladder and see the water foaming over the rocks.

Nobody can resist having a push at the heavy rock which sways when touched but has never yet toppled over. Look for the signs 'Roche Tremblante'.

Hôtel du Lac 🛏 ✗ S
> 9 rue du Général de Gaulle
> **tel:** 02 98 99 71 14
> **fax:** 02 98 99 70 91
> **closed:** Jan

A popular and always busy favourite stop for many years where the 15 rooms need some reviving but are reasonably priced at 40–48€, all with shower and TV. Breakfast is 6€ and meals 16–24€. Demi-pension is 52€ per person.

For a quick snack at lunchtime, the pizza at 6.5€ or the salad at 5€ are acceptable.

ÎLE TUDY

29980 (Finistère)
10 km SE of Pont l'Abbé

A narrow spit of land that juts out into the estuary of the Pont l'Abbé river, with a good view of all Loctudy's fishing boats opposite and of the Anse de Bénodet to the right. The *haute marée* is most impressive from this vantage point, when the spring tides flood the narrow winding alleys of the little village – with a magnificent beach.

This is a real fishing village, not an instant holiday resort, and is correspondingly picturesque. It tolerates the tourists in the summer, accepting that some of the residents gain their livelihood through them, but once the parking lot is empty, it settles back happily to the serious business of putting the world to rights in the bar.

Hôtel Moderne 🛏 ✗ S
> 9 place de la Cale
> **tel:** 02 98 56 43 34
> **restaurant closed:** mid-Nov to mid-Dec

A Logis de France in a splendid position overlooking the water.

Tables outside from which to observe all the fishermen coming and going. The locals drink in the bar and it's all very friendly and un-touristy. There are several other bars and a *crêperie* to choose from but the Moderne is the friendliest and liveliest.

Rooms with a shower cost 32€ and menus are from 12€.

JOSSELIN

56120 (Morbihan)
72 km E of Rennes
market: Sat

Here is a 'must' town to visit. At Josselin, you will see the finest example of medieval architecture in Brittany. Part castle, part fortress, this construction by Olivier de Clisson is best seen from the river which gives you a full view of the castle walls.

The original building is 12th century but was destroyed by an English army and rebuilt in the 14th century. Restoration was necessary after the Revolution.

During the War of Succession, the famous Combat du Trente (Battle of the Thirty) took place five kilometres from the castle where you will see a granite marker. This pitted in battle 30 French knights and 30 English knights.

The castle inside is, frankly, very disappointing. Only four rooms are open and they are crowded with uninteresting furnishings. It is open in July and August every day from 10 am–6 pm, from June to September every day 2 pm–6 pm and other months on Wednesdays, weekends and holidays 2 pm–6 pm. The stables contain an antique doll museum which requires separate admission.

The hill climbs up to the basilica of Notre Dame de Roncier. This means 'Our Lady of the Bramble' and is named after an incident in the 9th century when a peasant found a bramble bush which kept its leaves all year round. Inside it was a statue of the Virgin Mary and though the peasant took it away twice, each time it returned. A chapel was built on the spot and around it are several beautiful houses built in the 17th century. The chapel is the destination of a great *pardon* on the second Sunday in September.

Au Relais de l'Oust 🛏 S-M
route de Pontivy
tel: 02 97 75 63 06
fax: 02 97 22 37 39
closed: first two weeks of Jan

The 25 rooms are in a trim modern building with a chalet look. English is spoken and the comfortable, well-furnished rooms with television are 42–48€. Demi-pension is 39–42€.

Hôtel de France 🛏 ✗ M
6 place Notre Dame
tel: 02 97 22 23 06
fax: 02 97 22 35 78
closed: Sun eve and Mon o.o.s.; Jan

A small and simple hotel-restaurant, no frills but comfortable and reliable. The 25 rooms are 48–80€ and the cooking is equally simple and the quantities very generous.

Menus under 24€.

La Carrière (Cd'D) M
8 rue de la Carrière
tel: 02 97 22 22 62
closed: o.o.s.

M. and Mme. Bignon speak English and will make you very comfortable in this large and elegant house. The reception rooms are filled with antiques and the beautiful hall is exquisite with its gilt panelling. The six bedrooms are very charming and all have a shower. Four of the rooms have twin beds. Rooms are 56–64€ for two people with breakfast included. No meals are served but plenty of restaurants are in Josselin. It is located on the RN24.

LE JUCH

29100 (Finistère)
4 km SW of Douarnenez

LE JUCH

Kersantec (Cd'H) S
tel: 02 98 74 71 36
open: all year
no credit cards

An old white-painted farmhouse in the dairy-producing part of Brittany, Kersantec has been in the hands of the family of René and Yvette Renevot for generations. They live in a newer house, which has one upstairs and one downstairs double room, while in the farmhouse itself, a very comfortable apartment is usually booked for several days at a time. Each of the rooms has a private bath but a toilet is shared and they are 40€ with breakfast included.

It is just north of the D765 (look for the route Tar-ar) and only minutes from the coast.

JUGON-LES-LACS

22770 (Cd'A)
20 km W of Dinan
market: Fri am, Sun

Handy from the D176, Jugon-les-Lacs is well described as a 'City of Character'. It is a popular vacation spot for its architecture, as well as its rivers, woods and lakes that provide unlimited opportunities for hiking, fishing, cycling, sailing, canoeing, tennis and lots more.

Restaurant de l'Ecu ✗ S
25 place Martray
tel: 02 96 31 61 41
Closed: evenings from Nov to Mar except Fri and Sat
no credit cards

In a delightful old 17th-century house, this restaurant is a favourite with the locals and serves regional dishes cooked in traditional style. You can choose from the menus or *à la carte*. Either way, you can have a very tasty and satisfying meal for around 16€.

KERDRUC-EN-NÉVEZ

29920 (Finistère)
25 km W of Lorient

A picturesque old fishing port on the Atlantic coast.

Pen Ker Dagorn (Cd'H) S
chemin des Vieux-Fours
tel: 02 98 06 85 01
open: on demand only from Nov to May
no credit cards

This serene old house is close to the port and only 2 km from the beach. Two double rooms and two twin rooms, all with a bath and WC at 52€ for two people.

The wooden panelled walls furnish all the bedrooms which vary in style. Breakfast is included but a two-night stay minimum is required. The Brossier-Publier family are proud of the peaceful atmosphere in their house and its surrounding gardens.

LAMBALLE

22400 (Cd'A)
18 km SE of St-Brieuc
market: Thurs

An important livestock market town that really comes to life the second Sunday in July when they hold the Folklore Festival of the Ajoncs d'Or (the golden gorse).

La Tour d'Argent 🛏 ✗ S-M
2 rue du Dr Lavergne
tel: 02 96 31 01 37
fax: 02 96 31 37 59
restaurant closed: Sat o.o.s.

The hotel is located in a side street off the main square and away from the traffic noise. The 31 bedrooms are very comfortable and are 45–61€ for two people.

The restaurant is a short distance away down the hill in an ancient building. Through the cheerful bar is the smart dining room with menus at about 16€. Demi-pension is offered at 42–48€ per person.

Ferme de Malido (Cd'H) S
tel: 02 96 32 94 74
fax: 02 96 32 92 67
open all year
no credit cards

A completely renovated house among scores of farms yet only a few minutes from the sea. M. and Mme. Robert Legrand are welcoming hosts and speak English. The six bedrooms are simple but pleasing and comfortable. At 32–48€ for two people, they are attractively priced, especially as this includes breakfast. All rooms have a shower and one has a balcony. No restaurant but plenty nearby, as well as tennis courts, a golf course, fishing and a swimming pool.

It is just out of Lamballe – take the D791 north to St-Alban then the Ferme de Malido is just 2 km along the road towards St-Brieuc.

LAMPAUL-GUIMILIAU
29230 (Finistère)
4 km S of Landiviseau

This small village has a church which astonishes most visitors with the beauty and intricacy of its carvings. This is one of the most remarkable of the many *enclos paroissiaux*, parish closes, in Brittany.

De l'Enclos ⊨ ✗ S
tel: 02 98 68 77 08
fax: 02 98 68 61 06
closed: Fri pm, Sun pm, Sat lunch o.o.s.

A modern place with 36 comfortable rooms at 40–50€. The restaurant does a fine job and is reasonably priced at around 16€. Crab is usually one of the featured shellfish on the menu.

LAMPAUL-PLOUHARZEL

29229 (Finistère)
28 km S of Roscoff

This small village has one of the best fish restaurants in the area.

Auberge du Krugel ✕
tel: 02 98 89 35 89
open: all year
no credit cards

They have a way with fish that brings diners from all around. The salmon is particularly to be recommended. A little pricey but well worth it, 16–40€.

LANCIEUX

22770 (Cd'A)
7 km W of Dinard

A small village on the north coast looking across the water at the plage du Roureret. An excellent beach gets protection at both ends from rocks. It runs into St-Briac-sur-Mer.

Les Hortensias (Cd'H) S
40 rue du Moulin
tel: 02 96 86 31 15
open: all year
no credit cards

Eric and Jacqueline Cosson (who speak English) offer three rooms with a bath or shower at the modest price of 48€ for two people. The price reduces the longer you stay. All the rooms are prettily decorated and very comfortable. There are pieces of antique furniture and guests all agree that the breakfasts are exceptionally good (and included in the price).

LANDÉDA

29214 (Finistère)
28 km N of Brest

On Brittany's headland, the extreme northwest coast is rocky but low to the water. *Abers*, small estuaries, dot the coastline and at Landéda is Aber Wrac'h, one of the larger of these. It's popular with sailors but pleasingly desolate otherwise and a great spot for this lonely hotel.

Baie des Anges M
350 route des Anges
Port de l'Aber Wrac'h
tel: 02 98 04 90 04
fax: 02 98 04 92 27
closed: Jan

A wonderful place to get away from it all and enjoy the sea and the wind. The 18 rooms and 2 suites are 45–116€ so there are plenty of rooms at the lower end. All have been entirely renovated and all are large. Swimming, sailing, cliff walks, tennis, canoes and kayaks offer lots of outdoor exercise. Several restaurants nearby, even though the Baie des Anges is a solitary hotel.

LANDERNEAU

29800 (Finistère)
20 km E of Brest
market: Tues, Sat

The picturesque Rohan Bridge crosses the Elorn River here, one of the few bridges left in Europe on which occupied houses still stand. Every year, Landerneau holds the Kann al Loar cultural festival in this wonderful setting.

In the town, the church dedicated to St-Thomas of Canterbury is a reminder of the days when links with England were strong. The Tuesday market draws crowds and the *crêpes* and farmhouse cheeses are highly regarded. On the quai de Cornouaille, visit the Comptoir des Produits Bretons for authentic Brittany goods from music cassettes and books to cider, food and crafts. This is a good place to buy gifts and souvenirs that are not too touristy. Out of town, the Manoir de Keranden is open to the public and there are tours.

Le Clos du Pontic 🛏 ✗ M
rue du Pontic
tel: 02 98 21 50 91
fax: 02 98 21 34 33
restaurant closed: Sat lunch, Sun

It's a short walk up the hill from the centre of Landerneau and sits in tranquillity amid a shady garden. The 32 bedrooms are very well equipped, have a bath and TV and are in a modern building. Prices are 42–55€. The restaurant is charming and the chef tries hard to be different. Meals are 15–39€.

LANDIVISIAU

29400 (Finistère)
20 km NE of Brest

The city used to be the trading centre for horses. It is a convenient starting point for tours of the region, which contains many of the finest *enclos paroissiaux* – the parish closes that contain a church, a gated entrance, a calvary, an ossuary and a cemetery.

Before you take such a tour, however, see St-Thiviseau Church with its 16th-century porch and carved stone decoration. Its tower has a main spire and four smaller ones around it. Near it is the Chapelle de Ste-Anne, beautifully decorated and with a 15th-century fountain adjoining. The water from it is still piped to communal washing tubs!

Restaurant Le Foch ✗ S
94 avenue Foch
tel: 02 98 68 02 00
closed: Fri eve, Sat lunch, Sun eve o.o.s.
no credit cards

Unbeatable value for money in a simple but always busy place. Two starters, a main course, salad, cheese, coffee, dessert and a carafe of wine – all for 10€! In the adjoining restaurant, menus at 13€ and

16€ are available if you feel really hungry or want a wider choice.

Hôtel de l'Avenue 🛏 ✕ S
16 avenue de Coat Meur
tel: 02 98 68 11 67
fax: 02 98 68 96 62
closed: last week Sept to mid-Oct, Mon lunch Oct to end April

Don't be put off by the conventional name – the cooking is really authentic Breton. Seafood, of course, but also specialities such as tripe and on certain days, the ancient dish of '*kig ha fars*'.

M. Salmas keeps the prices down to 12–24€ which is very reasonable for the quantity and quality. (I thought you might ask ... '*kig ha fars*' is beef, pork and sausage with garlic, cauliflower, carrots, turnips and leeks. It is not a stew, but all are served together with buckwheat crumbles.)

LANDRÉVARZEC

29510 (Finistère)
11 km N of Quimper

Auberge de Quilinen ✕ S
Lieu-dit Quilinen
tel: 02 98 57 93 63
fax: 02 98 57 54 99
closed: Sun eve, Mon, Tues eve, Wed eve

This small restaurant has a devoted following and is always full. M. and Mme. Dufosse make sure you dine well on seafood and the meals vary according to the catch so could not be fresher. Menus range from 15–29€.

LANDUDEC

29710 (Finistère)
13 km W of Quimper

Mainly visited for its fine château – where you can stay.

Château de Guilguiffin (Cd'H) M-L
tel: 02 98 91 52 11
fax: 02 98 91 52 52
website: www.guilguiffin.com
open: only on demand from Nov to 1 Apr

You won't see many more striking châteaux than this. The spectacular columns, the imposing façade and the magnificent gardens make the building a perfect example of 18th-century architectural splendour.

The four rooms and two suites have great bathrooms and TV, and are all very tastefully decorated. The rooms are 104–160€ and the suites, which can accommodate three or four people, 176–208€. Breakfast is included.

Philippe Davy is a warm host, speaks English and is very proud of his château, as he should be. The public rooms are wood panelled and equally beautiful. In the dining room, meals are 16–48€.

The château is just on the south side of the D784 and about 10 km west of Quimper.

LANESTER

56600 (Morbihan)
between Lorient and Hennebont
market: Tues

Lanester occupies the peninsula between the two towns, which means that it is bordered on one side by the Blavet River and on the other by the Scorff River. It must be the busiest town in Brittany — there's so much going on all the time. Listen to this line-up ...

In April, a ten-day childhood festival has shows and displays, discussions and lectures. Also in April is the springtime festival with parades in traditional costumes.

The annual cycle race between Lanester and Quiberon takes place in early May. In late May and a few days at the beginning of June is a peculiar theatrical event called *Pleuropodia*. Each year, there is a different theme. Also in May and June (on dates that vary from year to year) are painting and sculpture exhibitions.

For ten days at the end of June and into July is the amateur theatre festival. This is run by the 'Fontaine de Chevaux', an association that propagates and encourages amateur theatre and it

LANESTER

is held in Kerhervy, at a place known as the Graveyard of Boats. In mid-June, the annual music festival is held.

Bastille Day, 14 July, comes in for its share of jollities with parades and fireworks. In November comes the *Festival Crock Chanson* with shows and concerts.

Hôtel Kerous 🛏 S
74 avenue Ambrose Croizat
tel & fax: 02 97 76 02 50
open: all year

In one of the 20 rooms you can rest up after all that excitement. Simple is the word for them — not quite spartan but they have TV and are a meagre 32€. They speak English here too.

Hôtel Le Bougainville 🛏 ✗ S
4 rue Jean Jaurès
tel: 02 97 76 15 86
fax: 02 97 81 15 02
open: all year
restaurant closed: Fri eve, Sat, Sun o.o.s.

Only 11 rooms and they are very popular at a price of 29–44€. All have TV and there is a restaurant which serves good Breton food. Demi-pension at 29–44€ is a good bet.

LANNILIS

29870 (Finistère)
22 km N of Brest

It dominates a small peninsula between two *abers*, the estuaries that dot the Brittany coast. The Château de Kerouartz is a fine sight but it is not yet open to the public. Lannilis is famous for its group specializing in Breton dancing.

Auberge des Abers ✗ M
5 place Général Leclerc
tel: 02 98 04 00 29
closed: late Sept to early Oct, Sun eve, Mon, Tues, and lunches except Sun

The prices are a little elevated but there is no denying that the food is excellent and so is the presentation. Seafood is dominant but lots of other choices too. Most diners are satisfied with the 24€ menu but other and more elaborate ones go up to 56€.

LANNION

22300 (Cd'A)
39 km NE of Morlaix
market: Thurs

The Thursday market takes over the district and it may be worth timing a visit to Lannion in order to take it in. Around the Place Général Leclerc are lots of narrow old streets and old houses but the main square is known as Place du Marchallac'h and is a little further up the hill.

The church of Brélévenez, built by the Knights Templar, is 12th century and has some attractive features but, otherwise, the best sights are out of town. The Chapelle de Kerfons above the Leguer Valley is an old Breton chapel with a lot of carved detail. The Château de Tonquédec is a splendid medieval castle from the 13th century and recent restoration work makes it possible for you to wander round inside the walls and be amazed. The Château de Rosambo and the Château de Kergrist are close too and represent work from the 16th to the 18th century.

Manoir de Kerguéréon (Cd'H) M
tel: 02 96 38 91 46
closed: All Saints to Easter (open only on demand)
no credit cards

An authentic Brittany manor house with a large central tower and arched doorways. It won first prize in a contest for the best restoration of an old house. It has been maintained in beautiful condition by M. and Mme. Gerard de Bellefon and converted into a bed and breakfast. The inside is just as charming as the outside.

The two bedrooms both have a bath and WC, are impeccably furnished, and are priced at 88€ for two people, with breakfast from home-made ingredients included. English is spoken and the welcome and service are warm and genuine.

LANNION

Manoir de Crec'h-Goulifern 🛏 M
tel: 02 96 47 26 17
fax: 02 96 47 28 00
open all year
no credit cards

This manor house was formerly an 18th-century farm and has been renovated with charm and care. It is just outside Lannion to the north-west.

The eight rooms have a bath or shower and all are in rural style, a little small but well appointed, 48–72€ for two people with breakfast included using homemade pastries. You can play tennis in between visits to the local sights. Mme. Droniou is a perfect hostess.

☆ La Ville Blanche ✗ M
route Lannion-Tréguier
tel: 02 96 37 04 28
fax: 02 96 46 57 82
website: www.la-ville-blanche.com
closed: 10 Dec to 1 Feb, Mon, Wed eve and Sun eve o.o.s. except Jul, Aug

For many years, a local favourite and increasingly known to visitors, La Ville Blanche has emerged to become one of the top restaurants on the Pink Granite Coast. The Jaguin brothers get their lobsters from M. Crocq in Trégastel and there are none finer. Naturally, these figure prominently on the menu and you can also expect to find fish dishes cooked in cider in Breton style. Menus at 20€, 32€ and 42€.

LARMOR-BADEN

56870 (Morbihan)
12 km W of Vannes

An exceptional spot on the coast jutting out into the Gulf of Morbihan with its scores of small islands. From here, boats go out to many of these – Les Vedettes Blanches Armor runs a fleet of particularly smart white boats all year round.

An exceptional spot demands an exceptional hotel and here is one ...

Kerdevan (Cd'H)
tel: 02 97 57 05 85
fax: 02 97 57 25 02
open: all year
no credit cards

The large white villa has opened quite recently but is already a hit with tourists from Britain, Germany and Spain. Marie-Claude Hecker speaks all of these languages (and even a little Italian) and is a gracious hostess.

Kerdevan's location, comfort, facilities and price are an unbeatable combination. Of the four bedrooms, three are on the ground floor on a terrace looking out to sea. The fourth room leads out to the gardens and in turn to the beach. All rooms have a bath and are 40–56€ for two people.

LARMOR-PLAGE

56100 Lorient (Morbihan)
5 km S of Lorient

An unpretentious village with a pleasant beach that looks across at Port Louis, once a powerful fortress. In the high season, it is busy with visitors and sailors.

Villa des Camellias (Cd'H) S
9 rue des Roseau
tel: 02 97 65 50 67
open: all year
no credit cards

This is one of those *chambres d'hôtes* that may be difficult to get into because it has a faithful clientele that comes every year. That isn't helpful if you need somewhere to sleep, but it tells you that the attractions of the villa are well known and appreciated.

So now that you have been advised to reserve well in advance, you need to know that M. and Mme. Allano run a very efficient, cosy and comfortable place. Three bedrooms are upstairs and a fourth (somewhat smaller) is downstairs. All are 39–44€ including breakfast.

LE LATZ

56470 La Trinite-sur-Mer (Morbihan)
6 km NE of Carnac

Right there amid the dolmens and the menhirs is Le Latz with a very convenient bed and breakfast.

La Maison du Latz (Cd'H) S
tel: 02 97 55 80 91
open: all year
no credit cards

What a spot! The finest location for prehistoric stones in the world and a river running into the ocean. That's where La Maison du Latz is and where Christian and Nicole Le Rouzic will welcome you and do everything to make you feel at home.

Two twin rooms, one double and one suite for three or four people are comfortable and peaceful and all have bathrooms. They are 45–52€ for two including breakfast which is served in the glassed-in verandah with great views. An evening meal of excellent seafood is available if you reserve the day before – 16€ but wine not included.

LESCONIL

29730 (Finistère)
9 km S of Pont l'Abbé

Grand Hôtel des Dunes 🛏 S
17 rue Laënnec
tel: 02 98 87 83 03
fax: 02 98 82 23 44
closed: mid-Oct to end March
no credit cards

Great views looking out over a huge sand dune at the sea. All the rooms have been refurbished and are large and well equipped, most of them with a view so ask when you reserve. All rooms are 52€ for two people.

LESNEVEN

29260(Finistère)
26 km N of Brest

Lesneven is an important market town and the capital of the county of Léon. Its age can be seen in the 17th-century granite houses and its history can be followed in the Museum du Léon which is in what used to be the Ursuline Convent.

Le Week End ⨌ ✕ S-M
Pont-du-Chatel
tel: 02 98 25 40 57
fax: 02 98 25 46 92
open: all year
restaurant closed: Sun, Mon

Extraordinarily good value, Le Week End is on the riverbank and has 13 rooms, all quiet and comfortable and nicely appointed are 34–53€. Regional cooking makes use of local ingredients and the fish is always fresh. Demi-pension is 36–40€.

LEZARDRIEUX

22740(Cd'A)
5 km W of Paimpol

It is located where the bridge crosses the wide estuary of River Trieux by means of the east-west D786.

Relais Brenner ⨌ ✕ M-L
6 rue Saint Julien
tel: 02 96 22 29 95
fax: 02 96 22 22 72
closed: 1 Nov to 1 Apr

A great location here, with lawns sloping down to the river. There are now 16 rooms (there used to be twice as many) and half a dozen very large rooms that can be called suites. The price range of 80–288€ gives you a wide choice, with plenty of good-sized rooms though at the lower end. The public rooms too are large and welcoming. Breakfast is 12€.

The cuisine is of a high standard and seafood is dominant though plenty of other dishes are there too. Lunches are 24€ and dinners 40–72€.

LOCQUELTAS

56390 Grandchamp (Morbihan)
12 km N of Vannes

Chaumière de Kerisac (Cd'H) S
tel: 02 97 66 60 13
closed: Feb
no credit cards

From Vannes, you drive north on the D767. Past Locqueltas, turn left and you will have no trouble finding the Chaumière, a long, low thatched-roof building. The dining room/salon is filled with souvenirs and mementoes of M. and Mme. Cheilletz-Maignan's years in the Far East and Africa.

The stone fireplace, the low wooden-beamed ceilings and the stone stairway are typical features of this old house. There are three bedrooms, two of them upstairs and the third in a separate building out of doors. All are furnished with antiques and are kept filled with fresh flowers. The price for two people is 61€, breakfast included. The Cheilletz-Maignan's daughter speaks very good English and the reception is cool but efficient.

LOCQUIREC

29241 (Finistère)
22 km NE of Morlaix

A small fishing port and a popular if rather quiet resort town, Locquirec occupies a fine position on the Corniche de l'Armorique and has a renowned church, dedicated by the Knights of Malta, with a bell tower adjoining an elegant turret. Any excursion from here usually heads west along the coast to St-Jean-du-Doigt. This village has in its church a finger of St-John the Baptist, believed to have miraculous curative powers.

Grand Hôtel des Bains 🛏 ✘ M
15 bis, rue de l'Église
tel: 02 98 67 41 02
fax: 02 98 67 44 60
hotel closed: Jan
restaurant closed: lunchtimes

Grandiose hotels like the Grand do not usually find their way into these pages (despite their name). This imposing hundred-year-old building has just been renovated and redecorated and the locals say it looks better than it ever did. A large covered and heated swimming pool has been added too.

It is a four-storey structure with all the bedrooms looking out to sea, mostly from balconies. It was used in the classic French film, *L'Hôtel de la Plage*, because of its exceptionally beautiful location and it is surrounded by carefully tended gardens. Further facilities include sauna and massage.

The 36 rooms vary in size and the pastel colours vary too. All have a bath and TV. Demi-pension is only 60–88€ for two or 76–104€ per person on a three-day minimum.

The restaurant has a menu at 23€, with *à la carte* specialties, and the main theme being seafood. The price is not unreasonable for the quality offered here.

LOCRONAN

29186 (Finistère)
17 km NW of Quimper
market: first Tues

A very picturesque town and named after St-Ronan, the 9th-century Irish monk, Locronan is one of the top candidates for 'the prettiest village in Brittany'. It is so picturesque with its cobbled streets and old houses that it now attracts enough visitors to border on the 'touristy'. Roman Polanski liked it enough to use it to film his *Tess of the d'Urbervilles*, believing it to be more like Wessex than any place in England.

The canvas industry used to be the mainstay of the town and nearly everyone worked in it. The textile tradition has been revived recently and craft centres are scattered throughout the

LOCRONAN

town where you can see people weaving and knitting. Quimper Faience at 2 rue du Prieuré is a boutique with a wonderful selection of Brittany linens for sale. On the place de l'Église is the shop of Monsieur Le Guillou with magnificent confections and candies. If you have not yet tasted the Brittany speciality, *Kouign-Amann*, this is the place to do it.

The imposing church on the square is named after St-Ronan. Before you go in, you will see the calvary and inside don't miss the ten medaillons around the pulpit that tell the story of St-Ronan and his travels.

On the second – sometimes the third – Sunday in August is the *Petite Troménie*, a procession that follows the route of the saint. Every six years, this becomes the *Grande Troménie* that stops at 44 places during the long procession, ending at a block of granite known as St-Ronan's Chair and declared by local legend to be the boat in which the saint sailed from Ireland to Armorica.

☆ Manoir de Moëllien ⊨ ✗ M
tel: 02 98 92 50 40
fax: 02 98 92 55 21
closed: 4 Nov to 20 Mar
restaurant closed: lunch Tues, Wed, Thur Mar to mid-Jun, and Tues lunch, Wed all day, Thur lunch Sept to Nov

This grey stone 17th-century manor house is 3 km to the northwest of Locronan on the C10. It is named after Thérèse de Moëllien who was one of Châteaubriand's lovers. The stone gateway and the long drive are impressive.

The 18 bedrooms are comfortable and quiet, all with a bath or shower and TV and very reasonable at 58€ for two people plus 8€ per person for breakfast. The dining room with its beams and log fire is attractive and the meals are very enjoyable and 20–48€, though demi-pension may be preferred at 60–92€. Their *rognons de veau au grain de moutarde* is locally renowned. In good weather, meals are served in the lovely gardens.

Le Prieuré ⊨ ✗ S
rue du Prieuré
tel: 02 98 91 70 89
fax: 02 98 91 77 60
closed: mid-Dec to mid-Mar

An attractive old granite building on the edge of the village. The 14 country-style rooms have a bath or shower and TV and are a good deal at 45–56€ and 6.5€ for breakfast. Most are in the main building, some in an annexe. There is a light meal special at 12€ and menus are 12–40€.

Au Coin du Feu ✗ S
rue du Prieuré
tel: 02 98 51 82 44
closed: evenings Sun, Tues, Wed

You can eat out on the verandah or indoors but you know from the name that this is a place that specializes in grills. Various kinds of fish are grilled, but the sautéed langoustines in curry sauce is different and so is the *lotte à l'Armoricaine*. The price range for such good food is very modest – 11–21€ – and Mme. Hardonnière-Nedelec packs them in.

LOGUIVY DE LA MER

22620 Ploubazlanec (Cd'A)
5 km N of Paimpol

One of the many attractive fishing ports in Brittany. It's on the Trieux River and has fine views out to sea.

Au Grand Large ✗ M
tel: 02 96 20 90 18
fax: 02 96 20 87 10
closed: Mon o.o.s. and all Jan

A modern building next to the old port. Rooms are large and well furnished and have a bath and TV. The view is great from the large windows in all of the six rooms, which are 56–64€. The restaurant is famous for its *plateaux de fruits de la mer* which are a surprisingly reasonable 16–32€.

LOMENER

56270 (Morbihan)
3 km S of Ploemeur

This village, which is a popular resort for the residents of Lorient, is on the rocky coast of Morbihan, with its small sandy beaches and rocky coves. The Île-de-Groix can be clearly seen.

Le Vivier 🛏 ✗ S
   9 rue Beg er Vir
   tel: 02 97 82 99 60
   fax: 02 97 82 88 89
   closed: Sun eve, 25 Dec to 10 Jan

A modern hotel built into the sea wall and making the most of the views. The rooms are basic and have only showers. They cost 48–58€. The cooking is reliable Breton and mostly seafood, with menus starting at 16€.

LORIENT

56100 (Morbihan)
58 km W of Vannes

By no means a tourist town, Lorient was established as a naval base and dockyard by Napoleon. This prominence grew and resulted in its being selected as the main base for the U-boat hunter-killer packs in World War II that preyed on Atlantic shipping. After being heavily bombed throughout the earlier years of the war, the German forces held out there after the Allied forces had occupied most of Brittany and the ensuing fighting destroyed what was left of the town.

Reconstruction has brought the population up to about 60,000 but it has little to offer the visitor – except for ten days at the beginning of August when a Celtic celebration is held. 5,000 musicians, dancers, singers and writers and over a quarter of a million people swarm into the city which already has a large student residence.

The Maison de Mer on quai de Rohan has an information centre showing the history of the town and its maritime involvement.

The Musée de la Compagnie des Indes, in a 17th-century citadel in the Port Louis area southeast of Lorient, gives the history of the French East India Company and its prosperous trade with the Orient (hence the name of the town). It is open every day except Tuesday from 10 am to 7 pm.

Hôtel Victor Hugo ⊨ ✕ S
36 rue Lazare-Carnot
tel: 02 97 64 26 54
fax: 02 97 64 24 87
restaurant closed: Sun, Mon lunch

Comfortable rooms with shower and TV are 37€ but a few double rooms with shared bath facilities go for 26€. Despite this frugality, the restaurant is very good and meals are 14–32€.

Hôtel d'Arvor ⊨ ✕ S
104 rue Lazare-Carnot
tel: 02 97 21 07 55
open: all year
restaurant closed: Sun
no credit cards

A small, friendly place that has rooms with a shower – and even some antique pieces of furniture – for 24€. Its restaurant is very good and has menus for 14€ and 20€.

L'Amphitryon ✕ M
127 rue du Colonel Müller
tel: 02 97 83 34 04
fax: 02 97 37 25 02
closed: early Jan, early May, early Sept; Sun, Mon

Recently completely renovated, L'Amphitryon, with Jean-Paul Abadie's personal and precise cooking, has become a Mecca for diners in the area. He brings his native style of cooking from the Pyrenees and blends it with Breton. Fish naturally dominates. Menus are 20€, 26€, 42€ and 56€.

LORIENT

The Royal Couscous ✗ S
65 rue Lazare-Carnot
tel: 02 97 64 45 78
open: all year
no credit cards

North African specialities and a good meal for under 16€. The tagines are especially good for upwards of 8€.

LOUANNEC

22700 Perros-Guirec (Cd'A)
4 km E of Perros-Guirec
market: Fri

On the northern coast, Louannec is a popular resort. You can take the boat trip out to the Sept Îles and walk along the cliffs by the old coastguard trails.

Le Colombier (Cd'H) S
8 Coat Gourhaut
tel: 02 96 23 29 30
closed: Sept to Mar
no credit cards

Here is a very economical but good-quality place for a short stay only minutes from the northern coast. It is a remodelled farmhouse in the midst of farming country and M. and Mme. Fajolles run a fine operation and speak English. The four rooms are bright and comfortable and each is decorated in a different colour. The price for two people is 37–45€ and breakfast is included. The large aquarium in the breakfast room is an unusual touch. Beside the sitting room is a well-stocked library and though there is no restaurant, plenty are nearby.

LOUARGAT

22540 (Cd'A)
14 km W of Guingamp

Louargat is the first village west along the N12 from Guingamp and conveniently located for exploring the forests to the south of the N12.

Manoir du Cleuziou 🛏 ✕ M
Le Cleuziou
tel: 02 96 43 14 90
fax: 02 96 43 52 59
closed: Jan, Feb
restaurant: open weekend only; o.o.s. lunch only

Remarkably good value here at this 15th-century manor house where the magnificent exterior is matched by the authentically medieval interior. In front, the neatly trimmed hedges indicate the care and attention extended throughout.

The great old stone fireplaces, the hanging tapestries and the carved wooden doors take you back in time and though the 28 bedrooms are not large, they are pleasant and attractive. They are 52–77€ for two people and it is worth spending the bit more on the higher-priced rooms. Breakfast is an additional 6.5€ and you may want to consider the good deal offered on the demi-pension plan at 54€ per person.

The restaurant offers menus at 15–36€ and chef Joseph Traon is getting a lot of compliments. The Costan family have put a bar in what was the old wine cellar. A swimming pool, tennis facilities at a minimal extra charge, billiards, a large lounge are all there and the mountains, the lakes and a golf course are all close.

LOUDÉAC

22600 (Cd'A)
25 km S of St-Brieuc
market: Sat.

Useful to the traveller for its handy location at the junction of the St-Brieuc-Vannes road and the Rennes-Morlaix road.

Les Voyageurs 🛏 ✕ S
10 rue de Cadélac
tel: 02 96 28 00 47
fax: 02 96 28 22 30
restaurant closed: Sat

The renovation of the 28 rooms, five years ago, has increased the popularity of this quiet and comfortable hotel. Rooms are 37–53€.

It is the restaurant that is the prime attraction though. The menu at 12€ is extraordinarily good and the 28€ menu includes such delicacies as home-made duck pâté and scallops provençale. Seafood and grills are the specialties but there is a fine selection of other dishes too.

MALESTROIT

56140 (Morbihan)
25 km NE of Vannes

This is a historic town (it celebrated its millennium recently) but sadly, it has not worn very well. The Church of St-Gilles is in the centre of town and was built in an unusual reddish stone in the 12th century. The pulpit is a fine example of carving and the stained-glass windows are noteworthy.

Le Canotier ✗ S-M
11 bis, place du Docteur Queinnec
tel: 02 97 75 08 69
fax: 02 97 75 13 03
closed: Sun eve and Mon

Very popular locally this restaurant is on split levels. The lunch menu is a mere 9€ and there are others at 12–32€. Most are fish dishes and include a seafood platter. Local products are used.

MELRAND

56310 (Morbihan)
16 km SW of Pontivy

One of the most unusual calvaries in Morbihan is here, decorated in gold and with a shaft ornamented with the heads of the 12 apostles.

Melrand, on the northern edge of the Carnac area of prehistoric stones, has its own share of them, but the big attraction is the Ferme Archéologique. The site dates from AD 1,000 and it has been excavated and rebuilt so that you can see it almost exactly as it was then. It is complete with thatched-roof houses, a garden of medieval herbs and lots of sheep – and even the smell of cow-dung has not been forgotten. It is open from June to August 10 am–7 pm and from September to May 11 am–5 pm.

La Tourelle ⊟ ✗ S
Place de l'Église
tel: 02 97 39 51 13
closed: one week in Sept
no credit cards

This friendly old village house has been turned into a very simple but comfortable wayside inn. The rooms are 21–24€ and the menus are 8–21€ and both are excellent value.

MOËLAN-SUR-MER

29350 (Finistère)
10 km SW of Quimperlé

Les Moulins des Ducs ⊟ ✗ M
route des Moulins
tel: 02 98 96 52 52
fax: 02 98 96 52 53
closed: mid-Dec to 1 Mar

The converted windmill theme is repeated here, though the 27 rooms are located in cottages of two storeys spread throughout the park-like grounds with beautiful flower-filled gardens. In the main building, there is a swimming pool and sauna. Hosts (and new owners) Thierry Quilfen and Angel Divovic will tend to your every need.

The rooms all have a bath or shower, TV and minibar and are 77–144€ plus 8€ for breakfast. The cooking is of an exceptionally high standard and meals are 24–56€. The dining room looks out at the turning water wheel of the mill which dates from the 16th century.

MOËLAN-SUR-MER

Manoir de Kertalg 🛏 M-L
route de Riec-sur-Bélon
tel: 02 98 39 77 77
fax: 02 98 39 72 07
closed: 11 Nov to Apr

A very romantic old house, nestling among the trees in its own substantial grounds, no restaurant but plenty of them only ten minutes away. Nine spacious and nicely furnished rooms are 88–176€ and there is a suite that accommodates four people.

Le Puit Gourmand ✕ S-M
13 rue Pont ar Laër
tel: 02 98 39 65 70
closed: Tues eve, Wed

The speciality of the house is a *Croustillant de Sarrasin aux Langoustines et Au Crabe* (langoustines and crab under a crispy buckwheat crust). Eels from Baye (claimed to be the best) are cooked in honey and lots of other dishes are just as different. Menus go from 9–37€ and M. and Mme. Peron make sure that you can't go wrong at either end of the range.

MOLAC

56230 (Morbihan)
25 km E of Vannes

À la Bonne Table 🛏 ✕ S
3 place de l'Église
tel: 02 97 45 71 88
fax: 02 97 45 75 26
closed: Sun eve, Fri eve o.o.s.

It was built in 1683 on the village square and this old coaching house is as inexpensive as you will find – only 18€ for a simple room or 24€ for one with a shower. All are clean and simply furnished but with good beds.

Food is more important here though it is just as inexpensive. The menu of the day is 10€ and other meals 16–29€. The first Tuesday of each month is Caribbean Day with dishes of that region and every

Thursday is Couscous Day. The atmosphere is happy and animated and the emphasis is on good food, well cooked and served.

MORLAIX

29600 (Finistère)
55 km NE of Brest
market: Sat

The city dates from the days of Roman Gaul. The Celts from Armorica built a fortress here and called it 'Mons Relaxus' which even us non-Latin scholars can translate as 'Mount of Rest'.

Its situation, at the end of a steep-sided valley, where two rivers, the Queffleuth and the Jarlot meet, made it a perfect place for a major port. Consequently, invasions by the Kings of France, the Dukes of Brittany and the Kings of England made it a strongly contended location.

Today, it does not have a great deal to offer the visitor but the same characteristics that attracted the invaders still prevail for the tourist and so Morlaix is an excellent base for trips elsewhere along that stretch of the northern coast.

If the town does not have a plethora of tourist sights though, it is pleasing with its boutiques, pretty Breton houses, lots of cosy cafés and flower-filled windowsills.

A peculiarity is the large number of Irish pubs. The Bar Ty Coz on Venelle au Beurre is one of the best.

The Maison de la Duchesse Anne on the rue du Mur is 16th century and is open 10 am–12 pm and 2 pm–6 pm. It is one of the many 'lantern houses' in Brittany – so-called because their design was such that a single lantern hanging from the very high ceiling would light the whole building. Other notable houses of the period are further along the rue du Mur and on the nearby Grande Rue and rue Ange-de-Guernisac.

The Musée des Jacobins has mementoes from homes in Morlaix that are no longer standing. It is in the Église des Jacobins which was built from 1238 to 1250. Its exhibits include displays of Breton life and there are some fine paintings of the last two centuries. It is open all year but times vary according to the season.

La Maison des Vins on the place Viarmes is worth a stop too. They have not only a wide selection of wines of all types and at all prices but *chouchen*, a Brittany liqueur with honey and fruits but the whisky of Brittany and lots of ciders, most of them hard.

In July and August, there is an 'Art on the Streets' festival every Wednesday night with clowns, mimes, singers and dancers. On the place de la Madeleine, La Brasserie des Deux Rivières is a brewery that brews an all-natural beer marketed as Coreff. Tours are free (Monday, Tuesday and Wednesday at 10.30 am, 2 pm and 3.30 pm) and tasting is on the house so you may want to time this for when you are thirsty after one of the self-guided walking tours that take you all around the town or around the port.

Hôtel Fontaine ⊨ ✗ S
ZA la Boissière, route Lannion
tel: 02 98 62 09 55
fax: 02 98 63 82 51
closed: 15 Dec to 10 Jan

It's about 3 km out of town but worth the short journey as Morlaix itself is not renowned for its accommodation. The 35 rooms are small but comfortable and priced at 37–42€. Meals are sound Brittany fare and run from 10€ to 26€.

Hôtel-Restaurant des Halles ⊨ ✗ S
23 rue du Mur
tel: 02 98 88 03 86
fax: 02 98 63 47 96
closed: last week of Dec
no credit cards

If you're really on a tight budget, this is unbeatable value. The 14 rooms all have a TV and are only 30€ with a bath (some cheaper rooms without private bath). Meals are 7–13€ but, though simple, are satisfying.

Crêperie Ar Bilig ✗ S
6 rue au Fil
tel: 02 98 88 50 51
closed: Sun, Mon
no credit cards

Possibly the best *crêpes* in town – and that's saying something in a town with a lot of *crêperies*. *Galettes* too and you can eat for 8€.

NÉVEZ

29920 (Finistère)
12 km E of Concarneau

Névez is renowned as the place chosen by Paul Gauguin when he left Paris and was contemplating going to the South Pacific.

Chez Gourlaouen (C. d'H) S
near Port Manech
tel: 02 98 06 83 82
open: all year
no credit cards

Dating from 1730, this brown stone farmhouse is just 300 metres from the sea. The six rooms are not large but are very nicely furnished and all have a shower. At 42€ including breakfast, these are keenly sought after.

The breakfast room has a low, beamed ceiling, an old stone hearth and lots of antiques.

NOYAL-SUR-VILAINE

35530 (Î-et-V)
12 km E of Rennes
market: Tues

Les Forges ⊨ ✗ S-M
22 avenue du Général de Gaulle
tel: 02 99 00 51 08
fax: 02 99 00 62 02
closed: Christmas eve

A modern building with 11 quite adequate rooms at 48–61€ plus 7€ for breakfast. The restaurant is popular and is mainly seafood, some dishes with a Breton touch. Meals are 16-26€.

PAIMPOL

22500 (Cd'A)
45 km NW of St-Brieuc
market: Tues

The fine harbour used to be full of fishing boats and a hundred or so years ago, the fishermen of the town would go off for six months at a time. Today, it is something of ghost port but reminders of those times are offered in the middle of July with the Fêtes of Newfoundland and Iceland, as these were the two principal fishing grounds for Paimpol's fishermen.

To the east are several beaches. Plage de la Tossen is the largest and most frequented. The biggest attraction locally is the Abbaye de Beauport. It is south of the town centre and about a half-hour walk. It is the oldest abbey on the Atlantic coast, dating from 1220. You can go through the ruins and identify the monks' living quarters and other areas. It is open 10 am–12 pm and 2 pm–5 pm all year round.

The 15th-century Château de la Roche-Jagu ought to be more of a tourist attraction than it is. The building is in good shape but somehow does not have the fascination of many castles. It is open every day 10.30 am–12.30 pm and 2 pm–6 pm all year round, but 10 am–7 pm in July and August. What it does have though is spectacular views of Le Trieux River, the viaduct and the river valleys.

Le Repaire de Kerroc'h ⊨ ✕ M

29 quai Morand
tel: 02 96 20 50 13
open: all year

An 18th-century stone house that has been expertly restored. The 13 rooms all have a bath, TV and minibar and are very nicely furnished, priced at 47–77€.

The new chef, Louis le Roy, is making a name for himself and already has one star. He will probably add a second. Meals are dominantly seafood and, for the quality, very reasonably priced at 18–58€.

Vieille Tour ⊠ M
> 13 rue de l'Église
> **tel:** 02 96 20 83 18
> **closed:** Sun eve and Wed o.o.s.

You can gather from its address that this is near the church – it is and at the top of the cobbled main street. The menu is mainly seafood but does have other dishes. The standard is above average and the prices reasonable at 16–40€.

La Ferme de Kerloury (Cd'H) S
> **tel:** 02 96 20 85 23
> **open:** all year
> **no credit cards**

An old farm, renovated as a bed and breakfast, this is a real find for families. In the large garden are a barbecue, a pond and a *crêperie*. Children are particularly welcome and all the guests eat together in the kitchen.

Two double rooms in the farmhouse have their own bathroom. In a converted stable next door, a double, a twin and a triple share a bathroom. The price is 40€ for two people, breakfast included.

Bab-El-Oued ⊠ S
> 17 rue des Islandais
> **tel:** 02 96 20 45 19
> **open:** evenings only
> **no credit cards**

The décor is overdone but then you can always sit outside and watch the passing crowd instead. It is one of those handy places, near the port, with light meals and snacks and inexpensive. The couscous tastes authentic and delicious and there are other ethnic offerings. You can always fall back on steak and frites. As much as you are likely to want for well under 16€.

PAIMPONT

35380 (Î-et-V)
40 km SW of Rennes

A small market town with an abbey church and a medieval gate and on the shore of a lake. It sits amidst the legends of King Arthur and Merlin the Magician in the Forest of Paimpont. The forest was previously called 'The Forest of Brocéliande' and this is where Merlin fell under the spell of the fairy Viviane, 'The Lady of the Lake', as he was sleeping by a fountain.

The legend says she kept him trapped inside the Merlin Stone which stands beside the Fairy Spring at Barenton, about 2 km west. A pleasant walk takes you to the small hamlet of Folle Pensée (Mad Thought) and on to the village of La Saudraie.

The Perron de Merlin is a large square stone where the spring flows into the fountain. The story says that water from the Fairy Spring sprinkled onto the stone will cause rain to fall and in 1835, the priest of nearby Concoret did so and ended a drought. Concoret at that time was called Konkored, the Valley of the Fairies.

The ruins of Comper Castle are three kilometres to the east and Les Forges de Paimpont is a particularly beautiful part of the forest. If you want stay amid these enchanted surroundings, you have two good choices.

Manoir du Tertre ⊨ ✕ M

Le Cannée
tel: 02 99 07 86 95
fax: 02 99 07 85 46
open: all year

A manor house, built in 1640, deep in the Brocéliande Forest. Its beautiful parkland grounds surround the manor containing six rooms and two suites, all magnificently furnished with antiques. They range from 96–120€ plus 6.5€ for breakfast.

In the kitchen, a team of accomplished chefs serve meals that pay tribute to traditional dishes while adding modern touches. Meals are 18€–40€.

La Corne de Cerf (Cd'H) S
Le Cannée
tel: 02 99 07 84 19
closed: Jan

M. and Mme. Morvan, the owners, are also painters and decorators so you can be sure they have done a good job of renovating this old stone house with a name reflecting its past – 'The Stag's Horn'.

The three bedrooms are comfortable and have modern bathrooms. They are 48€ with breakfast included. No other meals but there are restaurants nearby.

PÉAULE

56130 (Morbihan)
25 km W of Redon

Auberge Armor Vilaine 🛏 ✗ S-M
11 place Ste-Anne
tel: 02 97 42 91 03
fax: 02 97 42 82 27
closed: one week in Jan, two weeks in Feb, one week in Oct; Sun eve and Mon except in season

Only 17 rooms in this popular little inn, run by M. Boeffard, near the church. All have a bath or shower and TV and are 36–44€ plus 6.5€ for breakfast. The restaurant is a favourite with the locals and the meals are hearty and offer a wide range of choices. 12€ for lunch and up to 40€ for dinner but that includes wine.

PENMARC'H

29760 (Finistère)
30 km SW of Quimper

It sits at the southwestern most tip of France, boasting wind, sea and cliffs while daring the Atlantic Ocean to do its worst.

PENMARC'H

Le Doris ✕ S-L
port de Kérity
tel: 02 98 58 60 92
fax: 02 98 58 58 16
closed: All Saints to Easter

What a place for a restaurant! And such a good one! Mme. Le Palud cooks seafood specialities of fish and shellfish all caught off the inhospitable coast that almost surrounds Penmarc'h. The unusual range of prices, from 11–53€, reflects quality at all levels but caters for a wide range of customers.

PENVÉNAN

22710 (Cd'A)
40 km NW of Morlaix

It is not much more than a kilometre from the wild, northern coast and has a good, inexpensive hotel.

Grand Hôtel du Port Blanc ⌧ ✕ S
1 boulevard de la Mer
tel: 02 96 92 66 52
fax: 02 96 92 81 57
closed: mid-Nov to mid-Mar
restaurant closed: Oct

The hotel is near the windswept coast but English is spoken and the 29 rooms are a mere 36–42€. All have a bath or shower and are very clean and neat. Demi-pension is available at 40–45€.

PERROS-GUIREC

22700 (Cd'A)
12 km N of Lannion
market: Fri

This is the largest resort along this part of the coast, lively and popular. It becomes even more popular in mid-August, when first there is the *Pardon de Notre-Dame de la Clarté* (light) on the 15th then, on the next day, the Fête of the Hortensias.

Manoir du Sphinx 🛏 🍴 M
67 chemin de la Messe
tel: 02 96 23 25 42
fax: 02 96 91 26 13
closed: 3 Jan to 20 Feb
restaurant closed: Mon and Fri lunch

From the dining room and many of the bedrooms, you have great views of the sea along this stretch of the pink granite coast. The 20 rooms have a bath or shower and TV. All are carefully and tastefully decorated, large and very quiet even at the peak of summer. They are priced from 80–96€. The restaurant is closed Sunday evening and Monday during the off-season. The rest of the year, the cooking is attentive and mostly local ingredients, especially seafood. Menus are 21–47€.

Printania 🛏 🍴 M
12 rue des Bons Enfants
tel: 02 96 49 01 10
fax: 01 96 91 16 36
closed: mid-Dec to mid-Jan

A delightful old house, everything pink and blue, in a great location looking over the bay and towards Les-Sept-Îles. A tennis court and gardens are around the house which has 33 rooms at 112€ plus 9€ for breakfast. All are comfortable and well furnished. The restaurant is popular with locals. There is seafood but other choices too at 21–29€. Joel Inizan and Marie-Françoise Le Calvez run a fine operation.

Hôtel Gulf-Stream 🛏 S
26 rue des Sept-Îles
tel: 02 96 23 21 86
fax: 02 96 49 06 61
closed: Jan

An impressive location on top of a cliff near Trestraou. Doubles are only 27€ and rooms for three or four people are under 48€ and have a shower.

Au Saint Yvez ✕ S
rue Saint Yvez
tel: 02 96 23 21 31
fax: 02 96 23 05 24
open: all year

Traditional French cooking at a restaurant right in the centre of town. A very satisfying meal for under 16€.

PLANCOËT

22130 (Cd'A)
17 km SW of Dinan
market: Sat

The river Arguegnon rushes surprisingly through the centre of this undistinguished little town, with a bridge just opposite:

☆ Hôtel l'Écrin ⊨ ✕ L
20 les quais
tel: 02 96 84 10 24
fax: 02 96 84 01 93
closed: first two weeks in Oct, three weeks in Jan
restaurant closed: Sun eve and Mon, Tues lunch, Oct to Apr

Jean-Pierre Crouzil is one of the most celebrated chefs in the area. People travel far to eat the superbly crafted meals here. The price will be high (expect to spend 40–80€), but the meal will be a memorable experience.

How do you find it? It is opposite the railway station in Plancoët. The finest of local seafood, vegetables, poultry and meats are used. Hot oysters in a zabaglione of Vouvray wine and carrots, chicken sautéed in tarragon and served with pickled onions and fillet of turbot stuffed with crab are but three of the dishes served in the past and Jean-Pierre will have a whole new array of them by the time you arrive. (He may also have improved on his two Michelin stars!)

Rooms? Yes, there are seven of them at 72–152€ – and yes, this is double the price of five years ago. It's the food that people come here for though so check on when they are having the next 'Gastronomic Weekend'.

Ferme Auberge du Grand Trait ⊠ S
Le Grand Trait
tel & fax: 02 96 84 01 23
open: only for groups with reservations
no credit cards

Everything served comes from their own farm. Dishes include terrine of rabbit with shredded vegetables, ham and leek pie, rabbit cooked in cider and apples. Other dishes depend on what is available. Simple but delicious. You can have a fine meal in rustic surroundings for 12–20€.

PLANGUENOUAL

22400 (Cd'A)
27 km E of St-Brieuc

Domaine du Val ⊨ ⊠ M-L
tel: 02 96 32 75 40
fax: 02 96 32 71 50
open: all year

Handily located on the D786 and set in extensive grounds which sweep down to the ocean only 3 km away, the Domaine is an impressive building with a central spire and tall mullioned windows. Vines dangle bunches of grapes on the verandah.

The covered and heated swimming pool, the covered tennis courts, the squash courts and the sauna keep you healthy so you can enjoy the nearby golf course and a visit to the Château de Bienassis.

Most of the 38 bedrooms are in the main building, large and attractive, all with a bath and TV. Specify when you reserve if you wish to be there otherwise you may be in one of the outside rooms which are single-story granite houses, each with a terrace. Rooms are 72–160€ for two people and 122–184€ for two suites which accommodate up to six people.

Breakfast is 9€. You might want to consider the demi-pension arrangement for 72–112€, with smoked salmon, then lobster Breton-style or pigeon Valoise-style being typical dishes. Otherwise, menus are 23–37€ and *à la carte* items are available too.

PLÉDÉLIAC

22270 (Cd'A)
30 km W of Dinan

The Château de la Hunaudaye is the big attraction here. It is one of the most authentic-looking castles anywhere, built in the 14th century and in a nature reserve of 6,000 acres. It is open every day in July and August but from Easter to the end of June and in September from 3 pm to 7 pm.

A second attraction though is the Manoir de Belouze, a 15th-century manor house with gardens planted during the Middle Ages. Exhibitions are held frequently and concerts of Celtic and medieval music.

There's also a third attraction. The village of St-Esprit des Bois was a mass of ruins in 1974 then an association known as 'Ferme d'Antan', the farm of yesteryear, was formed mainly by younger people who wanted to be sure the memory of the village was not lost. They restored it and you can see the mill, the stables, the blacksmith's shop, the house where the family lived, the forge, the bakery ... in fact, everything that comprises a real working village. Open every day in season from 10 am to 12 pm and 2 pm to 7 pm. The phone number is 02 96 34 14 67.

Manoir-Auberge Belouze (Cd'H) S
tel: 02 96 34 14 55
fax: 02 96 51 21 07
open: in season
no credit cards

A lot going on here at this pleasing bed and breakfast – such as medieval and Celtic exhibitions during the summer. Marie-Christine Le Mee-Menard has a medieval herb garden and uses the products from it when she cooks medieval-style menus which are 15–20€. The comfortable rooms are 32–36€.

PLÉLO

22170 (Cd'A)
17 km W of St-Brieuc

Le Char à Bancs (Cd'H) M
    Moulin de la Ville Geffroy
    tel: 02 96 74 13 63
    fax: 02 96 74 13 03
    closed: last two weeks Sept
    no credit cards

From the British point of view, the name is unfortunate, conjuring up, as it does, images of busloads of drunken football supporters still furious over that disallowed goal or Morris dancers from Upper Downingdale. Nothing like that here.

The old mill has been converted into a very pleasing *auberge* by the Lamour family. The five bedrooms are all large and comfortable, have a bath or shower and can sleep up to four people. Breakfast is included in the price of 56–80€ for two, 72–88€ for three and 104–112€ for four. The beamed ceilings give them a medieval air and all are different.

It is easy to find, just north of the N12 autoroute, in the farming village of Plélo.

PLENEUF-VAL-ANDRÉ
22370 (Cd'A)
28 km W of Dinard

Long expanses of shining sand at this elegant resort town with a concert hall, a casino, lots of tennis courts, a promenade and flower gardens. Its restaurants are a big attraction too.

Le Biniou ☒ S-M
    121 rue Clémenceau
    tel: 02 96 72 24 35
    fax: 02 96 63 03 23
    closed: Feb, Tues eve and Wed

The name means bagpipe and though Scottish frugality might not prevail, meals are very high quality and thoughtfully prepared for 32€ with wine included.

PLERGUER

35540 (I-et-V)
25 km SE of St-Malo
market: Wed am

After informing you that Brittany is a *département* that is less cheese-minded than almost anywhere else in France, what do we have here? Nothing less than a Cheese Museum!

La Chevrerie du Desert is in a district called 'Le Desert', about 25 km from St-Malo but don't expect a mini-Sahara. Goats' cheese is, as you may expect, the focal point and Roselyn and Claude will be delighted to share their dedication with you. Raising goats and producing cheese are what this is all about at the Desert Goat Farm, and the boutique and the tasting room will satisfy your curiosity. (You can have lunch in the tasting room too.) In July and August, it is open every day 11 am to 6.30 pm and also from 1 April to 30 June, 1 September to 15 October, 2.30 pm to 6.30 pm.

PLEUDIHEN-SUR-RANCE

22690 (Cd'A)
15 km N of Dinan

The big attraction here is the Musée de la Pomme et du Cidre. You will find it at 'Ville Hervy' and the museum is open from April to September. You will learn everything you need to know about the history and technique of growing apples and making cider in the one-hour tour which is in most European languages including English. A typical Breton home of the past has been carefully re-created too. A tasting ends the tour and there is a boutique and a picnic area.

Manoir du Pont-de Cieux (Cd'H) S
tel: 02 96 83 36 61
open: Jun, Jul, Aug
no credit cards

This sturdy old 18th-century building is on the D29 just a couple of kilometres north of Pleudihen, heading toward St-Malo. The white-washed rooms are comfortable and reasonably priced at 32–40€.

La Petite Touche ✗ S
route Mordreuc
tel: 02 96 83 25 57
closed: Sat lunch, Sun eve, Mon

A small, family owned and operated restaurant that specializes in charcoal grills, chicken, beef, pork and fish – even lobster. The desserts are home-made. A log fire blazes away in winter and candles add to the atmosphere. You can eat well here for about 16€.

PLEUGUENEC

35720 (Î-et-V)
12 km SE of Dinan

One of the most spectacular sights in Brittany is here – the Castle of La Bourbonsais. It took a long time to build, from the 16th to the 18th centuries, and was the former residence of the members of the Breton Parliament. The formal gardens, the park and the castle are all national monuments and a zoo is on the grounds also. Shows of hunting are presented with huntsmen on foot and on horseback and 50 hunting hounds. The castle is open April to September 10 am to 7 pm, and 2 pm to 6 pm o.o.s..

☆ Château de la Motte Beaumanoir ⌨ ✗ L
tel: 02 99 69 46 01
fax: 02 99 69 42 49
closed: Christmas and New Year

La Bourbonsais is not the only castle around – here is one you can stay in, it's even moated. The construction of this one was begun about a hundred years earlier in fact and took at least as long to build as its larger neighbour.

La Motte Beaumanoir used to be a *chambre d'hôte* but it has grown in size and prestige. There are now 12 rooms and two suites and all are furnished in luxurious style with superb bathrooms. The suites are expensive at 160–216€, though the rooms are good value at 112–144€ for a very high standard.

The views over the trout lake and the substantial surrounding woodlands are magnificent, while the tennis court and the swimming pool add to the attractions.

The dining room has been steadily improved over recent years and is now rated very highly. Turbot and *daurade* are often on the menu and *gigot* of lamb in basil is a repeat favourite. Menus are relatively reasonable at 42–58€.

PLEURTUIT
35730 (Î-et-V)
15 km SE of St-Malo

The Château de Montmarin and its gardens is one of the reasons Pleurtuit gets a lot of visitors. It was built in the 18th century by a wealthy St-Malo shipowner as a home and is a majestic edifice with gardens and terrace looking on to the Rance River. Painting and sculpture exhibitions are frequently held in summer. The château is open only Sundays and holidays in April but every day except Saturdays, May to September from 2 pm to 7 pm.

The ruins of the old tidal mill can still be seen and the slipways down which ships were launched. There are numerous footpaths around that yield unexpected delights, as periodically you will find wonderful views of the Rance River.

☆ **Manoir de la Rance** ⇔ M
  Château de Jouvente
  Chemin du Manoir de la Rance
  tel: 02 99 88 53 76
  fax: 02 99 88 63 03
  closed: 20-Nov to Mar

A 19th-century manor house with a slender, graceful tower and a high roof, it faces the Rance River in a lovely wooded area.

Madame Jasselin is a delightful hostess and has ten rooms that are all comfortable and quiet with fine views of the sea, the cliffs and the countryside. They are priced at 72–128€ for two people and all have a bath and TV. Breakfast is 8€ per person. Two of these rooms can be considered as suites and are priced a little higher. Breakfast is an additional 8€.

A large lounge is very inviting and there is also a bar and a small living room. The gardens and terraces are used for refreshments too.

Jersey Lillie 🛏 S-M
cale de Jouvente
tel: 02 99 88 51 80
fax: 02 99 88 52 48
closed: end Nov to early March
no credit cards

On the banks of the Rance River and with great views of the water traffic. Named for Lillie Langtry who came here from her home in Jersey. The seven rooms are 56–64€ with breakfast at 5€. All have private bathrooms and TV. An unusual offering is balloon flights at 160€ per person.

PLEVEN

22130 (Cd'A)
37 km E of St-Brieuc

☆ Manoir de Vaumadeuc 🛏 ✖ M-L
tel: 02 96 84 46 17
fax: 02 96 84 40 16
closed: 1 Nov to Easter

A 15th-century manor house with all the trimmings – suits of armour, four-poster beds in massive bedrooms, wood-panelled baronial halls, enormous fireplaces and terrifyingly large and ornate chandeliers.

If you want to experience medieval living – but with all the modern comforts and amenities – then you have it all here. Friends found it too much, but after several days of Breton simplicity, it can be enjoyable. The 14 rooms are 96–160€ and during the high season, meals are limited to guests only. The quality and service in the dining room is extremely high and specialities include fresh salmon steak and *émincé d'agneau à l'oseille* (slivers of lamb with sorrel). Meals are 32–48€.

PLOËRMEL

56800 (Morbihan)
11 km E of Josselin
market: Mon, Fri

Its pivotal position at the junction of the D766, the N166 and the N24 makes Ploërmel a useful stop and handy for visiting Josselin Castle and the Forest of Paimpont. It is named after St-Armel who came from Britain in the 6th century and slew the local dragons. Inside the church, you can see him depicted with one of the defeated reptiles. The 12th-century ramparts unfortunately remain only as ruins.

Le Cobh ⊨ ✗ M
10 rue des Forges
tel: 02 97 74 00 49
email: lecobh@wanadoo.fr
open: all year

The Cruard family have done a fine job with this old Breton house, the name of which comes from their twinned town in Ireland. The 13 rooms have been renovated and are 24–52€. There are two restaurants, one on the first floor and the other in what was once the stables. The cooking is of a high standard with menus from 12€ to 40€.

PLOGOFF

29770 (Finistère)
4 km E of the Pointe du Raz

Hôtel de la Baie des Trépassés ⊨ ✗ S
Baie des Trépassés
tel: 02 98 70 61 34
fax: 02 98 70 35 20
closed: 15 Nov to mid-Feb

This large and popular hotel looks out on to a wide beach and is just three kilometres from the Pointe du Raz. The rooms are simple but adequate. All have a bath or shower and TV. They are priced at 29–55€. The food is well above average – the scallops *en brochette* are a favourite dish and the grilled prawns get a lot of takers. Menus include a starter of half a dozen oysters and are 24€, 31€, 39€ and 47€.

PLOMELIN

29700 (Finistère)
10 km SW of Quimper

On the banks of the River Odet, Plomelin sits amidst great tracts of wooded countryside. Legends abound here and have produced some strange names. Le Saut de la Pucelle is one of these and might be translated as 'The Virgin's Leap', as it is said that a young girl of Plomelin was able to jump across the River Odet to escape a menacing villain and thus preserve her virginity. Another is 'The Bishop's Chair', a little more hazy in its significance.

The distillery brings visitors and tasters and there is an old windmill at La Cale de Rosulien but, really, the countryside itself is the big attraction.

Château de Kerambleiz 🛏 M
tel: 02 98 94 23 42
fax: 02 98 95 31 01
closed: open on demand, for weddings and celebrations

Halfway between Quimper and Bénodet, the 19th-century château overlooks the Odet River. It sits in a large park surrounded by meadows and woodland. It has been fully renovated and the nine rooms and two suites all have fully equipped bathrooms and are comfortably furnished with antiques. There is no restaurant and rooms are 72–112€ and the suites 128–144€.

PLOMODIERN

29550 (Finistère)
17 km NE of Douarnenez
market: first Fri of month

The Chapel of St-Corentin is a more recent addition to Brittany's religious structures. It is in neo-gothic style and is near the

PLOMODIERN

fountain where the saint performed miracles. The Chapel of Ste-Marie du Menez-Hom is more the typical period (16th century) and its retables are famous.

That's not all the chapels. Plomodiern also has the Chapel of St-Sebastien (16th century) which has a statue of Christ with a child on each knee, and the Chapel of St-Suliau (17th century).

In August every year, the town puts on an exhibition of paintings and sculpture.

Relais Pors-Morvan 🛏 M
tel: 02 98 81 53 23
closed: 1 Oct to 1 Apr, school holidays and weekends

It's only a few minutes to the sea and some good beaches on the Bay of Douarnenez and in a quiet countryside setting. The 12 rooms are 48–52€ with breakfast included and all are well furnished and have pleasant bathrooms. There is a tennis court but no restaurant.

PLONEOUR-LANVERN
29167 (Finistère)
8 km NW of Pont l'Abbé

Manoir de Kerhuel 🛏 ✕ M
tel: 02 98 82 60 57
fax: 02 98 82 61 79
closed: 11 Nov to 15 Dec, 2 Jan to 15 Mar

The approach is breathtaking, along a private drive between rows of trees. The buildings are equally impressive – an authentic old manor house, thoroughly and carefully renovated, set in its large grounds consisting of woodland.

Each of the 20 rooms costs 96–112€ and is beautifully furnished with a fully equipped bathroom. Breakfast is 7€. After you have made use of the intimate bar, the dining room serves excellent meals at 40–56€. A heated swimming pool, tennis and a sauna are among the facilities

PLONEVEZ-PORZAY

29550 (Finistère)
18 km NW of Quimper

Only about 5 km from the beach at the bay of Douarnenez is this small village with a good bed and breakfast and a fine and reasonable *chambre d'hôte*. The crowds gather here every year on the first Sunday in August for the Pardon of Ste-Anne-la-Palud.

Trevilly (Cd'H) S
    tel: 02 98 92 52 25
    open: all year
    no credit cards

Close to the west coast is this old pig farm where Pierre and Hugele Rannou also grow cereal crops on their land.

One double room, one twin and one family suite, sleeping three to five, all have private bathrooms and are only 37–40€ for two including breakfast.

PLOUARET

22420 (Cd'A)
22 km E of Morlaix

Its Chapel of the Seven Saints is built around a megalith – yet another example of the church using pagan sites as is frequently seen throughout the former Roman Empire.

Le Presbytère Trégrom (Cd'H)S
    tel: 02 96 47 94 15
    open: all year
    no credit cards

Built in the early part of the 17th century, this grey stone edifice really was the presbytery and reconstruction in the past 20 years has been thoughtful and ingenious. The orchard and the walled gardens give an atmosphere of real privacy. One double and two twin rooms are all very well furnished and have luxurious bathrooms. The price of 48–56€ is very modest and it includes breakfast. Meals at 20€ are available on request and Mme. Nicole de Morchoven is an accomplished cook.

It is easy to find, being right in the centre of the village opposite the church.

PLOUER-SUR-RANCE

22490 (Cd'A)
8 km NE of Dinan

The village used to use the tidal waters of the Rance River to run their mills. Several of the mills are still here. A religious procession is held on the 15th of August every year to the even smaller village of Langrolay, just across the autoroute to the north. The procession goes to the chapel of La Souhaitier where, in the days that the fishing fleets set out for Newfoundland, wives would gather to pray to the Virgin Mary for the safe return of their husbands and sons.

☆ **Manoir de Rigourdaine** 🛏 M
   Route de Langrolay
   tel: 02 96 86 89 96
   fax: 02 96 86 92 46
   closed: 12 Nov to end Mar

Beautiful views of the Rance River valley are just one of the attractions of this thoroughly remodelled old farmhouse. They can be enjoyed from all 19 of the rooms, which also have a bath or shower and TV. All are well furnished and there are numerous personal touches. The ground floor rooms have a terrace. Prices are 48–64€ for two people and breakfast is 6€. M. Van Valenburg is young and enthusiastic.

PLOUGONVELIN

29217 (Finistère)
19 km W of Brest

Just a few more metres further and Plougonvelin would be the most westerly point in Europe. As it is, it overlooks a rocky bay with wild seas. The lighthouse is one of the most photographed along the coast.

The most extraordinary sight here though is the tiny fortified island of Bertheaume. It sits just offshore, connected to the mainland by two bridges and the fortifications comprise the entire top of the island.

Hostellerie de la Pointe Saint-Mathieu ⊨ ✗ S
tel: 02 98 89 00 19
fax: 02 98 89 15 68
closed: mid-Jan to mid-Feb

There are 21 rooms at a reasonable 45–68€ plus 6.5€ for breakfast or 45–56€ for demi-pension. It is a romantic and stormy location, facing the ruins of the old abbey of St-Mathieu and looking out towards the islands of Ouessant and Molene. The restaurant is medieval with its vaults, its staircase and the huge antique stone fireplace. Brigitte and Philippe Corre use only local products in the cooking and menus are 16–64€.

PLOUGONVEN

29640 (Finistère)
30 km SE of Morlaix

The main reason to visit Plougenven is to see and tour the Manoir de Mezedern.

La Grange de Coatelan (Cd'H) S
tel: 02 98 72 60 16
closed: 20 Dec to 25 Jan
no credit cards

Charlick and Yolande de Ternay have converted this weaver's cottage into a most unusual bed and breakfast. An open fireplace adds to the charm and the three bedrooms are nicely decorated, priced at 40–56€ for two people with breakfast included. The hosts speak English and make this a great place to stay, with the beach and the Arrée Mountains nearby.

PLOUGRESCANT

22820 (Cd'A)
7 km N of Tréguier

A tiny village on the north, pink granite coast.

Manoir de Kergrec'h (Cd'H) M
>on the D8
>**tel:** 02 96 92 59 13
>**fax:** 02 96 92 51 27
>**open:** all year
>**no credit cards**

This is the home of the Vicomte and Vicomtesse de Roquefeuil and they will welcome you to it (in English even). It is set in parkland close to the beach and has five rooms and two suites, all with a bath and WC. For two people, the price is 72–88€ for the rooms and 120€ and 136€ for the suites.

The interior, including all the rooms and suites, has been renovated recently. All are different and have antique furniture. Breakfast is included in the price and consists of home-made Breton *crêpes* and jams made from local fruits. An evening meal is available by reservation from 36€ and is served in a very impressive dining room with an immense fireplace.

PLOUGUERNEAU

29880 (Finistère)
29 km N of Brest

The village is considered a stronghold of Breton culture and its theatre company, the Strollad ar Vro Bagan, stages plays in both the Breton and French languages and based on Breton folklore. In the same building is the Musée des Goemoniers which tells you all about the seaweed business. Seaweed is a local commodity of importance with growing usage in pharmaceuticals, chemicals, cosmetics and foods. The museum is open in July and August, 3 pm-7 pm every day but Monday, April to June 3 pm-6 pm every day except Monday and the rest of the year Sunday only, 2 pm-6 pm.

North of the village are fine beaches, the Plage de Lilia being considered to be the best. From it, you can look out and see the lighthouse on the Île Vierge, the tallest lighthouse in Europe.

The lost village of Tremanac'h has been found! Buried under the sands off the coast north of Plouguerneau since the 17th century, it is the subject of local legends although the facts suggest inundation by shifting sand masses and encroachment of the sea. So far, over a hundred tombs have been uncovered and many belonged to members of the nobility as indicated by accompanying stone swords.

Le Castel Ac'h ⊨ ✕ S-M

Plage de Lilia
tel: 02 98 04 70 11
fax: 02 98 04 58 43
email: la.grand.voile@wanadoo.fr
closed: 20 to 24 Sept, mid-Nov to early Dec, Sun eve and Mon o.o.s.

It looks out at that tall lighthouse and M. Lescarret and Karine Prigent offer you 28 rooms, all very pleasant and brightly decorated at 28–48€ plus 7€ for breakfast. The service is attentive and genuinely helpful. A tennis court is available.

The restaurant has a reputation for its gastronomy and its seafood is notable. The chef makes occasional use of that local seaweed to excellent effect. Meals are 15–42€ and the outstanding dish is 'the plate of crustaceans' which includes the meatiest crabs I have ever encountered. Demi-pension is 42–55€. There is an inviting terrace adjacent to the bar.

Trouz ar Mor ✕ S

Le Corréjou
tel: 02 98 04 71 61
closed: Mon eve

It is just north of town and the terrace looks out over the sands. The building is not too prepossessing from the outside but inside it is very trim and cheerful. The food is dominantly seafood and you can enjoy a good meal for 16–32€.

PLOUHARNEL

56720 (Morbihan)
3 km NW of Carnac

A handy place to stay that is very convenient to Carnac and its prehistoric stones. It is on a sandy spit of land jutting off the Quiberon peninsula and it has two museums which are popular. The name of the Musée Galion tells you its prime exhibit – a replica of an 18th-century sailing ship. The museum is open 9.30 am –7 pm in July and August, Easter to June 10 am–12 pm and 2 pm–6 p m and is built inside one of the German bunkers left over from World War II.

The Musée de la Chouannerie deals with the anti-revolutionary uprising which had strong roots in these parts. The whole story of the Chouannerie is told – along with its sad ending when their forces were routed.

Along the sandy spit of the causeway are sandy beaches, some with rough water enough for surfers to gather here. The nude beach attracts even more visitors than the surfing beach or even the Plage de Penthievre which has sand-yacht-racing on its flat sands.

Hôtel l'Hippocampe ⊨ ✕ S
route de Carnac
tel: 02 97 52 39 51
fax: 02 97 52 39 66
closed: Oct to Mar

The 20 rooms here are fine for an overnight stay, have TV and are priced at 40–64€. English is spoken and the food is good enough that demi-pension at 48–64€ is a good idea.

☆ Hostellerie Les Ajoncs d'Or ⊨ ✕ M
Kerbachique
tel: 02 97 52 32 02
fax: 02 97 52 40 36
closed: 1-Nov to 15-Apr

A pink granite farmhouse formed by three adjoining buildings where Mme. Le Maguer welcomes you warmly and runs an extremely efficient operation. It's just outside the village and on the D781 between Carnac and Plouharnel.

The 17 rooms all have a bath or shower and TV and are 47–66€ or a suite for four people is 109€. Breakfast is extra at 6€. All the rooms have been recently renovated, all are different and are bright and cheerful with colourful fabrics and beautiful carpets.

The large restaurant has wooden beams, exposed stonework, paintings and a delightful fireplace. Menus are 15–24€. The breakfast room next door is just as inviting.

PLOUHINEC

56680 (Morbihan)
30 km W of Quimper
market: Sun

Hôtel de Kerlon ⊨ ✗ S
tel: 02 97 36 77 03
fax: 02 97 85 81 14
website: www.auberge-de-kerlon.com
closed: 1 Nov to 15 Mar

On the D781 from Lorient to Carnac, Plouhinec has sea coasts to the east, south and west and the Hôtel de Kerlon is perfectly situated only about 5 km from all of them. It is a very smart-looking, modernised building where M. and Mme. Coeffic extend a hearty welcome and keep the place immaculate.

The 15 rooms all have a bath or shower and TV. Several of the rooms have been renovated recently and you should ask for one of these. All are very reasonably priced at 39–52€, with breakfast additional at 6.5€. The cheerful dining room and the comfortable lounge bar are attractive.

Fish and shellfish of local origin command most of the menu and are always fresh and well prepared. Menus are 13–26€ or you may order *à la carte*.

PLOUIGNEAU

29010 (Finistère)
10 km E of Morlaix

Le Manoir de Lanleya (Cd'H) S
   tel: 02 98 79 94 15
   open: all year
   no credit cards

The 15th-century manor house that previously existed on this site has been rescued from extinction and very carefully restored and, although the result is a mixture of styles and periods, it is a very comfortable place to stay and M. Marrec deserves great credit.

The three bedrooms have a shower and one has an extra room. There are also four houses as accommodation. The rooms are bright and cheerful and breakfast is included in all the prices. Rooms for two people are 48€ plus 16€ for an extra person. The houses are 192–352€ for two people and range up to 288–512€ for seven people. Stone walls have been left here and there, and a stone fireplace and a wide staircase remain.

PLOUMANAC'H

22700 (C. D'A.)
6 km NW of Perros-Guirec

Some of the most magnificent walking scenery in Brittany is around Ploumanac'h, a small fishing port and seaside resort connected to the sea by a narrow inlet. The boulder-strewn shoreline has massive rocks and spectacular formations and the best way to see them is to take the short walking tour along the rue du Centre to the harbour, then along a coastal path through the Parc de la Bastille.

Staying on the coast, you walk to the plage St-Guirec where you will see the statue of the saint who landed here in the 6th century then up to Porz-Kamor and its lighthouse. The pathway curves past tiny coves and deep crevices. The Château du Diable is a rock formation that looks very much like a castle. At Porz Rolland, the path goes back to Ploumanc'h and the whole walk takes barely an hour.

PLOUMANAC'H

Close by is the spectacular Castle Costaeres, a towered and turreted delight even if you are not a dedicated castle fancier.

Les Rochers 🛏 ✖ M
> 70 chemin de la Pointe
> **tel:** 02 96 91 44 49
> **fax:** 02 96 91 43 64
> **open:** all year

A perfect spot on the port of Ploumanac'h, this old building has been completely renovated. The 14 rooms are large and well appointed. They cost 56–88€ and breakfast is 7€. Demi-pension is an alternative at 68–112€.

Hôtel de l'Europe 🛏 S
> 158 rue Saint Guirec
> **tel:** 02 96 91 40 76
> **fax:** 02 96 91 49 74
> **closed:** first two weeks of Jan

Its 18 rooms are comfortable and adequately furnished. All have TV. They are 55€ for two people and 5.5€ for breakfast.

Hôtel du Parc 🛏 ✖ S
> 174 rue Saint Guirec
> **tel:** 02 96 91 40 80
> **fax:** 02 96 91 60 48
> **closed:** 11 Nov to end Mar, Sun eve, Mon

Only 10 rooms here but all have TV and are a very modest 42€ plus 5€ for breakfast. Demi-pension is 40-45€ but if you prefer otherwise, lunch is good, sound Breton fare, about 12€ for lunch and 13–24€ for dinner including wine.

PLUMELEC

56420 (Morbihan)
12 km NE of Vannes

Moulin de Callac 🛏 ✖ S
tel: 02 97 67 12 65
fax: 02 97 67 12 65
open: all year
no credit cards

From the number of mills that have been successfully converted into hotel-restaurants, you will have concluded that Brittany must have had an awful lot of mills. This one is another such conversion, simple but very pleasant and with eight rooms at 28–36€ plus a mere 5€ for breakfast.

There is a nice garden and the restaurant is essentially a *crêperie* but with other dishes too. Meals are 8–24€ and you can eat out on the terrace in summer.

PLURIEN-FRÉHEL

22240 (Cd'A)
45 km NW of Dinan

On the Emerald Coast and with some spectacular views of the cliffs and the sea.

Manoir de la Salle 🛏 S-M
Route du Lac
tel: 02 96 72 38 29
fax: 02 96 72 00 57
closed: 30 Sept to 1 Apr
no credit cards

It's a large 16th-century stone manor house with spacious and cheerful rooms, all with modern furniture at 40–64€. A solarium and table tennis are there for recreation and a golf course is nearby.

PLUVIGNER

56330 (Morbihan)
32 km NW of Vannes

A hilltop village with a 12th-century church.

Le Cosquer-Trelecan (Cd'H) S
   tel: 02 97 24 72 69
   fax: 02 97 24 90 45
   open: all year
   no credit cards

Establishments don't usually get into these pages when they have only one room but exceptions have to be made and this lovely old thatched cottage deserves to be one of those. The room is a suite and sleeps four people. It has a bath and ranges from 44€ for two people to 56€ for three and 64€ for four with breakfast included. It is very well appointed and comfortable. Breakfast is served in the large living room full of antiques and with a big fireplace. There are restaurants in abundance around and Bernard and Françoise Menut are helpful and friendly hosts.

POLIGNE

35320 (Î-et V)
22 km S of Rennes

Château du Bois Glaume (Cd'H) M
   tel: 02 99 43 83 05
   fax: 02 99 43 79 40
   closed: 1-Oct to 1-Jun
   no credit cards

An 18th-century château in the middle of a wooded park with a lake – a beautiful setting for a very attractive building. M. and Mme. Bertheleme, who speak English, have just opened it after extensive renovation. It is located conveniently for the autoroute which goes south out of Rennes.

   The two suites and two bedrooms all have a bath or shower, the two suites have TV. The rooms are 64€ for two people and suites, also for two people, are 104€. All are large and very well decorated. Breakfast is an additional 8€ and lunch and dinner are available on request at 24€ (not including wine). All the public rooms are furnished with antiques. Tennis, golf and riding are all nearby.

POMMERIT-JAUDY

22450 (Cd'A)
9 km S of Tréguier

Château de Kermezen (Cd'H) M
tel: 02 96 91 35 75
open: all year (except Christmas)
no credit cards

The Comte and Comtesse de Kermel have had this château in their family for almost 600 years and continue to maintain it in magnificent condition. You know you are in for a treat when you pass between the great wrought-iron gates, drive along the tree-lined avenue with sweeping green lawns on either side and see that imposing façade.

Three double rooms and two twin rooms, charmingly furnished, all have their own bathrooms and are a bargain at 76–88€. This includes breakfast and you can have an evening meal on request at 16–32€ including wine.

PONT AVEN

29936 (Finistère)
15 km W of Concarneau
market: Tues

Famous as the place that Paul Gauguin, a 38-year-old stockbroker, left Paris and his wife and his five children to go to in 1886. He and his friend, Emile Bernard, painted there, Gauguin getting particular inspiration as he described 'When my wooden shoes ring on this granite, I hear the muffled, dull, powerful tone I seek in my painting'.

Gauguin did not discover Pont Aven – it was already filled with artists, mostly British and Scandinavian but a cosmopolitan crowd from many parts of the world. They lived in inns: the Julia which had largely French artists, the Des Voyageurs with Americans and the eclectic Pension Gloannec where Gauguin and others lived for 60 francs a month which included three meals and all the cider they could drink.

It was here that he painted '*Le Christ Jaune*', The Yellow Christ. He offered it free to the local priest who understandably refused it for it was not a conventionally Christian image. (The painting can be seen today in the National Gallery of Scotland.)

The town is just as picturesque now as it was then, maybe even more so for the three gushing streams that run through the town, bouncing and splashing over the rocks have had minor guidance. Now, they diverge and converge while enticing walks have been set up, beckoning the visitor. When the artists walked through the Bois d'Amour, arguing about art, there were more windmills than houses and, happily, some of these have been restored. The town has lots of galleries but you won't find any Gauguins in them.

On the first Sunday in August, the *Fête des Ajoncs d'Or* is held.

☆ Moulin de Rosmadec ⊨ ✕ M

Venelle de Rosmadec
tel: 02 98 06 00 22
fax: 02 98 06 18 00
closed: last two weeks in Nov, Feb, Sun eve and Wed o.o.s.

Yes, it really was a mill, built in the 15th century and one of 15. The Venelle de Rosmadec, where the mill is located, is a small lane running between two branches of a charming river.

The Sebilleau family run a very friendly and homely place and it is a pity it has only four rooms. All have a bath and TV and are 76€ for two people, with breakfast an additional 7€. They are comfortable and quiet (except for the slight rumble of the waterwheel which is still in operation).

The restaurant, however, gets primary recognition here – and has for 60 years. The Sebillau's son, Frédéric, runs it and his reputation is nationwide. (He was voted one of the handful to be '*Jeunes Restaurateurs d'Europe 2000*'.) Fish and shellfish are specialities, with the outstanding one being grilled Breton lobster. *St-Pierre* grilled with artichokes is another very popular dish and the flambéed *crêpes* are as good as any in this land of *crêpes*. Menus are 27€, 48€ and 64€ and *à la carte* choices are available. The dining room is something of a treasure too.

Le Châtel (Cd'H) M
tel: 02 98 06 00 04
closed: Nov to Mar
no credit cards

This bed and breakfast is a collection of old buildings which comprise a deer farm. You can visit the animals and M. and Mme. Gourleouen sell venison pâtés and other farm products. All the rooms are different and furnished in truly rural style. All have a bath or shower and cost 48€ for two people and, for that, a fine breakfast is included.

Auberge de la Taupinière ✗ M
Croissant Saint André
tel: 02 98 06 03 12
fax: 02 98 06 16 46
closed: 22 Sept to 15 Oct, Mon, Tues

You just know this restaurant is unusual from the outside – painted light green, lots of windows and a thatched roof. When you get inside, it's just as unusual, as the best tables are those that give a view of the kitchen where you can watch Chef Guy Guilloux in action. He is always trying for improvement and the menus at 43–75€ contain dishes such as crab *crêpes*, grilled langoustines and a winning combination – *rouget* and *daurade*. If you have room for dessert, I can recommend the rhubarb and strawberry crumble.

PONT-CROIX

29790 (Finistère)
20 km E of Brest

A delightful old town for just wandering around and getting a real feel of old Brittany.

Ty-Evan 🛏 ✕ S
18 rue du Docteur Neis
tel: 02 98 70 58 58
fax: 02 98 70 53 38
closed: Jan to Feb

A small but cosy place next to the town hall and on the main square. The rooms are comfortable and 40–43€. Even if you don't stay here, the restaurant is well worth a stop. The speciality is seafood and the scallops are a popular item and usually on the menu. Meals are 13€, 20€ and 29€ and if you do stay here, demi-pension is 38€ per person.

PONTIVY

56300 (Morbihan)
43 km N of Vannes
market: Mon pm

Almost in the centre of Brittany, Pontivy is a medieval town strategically located at a junction of roads, river and canal. The Rohan family dominated it during the Middle Ages and built the castle at the end of the 15th century then Napoleon redesigned it at the beginning of the 19th century. The Place du Martray has many houses from the 15th and 16th centuries and the rue du Docteur Guepin leads to the church of Notre Dame de la Joie.

North of it and looking down at the river, the castle is surrounded by incredibly high walls and has two massive towers and a deep moat. Every third Sunday in September, there is the *Pardon de Notre Dame de la Joie*.

Rohan Wesseling 🛏 S-M
90 rue Nationale
tel: 02 97 25 02 01
fax: 02 97 25 02 85
open: all year

No restaurant here but that keeps down the price of the 18 rooms, all with a bath or shower and TV, to 48–64€ plus 6.5€ for breakfast.

PORS EVEN

22620 (Cd'A)
5 km NE of Paimpol

A small fishing village that is still fully operational and disregards tourists, although it does still supply them with their oysters, mussels and lobsters.

Pension Bocher 🛏 ✗ S
44 rue Pierre Loti
tel: 02 96 55 84 16
closed: early Nov to early Apr

A grey stone house, covered with creepers, on the road leading to the port. The 16 rooms are all neat and clean and four of them have sea views. The prices range from 28–64€ according to the view and the size. The lounge has a big log fire when the Atlantic weather warrants it. In the restaurant, seafood dominates and meals are from 16€.

PORT-LAUNAY

29150 Châteaulin (Finistère)
30 km NE of Quimper

In the middle of July, crowds flock here for the *Fêtes de Port-Launay*. There is entertainment, shows and displays and a big fireworks spectacular to conclude the proceedings.

Au Bon Accueil 🛏 ✗ S
avenue Louison Bobet
tel: 02 98 86 15 77
fax: 02 98 86 36 25
closed: Jan, Mon and Sun eve o.o.s.

A popular and always busy place with 45 rooms, each with a bath or shower and TV, at 29–56€ plus 6€ for breakfast. Mme. Le Guillou runs a good operation and keeps everything spic and span.

The restaurant brings in a lot of locals, especially for the lunch on weekdays at 10€. Evening meals are 12–35€ with wine included.

Several fish dishes are featured plus other choices. Demi-pension is an alternative at 37–52€.

PORT-LOUIS

52690 (Morbihan)
5 km S of Lorient
market: Sat

This small fishing port and seaside resort was once a powerful fortress. Its 16th-century citadel and the 17th-century ramparts are still a delight and major renovations have recently been completed.

Building of the citadel started in 1591 and work continued until it was finished by Cardinal Richelieu in 1636. Tours take 90 minutes. Its bigger neighbour, Lorient, overtook it in importance but Port-Louis is still a pleasure to stroll around. Look for the rue de la Poste, the rue des Dames and the rue du Driasker where you can see many old houses.

Du Commerce ⊨ ✗ S-M
1 place du Marché
tel: 02 97 82 46 05
fax: 02 97 82 11 02
closed: Sun eve and Mon o.o.s.

A small quiet hotel despite its location in the village centre where it occupies a shady spot on the market square. There are gardens and, in the rear, an orchard. Small but adequate rooms are 24–40€.

The restaurant serves a lunch menu during the week at 11€ though there are other meals up to 40€. In the evenings, a 16€ special brings in all the villagers and is prepared from all local ingredients. The 36€ is a good price for demi-pension.

PORT MANECH

29920 (Finistère)
6 km S of Pont Aven

A tiny fishing port on the south coast of Finistère.

PORT MANECH

Kerambris (Cd'H) S
tel: 02 98 06 83 82
open: all year
no credit cards

A long, stone farmhouse building has been delightfully converted into a most welcoming bed and breakfast just a few minutes from the cliffs, while the beach is only a little further. Here, you can take sailing lessons, play tennis, climb the cliffs or hike along the paths and trails.

The three twin rooms and one double room all have bathrooms. The rooms are simple but more than adequate. The price of 40€ for two including breakfast is a rare bargain for such tranquillity. There are, however, no meals.

PORT NAVALO
56640 (Morbihan)
32 km SW of Vannes

A lively port and popular seaside resort, right out on the western tip of the Presqu'île de Rhuys, the peninsula that almost closes in the Gulf of Morbihan completely. The Tumulus of Thumiac is about 6 km east and, in the opposite direction, you are looking across a narrow strait at the Pointe de Kerpenhir.

Grand Largue ✕ M
on the port
tel: 02 97 53 71 58
fax: 02 97 53 92 20
closed: mid-Nov to 20-Dec, early Jan to early Feb, Mon and Tues Sept to Jun, Mon lunch Jul and Aug

It's right in the port and Serge Adam, he with the big moustaches and the jolly manner, was voted one of the *'Jeunes Restaurateurs d'Europe'* – one of only five chefs in Brittany to be thus honoured.

Seafood is predominant, with products coming from the day's catch and also from the restaurant's own fishponds. Meal prices start from 26€.

PORTSALL

29830 (Finistère)
30 km N of Brest

An extremely scenic port and highly photographable. The Côtes des Abers runs from Conquet to Brigognan – an *aber* is an estuary or a shallow muddy inlet and there are 120 kilometres of them here with Portsall right in the middle.

La Demeure Océane 🛏 S
    tel: 02 98 48 77 42
    fax: 02 98 80 52 64
    open: all year

The building itself is not remarkable, a light-coloured house topped with a sloping roof and lots of skylight windows in it. Inside though, the hospitality of M. and Mme. Richard more than makes up for it. The six rooms and two duplexes all have showers and are simple but very pleasant and recently renovated. The rooms are priced at 45–60€ and the duplexes at 76€ with breakfast an additional 5.5€. They are spread over two storeys.

An evening meal is served every day and is predominantly fish and shellfish. The price is 16–29€ and M. Richard has a cellar of fine wines.

POULDREUZIC

29710 (Finistère)
15 km N of Pont l'Abbé

From Pont l'Abbé, you can take the D2 northwest to Pouldreuzic.

Breiz Armor 🛏 ✕ S-M
    plage de Penhors
    tel: 02 98 51 52 53
    fax: 02 98 51 52 30
    closed: mid-Oct to mid-Dec, 2 Jan to mid-Mar (during holiday periods, will accept bookings for groups and conferences)
    restaurant closed: Mon o.o.s. (except residents)

POULDREUZIC

Right on the beach at Penhors is this modest but more than adequate modern-style hotel and restaurant. The 32 rooms all have a bath and are 52–66€. The very satisfying meals (lots of seafood) are 12–40€ and the hotel is very popular with the locals.

Ker Ansquer 🛏 ✗ M
village of Lababan
tel: 02 98 54 41 83
fax: 02 98 54 32 24
e-mail: keransquer.com/francoise.ansquer@wanadoo.fr
closed: 1 Oct to 1 Apr

A stone, sturdy-looking building with a massive tower and a slate roof. The 11 rooms are all very well tended by Françoise Duduyer who has taken over from her mother, Mme. Ansquer, under whose auspices this hotel rose to recognition.

Its popularity has increased the price range of the rooms, which are now 56–125€, though the value at the lower end of the range is very good.

Meals are 16–48€, though, once again, value is excellent at the lower end. I had a sauerkraut dish with fish, similar to one at a famous restaurant in Paris – this one was far superior. If you are lucky, you may also catch a meal of the *pré-salé* lamb which is such a Brittany speciality.

Should you be in a mood for an aperitif before dinner, don't miss the *Algane*. It is based on seaweed and is unexpectedly delicious.

QUEMENEVEN

29180 (Finistère)
18 km E of Douarnenez

Penfrout (Cd'H) S
tel: 02 98 92 21 58
closed: 1 Nov to Easter
no credit cards

A truly rural farmhouse, owned and run by two generations of the Bourveau family. The two double rooms share a bathroom and all are large and impeccably decorated and maintained. Only 37€ for a room for two and the included breakfast uses ingredients from the farm.

QUESTEMBERT

56230 (Morbihan)
20 km SE of Vannes

The magnificent covered market was built in the 16th century and is an interesting wooden structure. St-Michael's chapel has a fine carved calvary. The town was the site of the last historic battle between Alain Barbe-Torte and the Norman invaders in 938. Its hotel-restaurant is renowned throughout France.

Le Bretagne M-L, L
13 rue St-Michel
tel: 02 97 26 11 12
fax: 02 97 26 12 37
closed: Jan, one week in Mar
restaurant closed: Mon, Tues lunch, Wed lunch

The nine rooms are spacious and quite luxurious and range from 93–192€ but it is the restaurant that is the star here. Georges Paineau and his son-in-law Claude Corlouer run the kitchen, combining and competing, both creative, both talented. The grilled lobster with spices and the *coquilles St-Jacques* with shallots are two of the notable dishes but the two chefs blend tastes from numerous regions and countries. The magnificent old dining room with its panelled walls, candelabra and paintings is an added bonus. Menus are 48–84€, which makes the demi-pension price of 128€ per person very attractive.

Cadoudal S
6 rue Cadoudal
tel: 02 97 26 10 37
closed: Feb
no credit cards

You won't find a less expensive place to stay than this – five rooms at 23–26€. Naturally, you don't expect luxury but, for an overnighter, Cadoudal is perfectly adequate. It has a garden and the sea is only 15 km away.

The restaurant though – that is another matter, with 90 seats spread through three rooms. Seafood and regional specialities are cooked well and in hearty portions. It's good value with menus at 10–26€.

QUEVERT

22100 (Finistère)
2 km W of Dinan

The village is in a handy location in the middle of the small peninsula that has its northern end at Dinard. Thus it makes an alternative to staying in Dinard or Dinan and if you like B&Bs, you will love this one...

Le Chêne Picard (Cd'H) S
tel: 02 96 85 09 21
open: all year

M. Bouillier has three pleasant rooms, all with private bathrooms and one of them is family sized. Use of the kitchen can be arranged, although Dinan with its range of restaurants is only minutes away. Breakfast is included in the price of 31–45€.

QUIBERON

56170 (Morbihan)
46 km SW of Vannes
market: Sat

Once an island, the peninsula is now part of the mainland while the coastal stretches are more varied and interesting. The sardine-canning factory used to be much larger than it is now, but is still in operation and has not changed a lot.

The ferry goes out to Belle-Île from Port Maria while here in Quiberon, the Grand Plage accommodates large numbers in the summer. Some of these come to attend the thalassotherapy centre. The west coast is known as the Côte Sauvage and is pockmarked with coves, inlets, caves and jagged rocks.

Opposite the fishing port, the Maison Riguidel is a *boulangerie, pâtisserie* and *confiserie par excellence*. The family has been here

QUIBERON

since 1893 and if you have not tasted the Breton speciality, *Kouign-Amann*, then this is the place to do so.

The museum occupies three levels and is open July, August and September. It deals with the region, its history, geography and its characters.

Le Bon Accueil 🛏 ✕ S
  6 quai de Houat
  tel: 02 97 50 07 92
  fax: 02 97 50 41 37
  closed: mid-Nov to mid-Dec
  no credit cards

Very simple and inexpensive accommodation in a small and friendly hotel where the rooms are 24–29€. You can have a very satisfying meal for around 12€. It is located near the ferry building on the quai.

Hôtel des Druides 🛏 ✕ M
  6 rue de Port Maria
  tel: 02 97 50 14 74
  fax: 02 97 50 35 72
  closed: 1 Oct to 1 Apr

Its location only two minutes from the beach makes it popular and the docks for boats to Belle-Île are only a little further.

The 31 rooms are well maintained under the strict eye of M. Machabey. They range from 47€ to 95€ which gives you a wide choice of size, amenities, views of the sea and, if you like, a balcony. Breakfast is 8€.

The restaurant is up to the standard of the hotel and the speciality is seafood. Menus are 13–28€ or 52–72€ for demi-pension.

La Petite Sirène 🛏 ✕ M
  15 boulevard René Cassin
  tel: 02 97 50 17 34
  fax: 02 97 50 03 73
  closed: early Nov to end Mar

La Petite Sirène is almost on the rocky seafront, next to the massive Sofitel Thalassa (a luxury hotel with seawater treatments and rooms costing up to 416€).

The 14 studios, all with baths, and four apartments with kitchenettes, are 55-69€, plus 7€ for breakfast. The food is fresh and the chef de cuisine, Gerard Jarno, cooks regional specialities mostly seafood. One of his outstanding dishes is the *Petit Navarin de Homard Breton en Cocotte* and after eating it, you may change your mind about the best way to eat lobster. Meals are good value at 16–40€.

Le Verger de la Mer ✕ S-M
1 boulevard de Goulvars
tel: 02 97 50 29 12
closed: Jan and most of Feb, Tues eve and Wed o.o.s.
no credit cards

A delightful little restaurant with excellent seafood, of which the most popular dish is the *Vol au Vent de Langoustines*. Meals are 15–26€.

QUIMPER

29000 (Finistère)
52 km SE of Brest
market: Wed and Sat

A very upmarket town with chic shops where seasoned visitors to the area come to buy their gifts to take home. The River Odet runs through the town, crossed by numerous bridges which, together with the town's popularity, make it a parking nightmare, even o.o.s..

Don't miss the guided tour of the Musée de l'Alambic at 69 Chemin du Quinquis. It's open every day from 10 am till 6 pm and you can taste the ciders and the apple-based liqueurs. A visit to 9 rue du Salle will give you something to tell the people back home – at the Crêperie La Krampouzerie, you can eat seaweed *crêpes*!

The last week in July is a jolly time here with the *Festival de Cornouaille*, plays in the Breton language, folk music, dancing, a big procession and the Enthronement of the Queen of Cornouaille (Breton for 'Cornwall').

Despite its attractiveness and its strategic location, Quimper is not blessed with many hotels. The best is an old favourite which fell into disrepair but has now been renovated.

La Tour d'Auvergne 🛏 ✗ M
   13 rue des Reguaires
   tel: 02 98 95 08 70
   fax: 02 98 95 17 31
   email: www.la-tour-dauvergne.fr

The 38 rooms are of a good size, comfortable and with all amenities, priced at 82–95€ plus 9.5€ for breakfast. Since its renovation, Mme. Le Brun has been bringing the place back to its former popularity. The restaurant serves a nice selection of dishes including many seafood plates at 23–47€.

Le Clos de la Tourbie ✗ S
   43 rue Elie Fréron
   tel: 02 98 95 45 03
   closed: Wed and Sat lunch

Chef Didier le Madec brings his expertise from London, Dublin and the Tour d'Argent in Paris to this elegant yet welcoming and friendly restaurant. It is next to the cathedral and gaily decorated with flowers and plants.

Menus are 15€, 23€ and 29€ and use only fresh ingredients in the rapidly changing dishes offered. Pigeon, guinea fowl and truffles are among the items you may expect to encounter and the spiced duck fricassée is very popular.

L'Ambroisie ✗ M
   49 rue Elie Fréron
   tel: 02 98 95 00 02
   fax: 02 98 95 88 06
   closed: last week in Jun, All Saints; Mon

Just above the cathedral, L'Ambroisie serves contemporary Breton cooking using local fish with delicate sauces. Chef-owner Guilbert Guyon has a sophisticated touch and menus at 18€, 29€, 39€ and 56€ are good value.

QUIMPERLÉ

29300 (Finistère)
35 km E of Concarneau
market: Fri

At the Pentecost weekend, Quimperlé celebrates the fête of Toulfouen.

La Maison d'Hippolyte (Cd'H) S
2 quai Surcouf
tel: 02 98 39 09 11
open: all year
no credit cards

Not only is Mme. Lescoat a charming hostess who speaks English, but also you will be impressed by her collection of paintings and photographs by Breton artists that fill the house. In fact, La Maison d'Hippolyte is very popular with visiting photographers from abroad. It sits on the bank of the Isole River as it runs through the town.

The four bedrooms are clean and comfortable and nicely decorated. All have a bath or shower, but two of them have to share a WC. The price is 42€ for two people with breakfast included – and in good weather this is served on a terrace looking out at the river. It is easy to find, just behind the Office de Tourisme.

QUINTIN

22800 (Cd'A)
18 km SW of St-Brieuc

One of the more historic communities On the Côtes d'Armor, Quintin was a powerful city until the 18th century. Its position on the banks of the River Gouët flowing down to St-Brieuc is still surrounded by the medieval ramparts which guarded the city. The streets are lined with 16th-century and 17th-century half-timbered houses. The château is 17th century and the church contains a priceless relic – a piece of the Virgin Mary's belt which is venerated by childless women.

Le Clos du Prince (Cd'HR) S
>10 rue des Croix Jarrots
>**tel:** 02 96 74 93 03
>**fax:** 02 96 74 96 03
>**open:** all year
>**no credit cards**

Mme. Marie-Madeleine Guilmoto has personally chosen the many antiques that furnish this very old house near the centre of the town of Quintin. The enormous living room with its stone walls has a fireplace and is as inviting as the one bedroom and one suite. Both have a bath or shower and the price is a modest 61€ for two, breakfast included. An extra bed can easily be accommodated in the suite for a further 24€. Evening meals can be served on request at 16€ (wine not included).

There are tennis courts, fishing and riding close by.

RAGUÉNÈS-PLAGE

29139 (Finistère)
12 km SW of Pont Aven

The small island is joined to the mainland at low tide by a causeway and together with a rocky coastline and a small harbour, it all makes a photographer's delight.

The main beach has firm sand and, at both ends of it, walks along the cliff tops are very inviting.

Raguénès is out at the tip of the Névez Penisula and nearby Rospico is a sheltered inlet with fine sands, likened by many to the typical pirates' cove. The small village of Kerascoet, a little way inland, is another place that gets the camera shutters clicking with its picturesque granite cottages with thatched roofs.

☆ Men Du 🛏 M
>rue des Îles
>**tel:** 02 98 06 84 22
>**fax:** 02 98 06 76 69
>**closed:** 1 Oct to 25 Mar, but open over Christmas and all school holidays

The popularity of the very attractive beaches at Raguénès enhances the popularity of the hotels here and the Men Du is another place that deserves strong recommendation.

It is a white building, standing high above the beach in an almost lonely location and is, in fact, a modern though small hotel with a loyal clientele.

The rooms, like the hotel, are small and all have views of the sea. They are well furnished and very comfortable and have fully equipped bathrooms. At 44–52€, they are extremely good value.

The large glassed-in terrace has a much better view of the beach and the sea than do the rooms and there is a cosy bar adjacent.

The welcome and the service are of a high order and the lack of a restaurant allows the management to concentrate on running the hotel.

REDON

35600 (I-et-V)
65 km SW of Rennes
market: Mon

From mid-July to mid-August, there is the Festival of the Abbey with music, song and dance. The rest of the year, this is a pleasant little 18th-century town with well-preserved houses along the quays. The weekly market brings vendors from all around with their local produce. In the square, the main feature is St-Sauveur, the remains of the 9th-century abbey founded by Brittany's first ruler, Nominoë. The arcaded Romanesque lantern tower made of sandstone and granite is particularly notable. This was built in the 12th century and is considered to be the finest in all Brittany. Opposite it is the Gothic belltower.

The rivers and canals of this part of Brittany have always been of high importance to the region and the Riverboat Museum on the quai Jean Bart not only has a fine display of these but you can see how families lived and worked on them. During the high season, you can also go on to a barge. The museum is open mid-June to mid-September, 10 am–12 noon and 3 pm–6 pm, while o.o.s. it is open Saturday, Sunday and Monday from 2 pm–6 pm.

Bel Hôtel 🛏 M
    42 avenue J. Burel
    tel: 02 99 71 10 10
    fax: 02 99 72 33 03
    open: all year, except 26–30 Dec

This is really in St-Nicholas, a suburb about 2 km from the centre of town but it's the best choice as Redon itself is not well endowed with hotels.

    The 34 rooms are 32–52€ and are comfortable and well tended. All have a bath or shower and TV. Breakfast is 5.5€. There is no restaurant and this keeps the price down.

La Bogue ✗ M
    3 rue des États
    tel: 02 99 71 12 95
    closed: Sun eve

A very friendly restaurant with a warm atmosphere and renowned for its good service. You can enjoy an excellent lunch for under 16€ and dinners are up to 48€ with wine included. Oysters, salmon and snails are frequently on the menu and there are veal and beef dishes too. A dessert featuring the local specialty – chestnuts – is not to be missed.

RENNES

35000 (I-et-V)
market: Sat

The southern part of town is relentlessly modern and the nothern part is more appealing as it contains the old city, now pedestrianized. Here, the best parts to see are in the area around the cathedral. A disastrous fire in the 18th century destroyed nearly everything. The Rennes of today is known, in the main, as a university town.

    Still, it has been the capital of Brittany for nearly 500 years. The part that survived the fire contains the half-timbered houses between the quai Duguay Trouin and the place des Lices. The rue St-Michel and the rue St-Georges are particularly appealing. (Rue

St-Georges also has rows of inexpensive eating places where you can enjoy *crêpes*, pizza, Indian food, Chinese food and even Brazilian food.)

The big attraction though is brand new. The Parliament building, ravaged by fire a few years ago, has recently been opened to the public after millions of euros worth of restoration work. The ceiling paintings in the Grand Chambre and the sculpted wood ceilings in the Jobbe Duval room must be seen. Priceless Gobelin tapestries showing critical periods in Breton history were destroyed in another fire that occurred during restoration but some remain. Tours are available including in English.

At the end of June and the beginning of July, night-time concerts are held and tableaux depict *La Tombée de la Nuit – Création Bretonne*. To brighten up the winter months, Transmusicales is a French rock festival held the second week in December. The flea market in the boulevard de la Liberté brings crowds every Thursday from 8 am–4 pm.

The presence of so many students should mean plenty of inexpensive places to eat but it doesn't. Similarly, the quality of most of the hotels is mediocre. There are a few that are acceptable.

Garden Hôtel S

3 rue Duhamel
tel: 02 99 65 45 06
fax: 02 99 65 02 62
closed: Christmas

Modern but clean and pleasant with 24 rooms at 40–52€. It has a simplicity that is attractive and a bar and patio on the ground floor. English is spoken.

Les Canotiers S-M

35 avenue Janvier
tel: 02 99 31 69 11
fax: 02 99 31 40 11
open: all year

Its 28 very pleasant rooms are simply but charmingly decorated at 55€ plus 6€ for breakfast. Meals are similarly simple but adequate and demi-pension is 60€.

Le Corsaire ❌ M

>52 rue d'Antrain
>**tel & fax:** 02 99 36 33 69

Antoine Luce has been cooking here for 20 years serving lunch and dinner every day. His cooking is refined but traditional, no frills, no thrills, nothing complicated but high quality and consistency throughout. The braised ox tail with an escalope of *foie gras* gives an idea of the simplicity and menus are 18–32€.

L'Escu de Runfao ❌ S-M

>11 rue du Chapitre
>**tel:** 02 99 79 13 10
>**fax:** 02 99 79 43 80
>**closed:** three weeks Aug, Sat lunch, Sun

The old oak beams are part of the medieval remains of this building in the heart of the old town where Alain Duhoux will make sure that you have value for money. Its three dining rooms on two levels have pleased diners – locals and visitors – for years and standards have not only held but risen. Outside, the terrace by the fountain has charm in the summer and is popular for lunch.

When game is in season, you have plenty of choice of great dishes but when it is not, Alain Duhoux does wonders with fish. One of his specialities is sea bass stuffed with hot oysters and a real Breton plate is the veal sweetbreads and lobster in a cream and Sauternes sauce.

An interesting selection of wines from the south-west of France is on offer and the service is always discreet and efficient.

Hôtel de Léon 🛏 S

>15 rue de Léon
>**tel:** 02 99 30 55 28
>**fax:** 02 99 36 59 11
>**open:** all year

If you're looking for a reliable and really inexpensive place for an overnight stop, you can do no better than the de Léon. It's near the quai Richemont and the nine rooms (decorated by the owner) are 27–32€, plus a 5€ breakfast.

LA RICHARDAIS

35780 (Î-et-V)
5 km S of Dinard

On the west bank of the River Rance is this small village with a little boat harbour and sailing school. Painters love the views over the river from here.

La Soupière ✕ S
   14 rue des Genêts
   tel: 02 99 46 69 55
   fax: 02 99 88 16 16
   open: all year
   no credit cards

The locals swarm in here for the inexpensive seafood. The medallions of *lotte* are a popular and regular dish but the tray of *fruits de mer* gets plenty of takers. Menus are 13–18€.

RIEC-SUR-BÉLON

29340 (Finistère)
5 km S of Pont Aven
market: Wed

From its location on the Bélon River, you would expect this to be a great place to eat oysters – and so it is – the Mecca of oyster-lovers (in both meanings).

Domaine de Keristinec ⊨ ✕ M
   tel: 02 98 06 42 98
   fax: 02 98 06 45 38
   open: all year
   restaurant closed: Sun eve o.o.s.

Just 17 rooms and one apartment at 52–104€ but very well equipped and M. Soufflez keeps everything shipshape. This is the country that Gauguin loved to paint but really, those considerations are all secondary to 'Kerland', the restaurant here at the Domaine.
   Langoustines braised in champagne, shoulder of lamb roasted in

thyme and raspberry-champagne soup – these are just two of the delicious dishes at 18–56€. Seafood takes priority but everything on the menu is beyond reproach. English is spoken and the demi-pension should be considered at 63–84€.

☆ Chez Jacky ✗ S-M
   on the port
   tel: 02 98 06 90 32
   fax: 02 98 06 49 72
   closed: Christmas, Mon except holidays

A restaurant of renown, esteemed far and wide. It is a basic, authentic restaurant on the Bélon River and the oyster beds are right outside it. The *plateau de fruits de mer* is the most popular dish and though there have been criticisms of the lobster dishes, the place continues to pull the crowds and reservations are essential. The décor is rustic and the menus run from 16–64€.

LA ROCHE BERNARD
56130 (Morbihan)
40 km SE of Vannes
market: Thurs

A perfect anchorage, with old and new harbours, on the river Vilaine, upriver of the *barrage*. The river is particularly attractive just here, wide and tree-lined; two ancient cannons defend the entrance, many masts swim in the early morning mists beneath the great new bridge.

The main street is dull, but the old quarter leading down from the place du Bouffay to the creek is worth seeing as it is picturesquely cobbled and geraniumed.

Auberge des Deux Magots ⊨ ✗ M
   1 place du Bouffay
   tel: 02 99 90 60 75
   fax: 02 99 90 87 87
   closed: Sun eve and Mon, one week in Oct, 20 Dec to 15 Jan, one week in Jun

A smart, serious-looking building of stone, beautifully decorated and furnished throughout. The 14 rooms all have a bath or shower and TV. They range from 45-52€ but larger, family size rooms are available at 61–77€. The cooking is of a high standard and meals are 13–39€.

L'Auberge Bretonne 🛏 ✗ M-L

    2 place Duguesclin
    tel: 02 99 90 60 28
    fax: 02 99 90 85 00
    closed: 12 Nov to 1 Dec; 3 Jan to 26 Jan
    restaurant closed: Thurs; lunchtimes Mon, Tues, Fri

This is really a restaurant with eight rooms, and the two Michelin stars that Jacques Thorel has earned for his cooking affirms that. You may not want to pay 77–224€ for a room, even though they are spacious and well furnished in Breton style, when there is a wide choice of less expensive accommodation nearby. On the other hand, the meals are unquestionably worth their 24–72€ as they are a true dining experience. The roast lobster is high on the list of recommendations, and some of the desserts are truly staggering.

Domaine de Bodeuc 🛏 ✗ M

    tel: 02 99 90 89 63
    fax: 02 99 90 90 32

Strictly speaking, the Domaine is in the village of Nivillac which is on the other side of the busy A165 from La Roche Bernard, although the two are close. It stands in a large park of hundred-year-old trees. M. and Mme. Grandpère are the most gracious of hosts and the décor and furnishing are of a very high standard. The ground floor lounge is a popular meeting spot for guests. The swimming pool is heated and there is a library and billiards.

Eight rooms all have a bath or shower and TV and are 84–92€, while breakfast is an additional 7€. Monsieur Grandpère is the chef and his dishes are simple but tasty, priced at 28€ for three courses.

ROCHEFORT-EN-TERRE

56220 (Morbihan)
25 km NW of Redon

A photographer's dream – one of the prettiest villages in Brittany, surrounded by glorious countryside. Geraniums are everywhere and the main street is lined with 16th- and 17th-century granite houses. An elaborate calvary stands in the place de l'Église but the castle is in ruins except for its imposing gateway, part of the walls and some underground passages.

Its *pardon* on the third Sunday in August is famous and draws large crowds. The Park of Prehistory is only 3 km away.

A very popular local visit is to the Château et Musée de Rochefort-en-Terre. It is built on a high rock and is in Renaissance style, having been constructed during the 16th and 17th centuries. It is a genuine feudal castle though some restoration was done during the 20th century. This was through the intervention (and the money) of an American, Alfred Klots, and part of the castle buildings contain his art collection. The château and museum are open April to October every day. There is a small fee but guided tours are free and you can ask for one in English.

Château de Talhouet (Cd'H) M
tel: 02 97 43 34 72
fax: 02 97 43 35 04
open: all year

A real château in the traditional Breton style and very expertly restored and converted into a superior small hotel. The eight rooms are comfortable and border on the luxurious. Many have antiques and seven of them have very well-equipped bathrooms while the other has a shower. All have TV and the price range is 96–152€, including breakfast.

The games room, the salon and the dining room are as you would expect in a château. An evening meal is served at 39€, not including wine. Jean-Pol Soulaine is an attentive host.

ROCHE MAURICE

29800 (Finistère)
5 km SE of Landerneau

The ossuary in the church dates from 1640 and is one of the finest in Brittany. Outside, the carvings depict Satan, with a spear, menacing a selection of characters representing most of humanity.

Le Vieux Château ✕ S
    4 Grand Place
    tel: 02 98 20 40 52
    closed: evenings, except weekends
    no credit cards

By the church, on the village square and next to the ruins of an 11th-century château – what more could you ask?

What you get is perhaps the best value in the region. The weekday lunch costs 9€ and menus in the evening are 12€, 15€ and 20€. The *blanquette* of monkfish with saffron is one of the recommended dishes but there is a wide choice.

ROSCOFF

29211 (Finistère)
25 km NW of Morlaix

This old harbour town occupies the tip of a peninsula that stands on guard at the entrance to the Bay of Morlaix. Do not confuse it with the ferry port to the east which is modern and strictly practical.

The rue Amiral-Reveillère is lined with 16th- and 17th-century granite houses, many with classical dormer windows. Mary, Queen of Scots landed in Roscoff in 1548 as a child bride and stayed in number 25 on this street. Some 200 years later, Bonnie Prince Charlie landed here, escaping from his English pursuers and seeking military help from the French court.

You will also see here the Gothic Church of Notre Dame de Kroaz Baz with its extraordinary three-tiered steeple. The guns and ships carved on the outside are unusual and in the nature of 'a word from our sponsor', as the wealthy shipowners in Roscoff were largely responsible for the finances to build the church. Nearby is the Aquarium, a part of the marine biology research centre.

Across the harbour is the small Chapelle Ste-Barbe, sitting proudly on a rock at the Pointe de Blascon amid the giant saltwater pools full of crab, crayfish and lobster. You can visit these on working days 10.30 am–12 pm and 3 pm–6 pm.

In the 19th century, onions were a big export from this region and England was the main market. The sellers would spend six months or so there and return with English habits. The Musée des Johnnies tells this story in an episodic but amusing way. It is in a small chapel on the waterfront and is open June to September, every day except Tuesday 10 am–12 pm and 3 pm–6 pm.

From the ferry port, you can take a 15-minute ride out to the Île de Batz.

Hôtel Talabardon M

place de l'Église
tel: 02 98 61 24 95
fax: 02 98 61 10 54
closed: 26 Oct to end Feb

The Talabardon family has been running this place for well over a hundred years. It is a beautiful Breton-style building, right on the church square and facing on to the sea and the Île de Batz channel.

The 39 rooms are well equipped and 53–106€ plus 9€ for breakfast. The family are chefs and serve seafood specialities prepared from local ingredients in a sumptuous dining room from which you can watch the sea. Menus are 20€, 28€ and 44€.

Hôtel Brittany M

22 boulevard Ste-Barbe
tel: 02 98 69 70 78
fax: 02 98 61 13 29
closed: 21 Oct to end Mar

Be sure to ask for a room in the old part of the hotel which is right on the picturesque port. All the rooms are comfortable, but the older ones are better located and better furnished than those in the annexe. They are 60–120€ so you can tell they vary considerably in size and attractions.

The restaurant is known for its good food and the kitchen uses interesting approaches to fish dishes, which are 16–45€.

☆ Le Temps de Vivre ✗ M
19 place Lacaze Duthiers
tel: 02 98 19 33 19
fax: 02 98 19 33 00
closed: Sun eve, Mon and Tues lunch; three weeks in Oct, three weeks in Mar

This is one of the outstanding restaurants in Brittany and you don't even have to go out of your way to enjoy it. It is located on the waterfront, right in the centre of the picturesque port of Roscoff which you will certainly be visiting.

The chef makes it this renowned, of course. Jean-Yves Crenn is known all along the northern coast and he believes in using the traditional food of Leon as his base, then finding ingenious and delicious interpretations of it. As icing on the cake, a meal here is not that expensive.

Langoustines in various imaginative ways are always on the menu. A speciality which recurs often was happily on offer the day I ate there – *St-Pierre* with a cream sauce of cauliflower and almonds in a bouillon of tomatoes and white wine. But no matter what Jean-Yves cooks, he makes use of the fresh fish from the ocean and the fresh fruit and vegetables from inland. Menus are 28–60€.

ROSNOEN

29580 (Finistère)
28 km SW of Brest

Rosnoen's location on the River Aulne has always made it a regular stop for river traffic. In the 16th century, the raising of bees here saw the replacement of sugar with honey and the Écomusée de l'Abeille, just up river, tells you the story. At Térénez, near the museum are the fish ponds that were active at the time.

The powder magazine on the tiny Île of Arun was built in 1692 – showing yet another activity of these busy Rosnoenians.

The town is not endowed with hotels but Stéphane Brindeau's bed and breakfast place has six rooms, all with TV and one with a view of the river. She is on 02 98 81 06 90 or fax 02 98 81 08 81 and charges only 32-39€ with breakfast included.

ROZ-SUR-COUESNON

35610 (Î-et-V)
5 km W of Mont St-Michel

Just on the Île-et-Vilaine side of the border with Normandy is this village, almost on the beach. It is very handy for visiting the nearby famed island-castle.

From the perched position of the village, you have panoramic views of the 'polders', vast expanses of sandy beach reclaimed from the sea. You may see some of the flocks of salt-meadow sheep from whence comes the lamb *pré-salé*.

The importance of sheep to the region is emphasized by the *Pardon du Mouton*, the procession of the sheep followed by an open-air mass on the first Sunday in August.

Les Quatres Salines ⊨ ✗ S
  3 rue des Quatres Salines
  tel: 02 99 80 23 80
  fax: 02 99 80 21 73
  open: all year

This unorthodox-looking but trim hotel-restaurant surrounded by bright clumps of flowers has 18 rooms at a very modest 36–42€ plus 6€ for breakfast. English is spoken and the restaurant, which serves mostly seafood, is very popular. Demi-pension is offered at 3344€.

SABLES-D'OR-LES-PINS

22240 (Cd'A)
45 km W of St-Malo

A charming beach resort with sands just as golden as its name. Many say they are the finest in Brittany. There is also a nine-hole golf course and lots of hotels and restaurants.

It caters strongly for children too with pony rides, sand dunes and pedal cars. For less energetic children, the electric cars are popular. It is on an exposed stretch of the Emerald Coast so the wind can occasionally be annoying.

Hôtel de Diane ⊨ ✗ S-M
>avenue des Acacias
>**tel:** 02 96 41 42 07
>**fax:** 02 96 41 42 67
>**closed:** Nov to Mar

This large building a very agreeable ambiance, and more than half of the 28 rooms have fine views of the beach. The price of 56–60€ is agreeable, too, as you get a bath or shower and a TV in all the rooms. Breakfast is 10€ and demi-pension is 48–54€. Meals may be obtained separately at 11€ for lunch and 15–38€ for dinner.

Le Manoir St-Michel ⊨ M
>à la Carquois
>**tel:** 02 96 41 48 87
>**fax:** 02 96 41 41 45
>**closed:** 2 Nov to 1 Apr

A 16th-century manor house just over a kilometre out of Sables-d'Or on the D34 going north to Cap Fréhel. It has been well converted into a hotel with 17 rooms, not large but clean and smart, quiet and all with a bath or shower and TV. The gardens are delightful and though there is no restaurant, there are several nearby.

STE-ANNE-D'AURAY

56400 (Morbihan)
16 km W of Vannes

This is one of the holiest places in Brittany and the most famous *pardon* in Brittany is held here on the 25th and 26th of July. It pays homage to Ste-Anne, the mother of the Virgin Mary and the patroness of Brittany. The Basilica is a bit grim with its massive appearance but the grounds around it are expansive.

L'Auberge ⊨ ✗ S
>56 route de Vannes
>**tel:** 02 97 57 61 55
>**fax:** 02 97 57 69 10
>**closed:** Nov, Dec

Exceptional value for money here where M. and Mme. Jean-Luc Larvoir are friendly and helpful (he is the chef de cuisine) and they take a real pleasure in satisfying the customer. The nine rooms are spacious and comfortable, have bathrooms and TV and are a real bargain at 36–48€ (a price level that has been held for a number of years!).

Nevertheless, it is the cooking that is the star attraction. The beamed ceilings, the copper pans and the numerous implements of Breton life make the dining room a delight. Produce is always fresh and everything is cooked to order. The service is impeccable and the price of 16–56€ is exceptionally good value. Demi-pension is even a little better at 39–45€.

The food must be good because Pope John Paul came to lunch here when he visited Ste-Anne. 'What did he eat?' you ask eagerly. He had fish soup, langoustines and sea bass.

La Croix Blanche ⊨ ✕ M

25 route de Vannes
tel: 02 97 57 64 44
fax: 02 97 57 50 60
open: all year

A good alternative to L'Auberge (it's right opposite), with rooms at 32–60€ and the added advantage of a garden. The dining room serves very good meals at 14–40€ with a nice variety of choices.

STE-ANNE-LA-PALUD

29127 (Finistère)
16 km N of Douarnenez

A popular seaside resort with good sandy beaches that are great for walking along.

The *pardon*, or pilgrimage, is a feature of Brittany life and the most famous in the *département* is the *pardon* here in Ste-Anne-la-Palud (*palud* means marshland). It is held the last weekend in August and there are spectacular processions on both the Saturday and the Sunday with the destination being the Chapel of Ste-Anne, surrounded by green meadows and herds of grazing cows. This is the fourth chapel to be erected on the site since the first one in the 6th century.

ST-ANNE-LA-PALUD

The Hôtel de la Plage has a fine reputation and it is on the beach by the bay. Rooms are 160–224€ and meals 48–72€ in the one-star restaurant where Jean-Pierre Gloanec has been cooking high-quality meals for 30 years.

ST-AUBIN-DES-LANDES

35500 (Î-et-V)
9 km W of Vitré

Aubin was the Bishop of Angers in the 6th century. The church is one of the most visited in the region and has a Roman nave and a choir added in the 17th century. The tall, slim spire is exceptionally graceful and most attractive.

The village known as Les Lacs is named after the slate quarry which produces an unusual grey-green slate. It was re-opened in 1960 when restoration work was beginning on many historical monuments and this was the only source of the unusual stone.

Restaurant des Lacs ✖ S
Les Lacs
tel: 02 99 49 51 22
fax: 02 99 49 56 62
open: all year

The restaurant does most of the business in the neighbourhood and you know why when you see that it has 350 seats and menus that start at 9€. If you want only one course, the *plat du jour* is only 5.5€. Heartier eaters can be accommodated too, with menus up to 26€.

ST-AVÉ

56890 (Morbihan)
5 km N of Vannes

In case you don't want to stay in the relatively busy town of Vannes with its (relatively) teeming population of nearly 50,000, here is a close and very good alternative. In the village of St-Avé, you can visit the Chapel of Notre Dame du Loc and walk the old ramparts. The Château du Plessis-Josso and the fortress of Largoet are also close.

Moulin de Lesnéhué 🛏 S
Lesnéhué
tel: 02 97 60 77 77
fax: 02 97 60 78 39

An extremely attractive grey stone mill from the 15th century by the banks of a small river. The 12 rooms are simple but modern with modern furniture and very comfortable. It's all very rural and the rooms are only 40–45€ with breakfast an extra 5€.

Pressoir ✗ M
7 rue de l'Hôpital
tel: 02 97 60 87 63
fax: 02 97 44 59 15
closed: first two weeks in Mar, first week in Jul, first three weeks Oct, Tues lunch Nov to Apr, every Sun eve and Mon

A highly reputable restaurant and its clientele come out from Vannes to enjoy the outstanding cooking. One of chef Bernard Rambaud's specialities is the *Galette de Rouget* with rosemary potatoes and an unusual dish is the Baked Eel from Guémené with buckwheat tagliatelli. A meal is around 24€ for lunch but dinner is more at 32–64€ – very reasonable for food of this tradition and quality.

ST-BRIAC-SUR-MER

35800 (Î-et-V)
16 km W of St-Malo
market: Mon am Jul and Aug

A picturesque spot with beautiful bays, sandy beaches and small islands offshore. Around the 17th-century church are narrow streets and winding walks where many famous painters have put the scenes on canvas. There are eight beaches, all with fine sand.

The second Sunday in August sees crowds gather here for the *Fête des Mouettes* (seagulls). Dancers and entertainers from all over Brittany come for this event and there are dozens of bagpipers (taken by some as confirmation that there was some collusion between the prehistoric builders in Scotland and Brittany). A procession goes through the town and is followed by folk dancing and the *Fest-Noz* (night festival).

Then there is the *Pardon de la Mer* in the first two weeks of July and a pilgrimage to the Chapel de l'Epine in September.

Manoir de la Duchée (Cd'H) M
tel: 02 99 88 00 02
fax: 02 96 27 28 96
open: all year
no credit cards

An exceptionally smart 17th-century manor house with an extension at one end in timber, stone and sporting large windows. It has four bedrooms with a bath and TV. One is on the ground floor, the others upstairs and all are very comfortable. Breakfast is included at 56€ for two people, but there is also a suite at 80€ for three or four people.

The big fireplace, the chandelier and the antique furniture maintain the manor house atmosphere while M. and Mme. Stenou keep the place in tip-top shape.

Mme. Couplière (Cd'H)
Le Clos du Pont Martin
tel: 02 99 88 38 07
email: dcoupl@club.internet.fr
open: all year

A three-star bed and breakfast with three rooms although only one has a private bath and shower. All rooms have TV and refrigerator and mini-bar. All are priced at 52€.

De la Houle
14 boulevard de la Houle
tel: 02 99 88 32 17
fax: 02 99 88 96 11
closed: Mar
restaurant open: Fri-Mon evenings only
no credit cards

Renowned in the neighbourhood for its wide variety of well-prepared seafood dishes. The *fruits de mer* tray is very popular and the *plat du jour* is under 16€.

ST-BRICE-EN-COGLES

35460 (Î-et-V)
market: 2nd Sun in month

Le Lion d'Or ⨳ ✕ S
6 rue Châteaubriand
tel: 02 99 98 61 44
fax: 02 99 97 85 66
open all year

A small but smart little place, excellent for an overnight, inexpensive stop. The 24 rooms are fully equipped, including TV, and only 42–48€ plus 6€ for breakfast. Demi-pension is 42–52€ and meals start at 13€. English is spoken. The seafood is very popular.

ST-BRIEUC

22000 (Cd'A)
58 km W of Dinan
market: Tues and Fri

Its museum is open on the rue des Lycéens-Martyrs every day. The big event of the year though – held in mid-June – is the rock music festival. Artists from all five continents come for this and it's a biggie. Performances fill all the concert halls and there are numerous outdoor events.

Ker Izel ⨳ M
20 rue du Gouët
tel: 02 96 33 46 29
fax: 02 96 61 86 12

It's near the cathedral and the 12 rooms are comfortable and attractively decorated, priced at 39–52€. The single-storey annexe in the rear has chalet-type rooms. Not exciting but practical.

Le Sympatic ✕ S
9 boulevard Carnot
tel: 02 96 94 04 76
closed: Sat lunch, Sun and last three weeks Aug

A warm atmosphere with good food and the faint aroma of the vine shoots burning in the fireplace grill. Menus are 11€, 14€, 17€, 23€ and 36€. The service is efficient and Le Sympatic is open till 11 pm.

Aux Pesked ✕ M
5 rue du Légué
tel: 02 96 33 34 65
fax: 02 96 33 65 38
closed: before Christmas to mid-Jan and Sat lunch, Sun eve and Mon

Owner Thierry Martin and Chef Thierry Bernard prepare only the freshest of the fish catch and every dish shows the master touch of a culinary artist. The chef employs ginger, lemon, lime and vanilla, for example, to achieve unusual flavours. Check on when they are having a wine *soirée*. Menus are 19€, 31€, 47€ and 58€.

ST-CAST-LE-GUILDO

22380 (Cd'A)
32 km W of St.-Malo

It is not so much a town, more a tight cluster of villages. The seven well-protected beaches are popular and there are numerous small harbours for fishing and pleasure boats.

One of the villages making up St-Cast is Pen Guen, with a long beach fringed by pine trees and sand dunes. Further along is La Garde with perhaps the best beach of all and Le Bourg and L'Île are two more of these villages also with good beaches.

☆ Château du Val d'Arguenon 🛏 (L)
Notre Dame du Guildo
tel: 02 96 41 07 03
fax: 02 96 41 02 67
closed: 1 Oct to 31 Mar
no credit cards

The 16th-century building is very well preserved. The rooms are large and with high ceilings, well decorated and furnished with antiques. One room is named Châteaubriand after the famous writer who used to stay here when his uncle owned it. Olivier and Armelle de la Blanchardière are friendly, young hosts who speak

English and are anxious to please.

There are four rooms at 72–96€ for two people, and one suite at 128€ which sleeps three people. All have a bath or shower and an excellent breakfast is included in the price, which is served in the lovely large dining room.

Le Colombier de Galinée (Cd'H) M
>La Galinée
>**tel:** 02 96 41 19 77
>**fax:** 02 96 41 19 87
>**no credit cards**

A bed and breakfast that gets great reviews from everyone who stays here. Only two rooms, both large and very comfortable, one priced at 61€ and the other at 96€. Both have TV. A park is adjacent.

Le Biniou ✗ M
>route Dinard
>**tel:** 02 96 41 94 53
>**closed:** 20 Nov to 15 Feb; Tues 15 Sept to 15 Jun; school holidays; Mon eve in winter

A very popular eating spot, smart and busy. All those flames you see are from lobsters being flambéed at the table. It is one of the specialities of the house and extremely well prepared (they use whisky). Red mullet baked in fruit-flavored olive oil is another and if you've had enough seafood for a while, the *pigeonneau farci aux trois champignons* is the dish to order. Three-course meals run from 15–39€ and the view is great.

ST-DIDIER

35220 (Î-et-V)
6 km E of Châteaubourg

Pen'Roc ⊨ ✗ M
>La Peinière
>**tel:** 02 99 00 33 02
>**fax:** 02 99 62 30 89
>**closed:** Sun eve o.o.s., 26 30 Dec

ST-DIDIER

An attractive stone building, completely modernised and out in the countryside. The 33 rooms are in rustic style (even though they are modern), large and comfortable and start at 68€ out of season and range up to 80€ in peak season. Apartments are available at 136€. These prices are justified by the impressive array of amenities – a heated swimming pool, gymnasium and sauna.

The food is of high quality and many home-grown ingredients are used. Menus start at 21€.

ST-JEAN-DU-DOIGT

29228 (Finistère)
17 km NE of Morlaix

A strong candidate for the town with the strangest name in Brittany. The finger referred is that of John the Baptist, said to have been brought here from the Holy Land by a crusading knight. It is housed in the 15th-century church which is a few kilometres in from the coast and east of Plougasnou.

Naturally, such a holy relic draws large numbers of pilgrims on 23 and 24 June and, although you cannot see the finger, it is believed to effect cures, particularly on the blind.

Le Ty Pont ⊨ ✕ S
Le Bourg
tel: 02 98 67 34 06
fax: 02 98 67 85 94
closed: mid-Nov to Mar, Mon o.o.s.

A modest little place in the village centre and very popular with the locals. The prices have not changed in five years – rooms are still 23–37€ and menus start at 12€.

ST-JOUAN-DES-GUÉRÊTS

35430 (Î-et-V)
3 km W of St.-Malo

St-Jouan is located just a little way down the estuary from St-Malo and is an alternative to staying in the busy town. St-Jouan dates from the 13th century. Two old mills stand at the entrance to the town, the Moulin du Domaine and the Moulin Quinard. Le Bos is an 18th-century house built by a wealthy shipowner from St-Malo. It is open to the public.

La Malouinière ⊨ M
Les Longchamps
tel: 02 99 82 74 00
fax: 02 99 82 74 14
closed: All Saints to Easter

A long, stone, impressive-looking building with nine rooms all with a bath or shower and TV. English is spoken and the standard is high throughout. There is no restaurant but this keeps the price down to 58–88€ which is very good value.

Manoir de Blanche Roche (Cd'H)
tel: 02 99 19 11 11
open: all year
no credit cards

The owner, Mme. Bertin, describes the building as a 19th-century English manor house and it is on the road between Rennes and St-Malo, only 5 km from the sea. Everything about this bed and breakfast is top class and the five rooms are well furnished and all have bathrooms. The TV is in a large and comfortable lounge while around the place is a wooded park. Very good value and personalised attention for 32–63€.

ST-LORMEL

22130 (Î-et-V)
15 km SE of Dinard

La Pastourelle (Cd'H)
tel: 02 96 84 03 77
closed: 15 Nov to Easter
no credit cards

Near the town of Plancoët, almost on the banks of the Arguenon River, lies this long, low, stone farmhouse that typifies the Brittany region. M. and Mme. Lede live in a separate wing of the house so that guests have their own part of it. Antiques abound and Mme. Lede has decorated the five bedrooms with flower-print wallpaper and pastel-coloured carpets. Each bedroom has its own bathroom and costs 44€ for a double or 28€ demi-pension.

Dinner is served in the pleasant dining room and fresh local ingredients are used. Being so close to the sea, fish and shellfish feature much of the time.

ST-MALO

35400 (Î-et-V)
market: Tues, Fri

After being a vital seaport for centuries, St-Malo was almost completely destroyed in 1944 by Allied bombing. Rebuilding has been expertly done though and if you follow the signs for 'Intra Muros' (within the walls), you enter the walled city of the past.

Walk along the ramparts (which survived the bombing) and the gate you see with enormous drum-shaped towers dates from the 15th century. By the porte de Dinan, ferries run to Dinard across the Rance River. The Mole des Noires is a jetty which stretches 500 metres out to sea.

For a tour of the best historical sights follow the signs that start in the place Châteaubriand. The cathedral of St-Vincent goes back to the 12th century and its tall spire is a landmark. The Demeure des Magon de la Lande is an 18th-century mansion built for one of the town's wealthiest merchants and is worth seeing for its architecture. Open in summer 10 am–12 pm and 2 pm–6.30 pm.

The cobblestone streets and the small squares have inviting little cafés and gift shops. The Museum in the Château is open every day except Tuesdays. In season, there are guided tours at 10.45 am, 2 pm, 3.15 pm and 4.30 pm. One of the biggest flea markets in Brittany is held every Tuesday from June to September, 8 am–6 pm. Nearby Paramé has some fine beaches and the ferry ride to Dinard is very popular.

A good approach here is to stay outside the walls for the best accommodation and stroll into town for dinner. The French call 'in town' *intra muros* but in case you really want to stay inside the walls, the following choices are listed.

INTRA MUROS

De La Porte St-Pierre 🛏 ✖ M
   2 place du Guet
   tel: 02 99 40 91 27
   fax: 02 99 56 06 94
   closed: Dec, Jan

It looks exactly like one of those little hotels you see in French movies or even a Hollywood movie that is supposed to be in France. The glassed-in front on the ground floor with tables and chairs outside on the pavement, then the bedroom windows above for two or three storeys. The 25 bedrooms in this case are all comfortable, fully equipped and 48–61€. English is spoken and the restaurant – which is popular with locals – serves reliable meals at 16–28€.

France et Châteaubriand 🛏 ✖ M
   place Châteaubriand
   tel: 02 99 56 66 52
   fax: 02 99 40 10 04
   open: all year

Châteaubriand was born here and some of the rooms look as if they have not changed much since that time. Still, there's no denying that this is a landmark building and it has character oozing out of the walls. From the third floor up, the view of the bay is great over the city ramparts. The 80 rooms are 68–88€ and quite comfortable, while the café-terrace is a magnet for tourists, residents and locals. Demi-pension is 56–64€.

☆ La Duchesse Anne ✖ M-L
   5 place Guy La Chambre
   tel: 02 99 40 85 33
   fax: 02 99 40 87 53
   closed: Dec, Jan; Sun eve, Mon lunch, Wed o.o.s.

It's almost as well-known as the Louvre and it seems as if everyone who has been to Brittany has eaten here. All have such good memories of it, though, that a word or two of assurance that this restaurant is as good as ever is justified.

At 32–48€ the price of a meal is worth every penny. The food is excellent, cooked to order (and to perfection), the service and the very Frenchness of it all plus the 1920s décor make it an experience to eat here. Their *sole meunière* is rightfully renowned and all the shellfish out of the nearby Bay of Mont St-Michel are superb.

Le Chalut ✗ M
8 rue de la Corne de Cerf
tel & fax: 02 99 56 71 58
closed: Sun eve, Mon, Tues o.o.s.

Small and very popular, Le Chalut is in the town centre and has a very pronounced nautical atmosphere. The accent is naturally on seafood, using high-quality ingredients, well cooked and smartly served. These factors make this one of the best places to eat anywhere around St-Malo and meals are 16–40€.

À l'Abordage ✗ S-M
5 place de la Poissonerie
tel: 02 99 40 87 53
fax: 02 99 56 66 74
closed: Thurs

A restaurant that is opposite the *Halle aux Poissons* naturally has the freshest of fish. The *plateau* of seafood is a favourite, lobster is too and the *lotte* with apples in cider is a delicious Normandy dish. Meals are 12–32€.

Brasserie Armoricaine ✗ S
6 rue du Boyer
tel: 02 99 40 89 13
fax: 02 99 40 46 42
closed: Sun eve and Mon o.o.s.

Seafood that is hard to beat and at great prices – that is the Brasserie, busy, bustling and popular. The cooking is highly traditional and always reliable. Meals at 10–20€.

La Coquille d'Oeuf ✗ S
20 rue de la Corne de Cerf
tel: 02 99 40 92 62
closed: Mon

Looking for a change from seafood? Here it is and meals at 11–16€. The *filet mignon* of pork in a red beetroot sauce is a good choice and so are the strips of duck breast in acacia honey.

OUTSIDE THE WALLS

Most of the places to eat and stay that are outside are still very close to the town. The best locations are along the beach, around La Grand Plage and along the beach of Rochebonne as far as Rothéneuf – that's going east. Going west, the adjoining town of St-Servan (the original settlement for St-Malo and listed separately in this book) has many good places.

Manoir de La Grassinais 🛏 ✖ M
12 rue de la Grassinais
tel: 02 99 81 33 00
fax: 02 99 81 60 90
closed: end Dec to end Jan
restaurant closed: Sat lunch, Sun eve and Mon

When you drive through the wrought-iron gates and into the grounds, you know from the look of the old stone manor house that you are in for a pleasant stay. What's more, Christian Bouvier will make sure of it.

The 29 rooms are modern and functional, bright and cheerful and a very modest 48–68€ plus 6.5€ for breakfast. The restaurant brings gourmands from all around for the original cuisine. The couscous with green cauliflower gives you an idea of the ingenuity you can expect from the kitchen. The wine list has some very good and quite reasonable Loire wines. Meals are 16–45€.

Les Charmettes 🛏 S
64 boulevard Hébert
tel: 02 99 56 07 31
fax: 02 99 56 85 96
closed: 12 Nov to early Feb

Its fine location on the beach at Rochebonne makes it very popular, especially if you want a simple hotel and eat elsewhere. The 17 rooms are a bargain at 26–52€, most rooms face the sea and some have balconies. English is spoken.

ST-MALO

Grand Hôtel de Courtoisville 🛏 ✕ M
69 boulevard Hébert
tel: 02 99 40 83 83
fax: 02 99 40 57 83
e-mail: gd.hotel.de.courtoisville@wanadoo.fr
closed: mid-Nov to mid-Feb

Quite a grandiose building with neat gardens and trees in front. The 47 rooms are 60–108€ and all are very well furnished. Breakfast is an additional 8€, though demi-pension at 53–85€ is a good alternative as the food is way above average.

ST-MARCEL

56140 (Î-et-V)
10 km NE of Redon

The principal attraction is the Musée de la Resistance where the exhibits recount the story of France's fight against the German occupation during World War II and Brittany's part in it. Try to see the film first as this will refresh your memory and help you understand the reasons for the importance of the museum. This area was ideal as a Resistance centre due to being well wooded and having lots of hiding places but also landing areas for small aircraft. It is open all year round and every day (except Tuesday from mid-September to mid-June). Commentary in French, English and German!

STE-MARINE

29120 (Finistère)
5 km W of Bénodet

L'Agape ✕ M
52 rue de la Plage
tel: 02 98 56 32 70
fax: 02 98 51 91 94
closed: Jan, Feb; Sun eve, Mon, Tues lunch

Patrick le Guen is a butcher's son who has been cooking all his life.

Inspirational rather than disciplined, he prefers to cook fish and does it with a distinct flair. His portions are generous and the prices of 26–63€ are fair for such quality.

ST-MARTIN-DES-CHAMPS

29600 (Finistère)
1 km N of Morlaix

St-Martin (this particular one, as there are lots of them) is almost a suburb of Morlaix on the north side, just past the Ste-Sève road.

Kerelisa (Cd'H) S
tel: 02 98 88 27 18
open: all year
no credit cards

A big house, homely and comfortable with two twin rooms and four double rooms, all nicely decorated and with shower. They are 36€ including breakfast. Christian and Marie Noëlle Abiven-Gueguen are efficient hosts and the public rooms consist of a comfortable sitting room and a dining room.

ST-MARTIN-SUR-OUST

56200 (Morbihan)
48 km N of St-Nazaire

A quiet little village but in the middle of a number of attractions – the Park of Prehistory, the castle of Josselin, the Oust Canal, boat rides in Morbihan Bay and the artisans' village of La Gacilly.

Château de Castellan (Cd'H) M
tel: 02 99 91 51 69
fax: 02 99 91 57 41
open: all year
no credit cards

An authentic 18th-century château where the outbuildings have been converted into four bedrooms and one suite, all with a bath or shower. M. and Mme. Cosse speak English and are very welcoming. The five rooms are bright and cheerful, very colourfully decorated and priced at 80–104€, breakfast included. Meals at 16–24€ are served in the enormous dining room.

ST-MÉDARD-SUR-ÎLLE

35250 (Î-et-V)
20 km N of Rennes
market: Sat am

The world pancake and *crêpe* festival may not quite rank second to the Olympics but, towards the end of July every year, contestants come to St-Médard from 40 countries spread over four continents to show off their pancake and *crêpe* recipes and offer them for tasting. Brittany-style pancakes are made with buckwheat and you will be able to eat lots of those, as well as pancakes made with millet, rice, manioc, sorghum and grains. Music and dance from all the four continents represented make this an entertaining and unusual (not to mention filling!) event.

ST-MÉEN-LE-GRAND

35000 (Î-et-V)
39 km W of Rennes
market: Sat am

This small town, just off the N12, has a church tower dating from the 12th century and the statue inside dates from a century later and is of St-Méen himself, the monk who founded the abbey in the 13th century.

To the northeast, 11 km away, are the ruins of the Château de Montauban, built in the 13th century and expanded into a powerful fortress in the 15th century. There are enough remains to make it worth a visit.

It seems extraordinarily specialized to have a museum devoted to cycling but in France the sport is much more avidly followed than in any other country. At number 5 on rue de Gaël is the

Louison Bobet Museum, established by the association to keep alive the memory of that great exponent of the sport. It is open all year, 2 pm to 5 pm.

ST-MÉLOIR-DES-ONDES
35350 (Î-et-V)
8 km E of St-Malo
market: Thurs am

Out on the small peninsula that contains St-Malo and Cancale, St-Méloir is a good alternative to staying in St-Malo itself and also very handy for Mont St-Michel.

The town describes its location as being at 'the heart of Corsair Country'. It is also at the heart of oyster country and just off the coast, you can see the extensive oyster beds.

If you are interested in glass and glass-blowing, you will want to see the Glass Workshop at number 4 rue de Radegonde where you can watch the artists at work and see their wares. It is open Easter to early January (except Sunday mornings and Mondays) 10.30 am –12.30 pm and 2.30 pm–6.30 pm.

Tirel-Guérin ⊨ ✕ M-L
gare de la Gouesnière
tel: 02 99 89 10 46
fax: 02 99 89 12 62
closed: mid-Dec to mid-Jan
restaurant closed: Sun eve o.o.s.

Roger and Guillaume Tirel with Jean-Luc Guérin have brought this place up into the higher ranks of hotel-restaurants in the area. The building has been around a long time and has had its ups and downs. At the moment, it's up and the 63 rooms at 48–192€ cater to all wallets. Most rooms are at the lower end (that is, up to 93€) and all are very comfortable and well equipped.

Sauna, a gym and a covered, heated pool are among the additional attractions. The restaurant is rightly very popular and Jean-Luc's braised Breton lobster is a speciality in all senses of the word. The *coquilles St-Jacques* is cooked in champagne and is nearly irresistible. Menus are 20–64€.

ST-MÉLOIR-DES-ONDES

Le Coquillage ⊨ ✕ M
Château Richeux le Point du Jour
tel: 02 99 89 25 25
fax: 02 99 89 88 47
hotel open: all year
restaurant closed: all day Mon and Tues lunch in season, all day Mon, Tues lunch and Thurs lunch o.o.s.

You can not only come here by boat but you can fly your chopper right on to the restaurant heliport. The surroundings also include a boutique and a park and there is a large terrace.

The wide selection on the seafood platter includes every fish and shellfish you might want and is far the most popular dish. The price is a very reasonable 18–36€.

ST-MICHEL-EN-GRÈVE

22300 (Cd'A)
18 km SW of Lannion

High cliffs curve around the attractive bay and the wide flat beach is very popular, not only with swimmers and impromptu soccer players but as a race track for nearby Lannion.

Hôtel de la Plage ⊨ ✕ S
tel: 02 96 35 74 43
open: all year

Ideal for families that want to take advantage of the excellent beach for games and sports. The hotel is located high on top of the cliffs and the rooms have superb views. They are 29–48€ with a bath.

The restaurant is very good value too with tasty, reliable cooking. Its proximity to the sea tells you that seafood is a prominent feature on the menu. Crab, lobster, mussels, langoustines are all popular and the *plateau de fruits de mer* is great value at 23€. There are plenty of other choices too though at 16€ and these include sea trout and *lotte*. The house wine is 8€ and very palatable.

ST-NICHOLAS-DES-EAUX

56930 (Morbihan)
16 km S of Pontivy

A small village (with a population of only 300) above the Blavet River. It has a 16th-century church surrounded by thatched cottages. A convenient stop in a peaceful wooded area.

Le Vieux Moulin 🛏 ✕ S
   tel: 02 97 51 81 09
   fax: 02 97 51 83 12
   closed: Feb; Sun eve, Mon

An old farmhouse converted into a small hotel with nine rooms. It is smart and well run by M. Troudet and very good value at 40–48€ plus 5.5€ for breakfast. The food is good, with a range of seafood, veal and chicken dishes. Menus are 13–24€. Demi-pension is an option at 45€.

ST-OUEN-DE-LA-ROUERIE

35406 (Î-et-V)

Château des Blosses (Cd'H) M
   tel: 02 99 98 36 16
   fax: 02 99 98 39 32
   closed: early Nov to early March

A charming little château, built in the 19th century and in the middle of a large, wooded park. It is furnished like a hunting lodge with old furniture and trophies. The seven rooms all have a bath and are very comfortable. Breakfast is included in the price of 88–136€ or demi-pension is available at 72–93€. If you prefer, you can dine in the evening for 40€ with wine included. You will find M. and Mme. Jacques Barbier attentive hosts.

   The château is just north of the D155, west of Fougères and south of Mont St-Michel.

ST-PHILIBERT

56470 (Finistère)
5 km S of Tregunc

It is on the banks of an estuary of the oyster-filled River Crac'h and very convenient for visiting both Carnac and the Gulf of Morbihan region. The peninsula of St-Philibert is covered with pines and the village is peaceful with a chapel and a weathered fountain. The chapel has a nautical theme with models of boats hanging from the ceiling, while on the altar there is a painting of a saint arriving from Britain in the traditional stone coffin-boat.

Hôtel aux Algues Brunes 🛏 ✖ S
Route des Plages
tel: 02 97 55 08 78
fax: 02 97 55 18 59
closed: mid-Sept to mid-May

English is spoken in this small hotel of 20 rooms at a reasonable 47–58€. It is clean, comfortable and the food is popular with the locals. Demi-pension is 55–85€.

ST-PIERRE-DE-PLESGUEN

35720 (Î-et-V)
12 km E of Combourg

Le Petit Moulin du Rouvre (Cd'H) S
tel: 02 99 73 85 84
fax: 02 99 35 16 71
open: all year
restaurant open: evenings
no credit cards

Yes, it used to be a windmill. On the edge of a forest, it is an old stone building with a large fireplace in the tiled floor dining room as you enter. The lounge next to it leads out to the pond.

The four bedrooms are small but immaculately kept and priced at 61€ for a double. One of them looks out on to the old water wheel. Unfortunately, owner Annie Michel-Quebriac no longer cooks dinner, which is a shame because she specialized in dishes of the region and has been featured in several magazines. She will direct you to the several good restaurants in Dinan, only ten minutes away, however. The mill is just off the D10 near Lanhelin.

ST-POL-DE-LÉON

29250 (Finistère)
5 km S of Roscoff

Your first glimpse of St-Pol will be the magnificent steeple of the Chapelle du Kreisker, the name means 'lower town'. At 77 metres, it is the main attraction of the town and was the former seat of the Bishop of Léon. The tower is not as tall but you can climb it and get a fine view of the town.

The old cathedral is near it and from it runs the rue du Général Leclerc with some interesting old houses. St-Pol is at the heart of an agricultural area, artichokes being the main produce.

Just 8 km outside town to the west is the Château de Kerouzere, an excellent example of French military architecture surviving from the 15th century.

Auberge Pomme d'Api ✗ S
   49 rue Verderel
   tel: 02 98 69 04 36
   fax: 02 98 69 01 20
   closed: last two weeks in Nov, Feb; Sun eve, Mon, Tues eve o.o.s.

A rustic environment and real Breton food. You can have a satisfying lunch for under 13€ and a dinner for 16–32€.

ST-QUAY-PORTRIEUX

22410 (Cd'A)
22 km N of St-Brieuc

Happily situated on the Bay of St-Brieuc, people flock here at the end of July for the *pardon* of Ste Anne. If you don't happen to be here at that time of year, the fish auction at the quayside can be interesting to watch as buyers nod, flip a hand or wiggle an ear to indicate they want to buy a few baskets full. Be there early though.

ST-QUAY-PORTRIEUX

If you can't rise with the birds (or in this case, the fish), you will be able to sample the catch because St-Quay is famous for its scallops and you will find them on sale everywhere.

☆ Ker Moor 🛏 ✗ M
13 rue du Président le Sénécal
tel: 02 96 70 52 22
fax: 02 96 70 50 49
closed: 6-23 Dec, early Jan

A popular spot and hard to get reservations. The hotel is quite spectacular, with flamboyant architecture and has fine views of the sea and the coast. Its 29 rooms all have a bath or shower and TV and are 72–88€ and 10€ for breakfast. Meals are 24-48€ and the restaurant has a good reputation. Demi-pension at 80–92€ is a good buy.

ST-RENAN

29290 (Finistère)
10 km NW of Brest
market: Sat am

This is the Pays d'Iroise, the sea between the Atlantic Ocean and the Channel. St-Renan is situated right in the middle of the peninsula and is a hub for visiting the wild and picturesque ports along the coast.

The Saturday morning market is one of the biggest in the region and worth attending, bringing in merchants and farmers from afar. Clustered around the place de la Marché are some magnificent old houses.

Renan was founded by an Irish monk named Ronan who arrived here in the 5th century. He finally had to leave when the demand for miracles put too much pressure on him.

The Musée d'Histoire Locale is open in July and August 3 pm–6 pm and tells you the story of the town.

Voyageurs 🛏 ✗ S-M
16 rue de St-Yves
tel: 02 98 84 21 14
fax: 02 98 84 37 84

M. Le Dot operates a 24-room hotel with a restaurant so well known that everybody knows about it. Renovation has now been completed to upgrade it, making it even more popular. The rooms are 45–71€, plus 8€ for breakfast and it is just as busy as the restaurant which has six rooms. The 4,000-litre fish and lobster tank tells you what to expect there. The menus are 16–40€. Demi-pension is 47–56€.

ST-SERVAN

35400 (Î-et-V)
3 km S of St-Malo
market: Thur, Fri

The Celts built a port here, probably in the 2nd century BC and it was called Aleth. Later, the main town became Corseul, up the Rance River near Dinan. As the Roman Empire crumbled, Aleth was protected by a powerful fortress. Then in the 6th century, the Welsh monk, Mac Low came and reached the rank of bishop. Viking raids began soon after, forcing the population to move from St-Malo further into the mainland where St-Servan ultimately became a town in the 18th century. It is almost a suburb of St-Malo today, with the invasions consisting of peaceful tourists.

A path goes all the way round the small peninsula and you have great views of the Rance Estuary, the bay and Dinard. The ruins of the Romanesque Cathedral are on the place St-Pierre, which makes a good starting place for this walk. You will be able to see the Île du Grand-Bé and the Île de Cézembre out to the northwest and you will pass the Fort de la Cité, built in 1759 and converted by the Germans in World War II into the headquarters of the German command with about three kilometres of underground galleries.

The Tour Solidor is a much photographed building. It was erected in the 14th century and in it today is the Musée International des Cap-Horniers which you can translate without difficulty into meaning a museum demonstrating the history of sailing around Cape Horn.

With St-Malo and St-Servan so close together, you can stay and you can eat in either one, in town or out, but the following are in St-Servan.

ST-SERVAN

L'Ascott 🛏 M
>35 rue du Chapitre
>**tel:** 02 99 81 89 93
>**fax:** 02 99 81 77 40
>**open:** all year

A little bijou of a château with a most impressive entrance through wrought-iron gates and showing lots of wrought-iron balconies. The smart white and grey adds even more character. There are 10 rooms – all bright and cheerful and well equipped. Prices are 400-106€ with 8€ for breakfast.

Le Valmarin 🛏 M-L
>7 rue Jean XXIII
>**tel:** 02 99 81 94 76
>**fax:** 02 99 81 30 03
>**open:** check Christmas dates in advance

A classy little hotel converted from a private home. The 12 rooms have all you could want from a three-star hotel and are 88–120€. It is in a quiet area near a park and has its own shady garden. Breakfast is a sumptuous affair.

Hôtel de la Rance 🛏 S-M
>15 quai Sébastopol
>**tel:** 02 99 81 78 63
>**fax:** 02 99 81 44 80
>**open:** all year, except Christmas

The 11 pleasant rooms overlook the beautiful estuary of the Rance, most have balconies and at 53–84€ are well priced. Breakfast is 8€. The quai Sébastopol runs around the port to the Tour Solidor.

☆ Le St-Placide ✕ S-M
>6 place du Poncel
>**tel:** 02 99 81 70 73
>**fax:** 02 99 81 89 49
>**closed:** Tues eve, Wed

Many say this is the best food in the entire St-Malo area but don't be put off by the outside which is not too enticing. The basis of the cooking is classic Breton but with some intriguing touches such as Eastern spices like curries. At 16–32€, it is extremely good value.

☆ La Korrigane 🛏 M
39 rue Le Pomellec, St-Servan
tel: 02 99 81 65 85
fax: 02 99 82 23 89
open: all year

To be highly recommended and everyone who has stayed here will describe it as one of the most delightful hotels in all France, not just Brittany.

Comfort and welcome are the two key words for this century-old residence with 10 rooms, all with a bath or shower and TV. All are beautifully furnished and decorated and no two the same. They are remarkably priced at 64–80€ plus 9€ for breakfast. The book-filled living room, the tea room, the bar and the gardens – all are exceptionally inviting and M. Marchon deserves great credit for keeping the place that way.

It is in the centre of town and there are good restaurants to try all around.

ST-SULIAC

35430 (I-et-V)
9 km S of St-Malo

Almost close enough to St-Malo to be a suburb of it but it is an old village built around a 13th-century church and with a very busy harbour. St-Suliac founded an abbey here in the 6th century and you can see a statue of him in the north porch of the church, slaying the three-headed dragon that terrorized the district.

La Goëlette (Cd'H) S
2 rue Besnier
tel & fax: 02 99 58 47 03
open: all year, except two weeks in winter – check dates
no credit cards

Comfortable, welcoming and a very reasonably priced overnight stop bed and breakfast just outside St-Malo. Only two rooms, a single at 40€ and a double at 56€. Peter Sobek will make sure of your satisfaction. (Not to be confused with the *crêperie* in town of the same name.)

Les Mouettes (Cd'H) S
17 Grand' Rue
tel: 02 99 58 30 41
fax: 02 99 58 39 41
open: all year
no credit cards

The five bedrooms in this well decorated (in pastel colours) and nicely appointed (with light wood furniture) bed and breakfast are 40€ but 47€ in July and August – and excellent value either way.

The name means 'seagulls' and you will see lots of them from the river inlet which, with its beach, is only a couple of hundred metres away. Isabelle Rouvrais runs a fine operation and every guest raves about the breakfasts which are included in the price. No evening meals are served but there are lots of restaurants nearby.

☆ La Grève ✗ S
tel: 02 99 58 33 83
fax: 02 99 58 35 40
closed: Sun eve, Mon

A little place right on the port and with very nicely done nautical atmosphere. The seafood is as good as anywhere around and excellent value at 16-29€.

ST-THÉGONNEC

29410 (Finistère)
9 km SW of Morlaix

With a population of about 2,000, St-Thégonnec does not have much to offer the visitor beyond its *enclos paroissial*, but that would be more than enough for many villages. Some of the *enclos* images are particularly elaborate. This is because St-Thégonnec arrived on the scene later than many other villages, so techniques had already been developed. Also, during the 17th century,

ST-THÉGONNEC

villages were constantly vying with one another for the most elaborate and expensive memorials.

The calvary built in 1610 intensified the rivalry with neighbouring Guimiliau. It incorporates the grotesque grin of King Henry IV who remarked 'Paris is worth a Mass' when he insincerely converted to Christianity and the subtle sculptor has portrayed him as one of the tormenters of Christ on the cross. The ossuary here (where bones were exhumed to make room for the newly dead) is without equal. Be sure to take a look in the church at the intricately carved pulpit, dating from 1683.

A number of walks leave from St-Thégonnec. One of the most popular is the Pont Hir walk, which follows a well-marked trail across rural landscapes to a tunnel that takes the River Coatoulsac'h through a railway embankment. You will see deer grazing in the woods along the way.

Some ruins of the old Château de Penhoat still remain.

☆ Auberge St-Thégonnec ⊨ ✕ M

place de la Mairie
tel: 02 98 79 61 18
fax: 02 98 62 71 10
closed: Christmas and New Year
restaurant closed: Sat lunch, Sun eve, Mon

Its 19 rooms at 48–72€, all very nicely furnished, are increasing in popularity and the food has been upgraded more than once so that this *auberge* is now excellent value for the money. Breakfast is an additional 6.5€ and meals 16–40€ offer unusual dishes, enticingly presented. Demi-pension is good value too at 60–64€ per person.

Prospital Coz (Cd'H) S

18 rue Lividic
tel: 02 98 79 45 62
fax: 02 98 79 48 47
no credit cards

A fine bed-and-breakfast establishment, cleverly built into the presbytery of the old church. The six rooms are of a good size and only 39€.

ST-YVI

29140 (Finistère)
14 km SE of Quimper

Right on the D765 from Quimper to Quimperlé, not an extraordinary village but with a very good bed and breakfast.

Kervren (Cd'H) S
tel: 02 98 94 70 34
fax: 02 98 94 81 19
open: all year
no credit cards

A farmhouse of Breton stone that looks capable of surviving centuries. It is a working farm and two of the bedrooms are in the house and four are separate. Four of the rooms are doubles and two are twins, all have a bathroom and cost 39€ including a hearty breakfast made from farm ingredients. Beautiful views of the hills surrounding the area.

SARZEAU

56640 (Morbihan)
32 km S of Vannes

Presqu'île de Rhuys, the peninsula that reaches out to the west on Brittany's south coast and almost encloses the Gulf of Morbihan has a number of pretty fishing villages but the largest village is Sarzeau. It is about 1 km from the Gulf coast and less than 3 km from the Atlantic coast so is a perfect location if you want a base to cover the whole peninsula.

On the main square are 17th- and 18th-century granite houses that were built when this was a busy market town and the hub of a prosperous agricultural area. In the square, you will also see a statue of Alain-René Lesage, the author of *Gil Blas*, the outstanding classic of Breton literature.

About 2 km south is the Château de Suscinio. It is close enough to the Atlantic coast that tidal waters used to replenish the castle moat and the Duke of Brittany built it in the 15th century as his summer home. It survived intact until the French Revolution and although only five of the original eight defensive towers remain and the living quarters have lost their roof, it is still a majestic sight.

A festival, *Les Creneaux de Suscinio* (*creneaux* means battlements), is held every August, but, during the high season, you can take guided tours.

SCAËR

29390 (Finistère)
30 km E of Quimper

At a junction of a large number of minor roads, Scaër has a castle, the Château de Kergoaler, which is open to the public. The ostrich and emu farm brings in visitors and Scaër also has a highly recommended bed and breakfast.

Kerloai (Cd'H) S
tel: 02 98 59 42 60
open: all year
no credit cards

Thérèse and Louis Penn have three large double rooms and one twin, all with bathrooms in this smart, large white house. A dairy farm still operates and there are ponies to ride.

Included in the 40€ for two people per room is a hearty breakfast that usually includes Breton *crêpes*. Evening meals at 20€ may be taken if you like.

Hôtel-Crêperie des Trois Dauphins S
16 quai des Paimpolais
tel: 02 98 70 92 09

A comfortable little inn in the harbour. The wood-panelled walls of the rooms are probably made to resemble a ship's cabins. Several rooms have baths and are 50€; the few without are 40€. Views of the sea and the Pointe du Raz are great.

SIZUN

29670 (Finistère)
32 km S of Morlaix

It sits on the banks of the Elorn River and it has a fine *enclos paroissial* of which the triumphal arch is particularly impressive.

Des Voyageurs 🛏 ✗ S
2 rue de l'Argoat
tel: 02 98 68 80 35
fax: 02 98 24 11 49
closed: three weeks in Sept
restaurant closed: Sun eve, Sat all day from Oct to Easter

Strictly basic and functional, this small but comfortable and inexpensive inn is fine for an overnight stay and a satisfying meal. It is convenient too – on a square in the centre of town and next to the church.

The rooms are 45€ and have been recently renovated. The restaurant serves home-made *pâtisserie, pâtés* and *terrines* and the cooking is good and wholesome. The 12€ lunch is a bargain and evening meals are 13€, 19€ and 22€ or demi-pension at 39€.

SPÉZET

29540 (Finistère)
40 km NE of Quimper

On Trinity Sunday, crowds pour in for the *pardon*, the procession that goes to the church of Notre Dame de Crann.

Pendreigne (Cd'H) S
tel: 02 98 93 80 32
open: all year
no credit cards

A typical Breton white and grey stone farmhouse set invitingly among the woods, pastures, hills and gurgling streams of the Finistère countryside. The front terrace approaching the house is bordered by gardens.

Two flights of stairs lead up to the attic where two bedrooms and a small sitting room are located. All are furnished in contemporary style, simple but very pleasant. A shared bathroom with wood-panelled walls serves both bedrooms. The price is 32€ for two people and the massive breakfast is almost worth that much alone! Fresh fruit juice, home-made jams and preserves, coffee cakes, hot *crêpes* and a choice of coffee, tea or hot chocolate – what a spread!

THEIX

56450 (Morbihan)
10 km W of Questembert

The draw here is the great Château du Plessis-Josso. It is a fortified manor house dating from the 14th and 15th century and provides a real insight into of the life of a lord of the manor. This is how they lived under the rule of the Dukes of Brittany. You can walk around the ramparts, see the great rooms and be fascinated by the four kitchens. It is open during July and August from 2 pm to 7 pm every day. Tours are also in English. There is a small fee. The phone number is 02 97 43 16 16.

Le Petit Clerigo (Cd'H) S
tel: 02 97 43 03 66
closed: 1 Nov to 1 Mar
no credit cards

The entrance to the five guestrooms in this modern farmhouse is at the rear. All rooms are large and there is a well-equipped kitchen for the use of guests. M. and Mme. Le Gruyere serve breakfast in their dining room and this is included in the modest 32€.

TONQUÉDEC

22140 (Cd'A)
10 km SE of Lannion

TONQUÉDEC

Le Queffiou (Cd'H) S-M
route du Château
tel & fax: 02 96 35 84 50
closed: 25 Sept to 1 Apr
no credit cards

You will probably be visiting the fortress of Tonquédec and if so, this is a perfect place to stay, being only a few hundred metres away. Odette Sadoc is an authority on the region and speaks very good English. The four large and airy bedrooms are all differently decorated and have a bath or shower and, with breakfast included, cost 56–60€ plus 20€ if you have an extra person with you.

TRÉBEURDEN

22566 (Cd'A)
9 km NE of Lannion
market: Tues

A fine seaside resort with some excellent beaches. It looks out at the Île Milliau, a small rocky peninsula that sticks out between two large beaches. From the tip of the peninsula, you have a wonderful view of the Bay of Lannion.

This is where the Pink Granite Coast begins, the *Côte de Granit Rose*. The hilly streets of the town look down on the beaches and you can fully appreciate the rosy glow of the rocks when it is accentuated by the sun.

Only a little over a kilometre inland, the enormous white sphere of the Plemeur-Boudou telecommunications centre is visible from here too.

Manoir de Lan Kerellec ⊨ ✗ M-L
allée Centrale
tel: 02 96 15 47 47
fax: 02 96 23 66 88
closed: mid-Nov to mid-Mar
restaurant closed: Mon and Tues lunch o.o.s.

Members of the Relais et Châteaux chain seldom find their way into these pages. Luxurious and spectacular as most of them are, they are priced out of the reach of many travellers – but here is a welcome exception.

It sits on the edge of a promontory that sweeps down to the sea, a charming old family home with antiques and natural wood panelling that has been carefully restored so as to incorporate modern conveniences without sacrificing traditional elegance.

The 16 rooms are large and beautifully decorated. All look out to sea from a private terrace. The rooms from 128–192€ are excellent value. There are other larger rooms up to 256€ and two really magnificent suites at over 320€.

The quality of the food and the cooking is near perfection. Fish and lamb figure prominently on the menu which is 23€ for lunch and 29–40€ for dinner.

☆ Ti al Lannec 🛏 ✗ M
14 allée de Mézo-Guen
tel: 02 96 15 01 01
fax: 02 96 23 62 14
closed: mid-Nov to mid-Mar

It's been around a long time and has gained a deserved reputation and a devoted clientele. M. and Mme. Jouanny run a fine operation that is hotel, restaurant, fitness and beauty spa all at the same time.

The 29 rooms are all beautifully furnished and decorated. All have a bath and TV and most of them have a verandah or terrace. 20 of the rooms are doubles, two are singles and seven are family rooms. They cost 104–176€ plus 15€ for breakfast. The cuisine is renowned and you may encounter roast duckling with blackcurrants or *coquilles St-Jacques* with curry sauce. Menus are 32–64€. Demi-pension is 96–132€.

Hôtel-Restaurant Ker An Nod 🛏 ✗ S
2 rue de Pors Tremen
tel: 02 96 23 50 21
fax: 02 96 23 63 30
closed: Jan to Mar

It is on the beach looking out at Île Milliau and if you're looking for a place at a more modest price than the foregoing admittedly upmarket establishments, this is it.

The 20 rooms (most of them look out to sea) are large and

comfortable. They are 56€ during the peak season, 40€ the rest of the year.

In the restaurant, a dish of mussels, a fish course and dessert make a very acceptable meal and will cost you a mere 14€. If you are hungrier than that, try one of the menus at 16€, 20€, 24€ or 27€. You can't go wrong.

TRÉDUDON-LE-MOINE

29690 (Finistère)
20 km S of Morlaix

La Ferme de Porz-Kloz (Cd'H) S
    tel: 02 98 99 61 65
    fax: 02 98 99 67 36
    closed: Dec to Mar

The buildings that now comprise the farm – and it is still a working farm – were once part of the Abbaye de Relecq, built in the 13th century. The location is a very romantic one, in the Arrée Mountains with its many legends of Celtic times.

The nine bedrooms are contained in three old houses and are thoroughly rustic with Breton fabrics and antique furniture. All have a bath or shower and TV and minibar. Prices are 43–52€ for two people, 61€ for three. Demi-pension is available at 44–48€ per person and breakfast is an additional 6.5€.

An evening meal is served in a rural dining room and dishes include shoulder of lamb with pears and – a rarely encountered treat – roast kid. M. and Mme. Berthou are thoughtful and conscientious hosts and a pleasant stay can be assured.

TRÉGASTEL

22730 (Cd'A)
9 km W of Perros-Guirec

It is out on a rocky tip of the northern coast amid the pink granite shapes with a variety of fairytale names. Its well-known Aquarium is open every day from June to September until 10 pm. The nearby Prehistoric Museum has the same hours.

Hôtel Bellevue 🛏 ✖ M
20 rue des Calculots
tel: 02 96 23 88 18
fax: 02 96 23 89 91
closed: end Sept to Easter
restaurant closed: end Sept to 2 May

A popular family hotel, noted for the high quality of its food. The 31 rooms are comfortable and well furnished and 64–88€ with 8€ for breakfast. Meals are 16–40€ including wine and demi-pension is 64–84€.

TRÉGROM

22420 (Cd'A)
14 km S of Lannion

L'Ancien Presbytère (Cd'H)
tel: 02 96 47 94 15
open: all year
no credit cards

This former rectory is opposite the church and has been cleverly converted into a fine bed and breakfast. The grey stone of its 17th-century construction is perfectly complemented by the blue shutters and the roses climbing everywhere. Through the arch, you can go into the enclosed courtyard with a well.

There are three rooms, all with a bath or shower. The price is 40–52€ for two people with breakfast included. Each is different and furnished with antiques.

It is a very homely place to stay and Nicole de Morchoven does a fine job of running it (she speaks English). Meals other than breakfast can be served on request and this means taking pot luck – but it is a very superior pot as Madame is a most accomplished cook. Otherwise, it means going 5 km or so to one of the neighbouring villages or east to Guingamp which has good restaurants.

TRÉGUIER

22200 (Cd'A)
16 km E of Lannion
market: Wed am

Tréguier was the historic capital of ancient Trégor and had a major university and a cathedral. The latter still stands, built in the 6th century by St-Tugdual, with a network of narrow streets and old houses around it.

One of the excursions from Tréguier that cannot be too highly recommended is the short drive north out to La Pointe du Château. Strange-shaped rocks poke out of the water and the whole ambience is eerily fascinating and perfectly suited to this legendary land.

These rocks are close to the shore while further out, you can see small islands, most of them uninhabited. One of these is Sagildas – it is where Colonel Charles Lindbergh went to meditate in solitude after his kidnapped son had been found murdered.

Despite the extraordinary atmosphere, this is a good place to picnic. If you go out there in the evening, you will see some really dazzling sunsets.

On the third Sunday in May, you can see the *pardon de St-Yves*, the patron saint of lawyers. In the cathedral, you can see a likeness of the saint himself.

The Renan Museum is open every day except Tuesday and Wednesday from Easter to the end of September.

Kastell Dinec'h 🛏 ✖ M

route de Lannion
tel: 02 96 92 49 39
fax: 02 96 92 34 03
closed: 31 Dec to 20 Mar
restaurant closed: lunchtimes, Tues eve, Wed eve

A long-time favourite where M. and Mme. Pauwels keep up their own high standard. It's a 17th-century manor house with some of the 15 bedrooms in the main house and others in the two annexes. The rooms are small but very tastefully decorated, many with antiques. All have a bath and most have TV. Prices run from 72–88€ and breakfast is 10€.

Menus are 21–48€ but *à la carte* is available too and the food is mostly seafood. M. Pauwels does the cooking and has some excellent recipes for mussels, *bar* (sea bass) and lobster. This makes the demi-pension at 70-80€ a very good choice.

TRÉGUNC

29910 (Finistère)
28 km SE of Quimper

The *pardon de St-Philibert* takes place on the last Sunday in August.

Les Grandes Roches 🛏 ✕ M
Route des Grandes Roches
tel: 02 98 97 62 97
fax: 02 98 50 29 19
closed: early Nov to end Mar

This huge old farmhouse has been fully renovated to make it into a fine country hotel. It sits surrounded by charming gardens. There are two dining rooms, a lounge with TV and a bar with an umbrella-shaded terrace.

Thatched cottages have been fully converted into 22 rooms, all furnished in traditional style and all containing bath or shower. They range in size and prices run from 40–88€ with breakfast at 7€. Demi-pension is available for three days minimum stay at 48–72€ per person.

There is a menhir on the grounds (how many hotels can make that claim?) and many other prehistoric stones can be found in the neighbouring countryside.

M. Henrich is German and the hotel is popular with German tourists. He and his wife have made this farmhouse into a fine hotel, convenient for Concarneau, Névez and Pont Aven. Meals are mainly seafood but duck often features as a change of pace. Menus are 16–40€ but there are also *à la carte* choices.

LE TRÉHOU

29450 (Finistère)
33 km SW of Morlaix

Mescouez (Cd'H)
tel: 02 98 68 83 39
fax: 02 98 68 86 79
open: all year
no credit cards

A fairly modern and not extraordinary house from the outside, it is an excellent bed and breakfast on the inside. The five rooms are cheerfully decorated in a variety of styles and look out into the courtyard or on the gardens.

The price of 39€ for two people including breakfast is a real bargain and an evening meal is available, cooked from local produce, at 13€ including wine. Elizabeth Soubigou runs the place very efficiently and speaks English. Her parents own the farm and remodelled the house.

LA TREMBLAIS

35320 La Couyère (Î-et-V)
25 km SE of Rennes

The village itself is not remarkable but it does have a fine, inexpensive bed and breakfast that is convenient if you are visiting the Château de Vitré or the famous megaliths at La Roche aux Fêtes.

La Tremblais (Cd'H) S
tel: 02 99 43 14 39
open: all year
no credit cards

This old stone farmhouse has been beautifully restored and bears the same name as the village. There is one large bedroom for two people at 40€ and a duplex suite for three people at 48€. Both are brightly decorated and very cheerful. M and Mme. Raymond Gomis are hospitable hosts and speak English.

TREMBLAY

35460 (Î-et-V)
16 km E of Combourg

Considered to be among the top few churches you should see in this area is the church of St-Martin in Tremblay. It was founded in the 11th century and is largely Romanesque. Its choir is widely renowned and it has a tabernacle that came from the even older abbey of Rille.

Roc Land 🛏 ✕ M
La Lande
tel: 02 99 98 20 46
fax: 02 99 98 29 00
closed: Sun eve and Mon, one week in Feb

Set amid the pine trees, this is a modern hotel-restaurant and a very handy overnight stop on the north-south E3 Euroroute. The 16 comfortable rooms are 45–52€.

TRÉMEUR

22250 (Cd'A)
22 km SW of Dinan

Les Dineux 🛏 ✕ S-M
ZA Les Dineux
tel: 02 96 84 65 80
fax: 02 96 84 76 35
closed: Feb
restaurant closed: Sat eve and Sun o.o.s., Christmas

A popular stop, as it is by the N12 autoroute. The 15 rooms are nicely appointed and comfortable, have a bath or shower and TV, and are very reasonably priced at 52€ with 6.5€ for breakfast. There is a swimming pool and gardens. The food is sound Breton fare, well-prepared and with a wide range. The place has a reputation for modest pricing. Lunch is 11€, meals are 15–26€ including wine and demi-pension is a good bet at 50€.

TRÉVOU-TRÉGUIGNEC

22660 (Cd'A)
12 km E of Perros Guirec

It is up on the northern coast and on a small bay with sandy beaches.

Ker Bugalic 🛏 ✕ M
   1 Vieille Côte de Trestel
   tel: 02 96 23 72 15
   fax: 02 96 23 74 71
   closed: 5 Nov to Easter

This creeper-encrusted old Breton house looks out over the sea and has 18 rooms at 44–75€ which is very good value. The service is friendly and helpful and the gardens are pleasant. Demi-pension is available at 56–72€ or you can have meals separately at 16–23€.

LA TRINITÉ-SUR-MER

56470 (Morbihan)
30 km SW of Vannes

At the mouth of the Crach River and a great place for boat-watching. The port and the fish market are popular and so are the delightful old houses in the town and the calvary.

A path used by the customs officers runs along the clifftops and from the Bridge of Kerisper, there is an exceptional view of the river and the bay.

Le Petit Hôtel des Hortensias 🛏 ✕ M
   place de la Mairie
   tel: 02 97 30 10 30
   closed: Dec, Jan

An outstanding location on the port with fine views of the fishing boats, the racing trimarans, the yachts and the oyster boats. The leading yacht captains gather here at Le Petit Hôtel which has five rooms, all with a bath and TV, and priced at 80–104€ off season and 120–136€ in season.

☆ L'Azimut 🛏 ✕ M
1 rue Men-Du
tel: 02 97 55 71 88
fax: 02 97 55 80 15
restaurant: closed Tues eve and Wed o.o.s.; Mon lunch only in summer

A fine view of boats and the water from M. le Calvez's popular restaurant where he grills on the wood-burning fire there. Lobster is not to be missed, served with coral sauce and the *coquilles St-Jacques* with *foie gras* salad is a close second. Plaice, sole and trout are often on the menu too and farm-raised quail features as an alternative to the seafood. It's about 16€ for lunch and 32–40€ for dinner and very good value for ambiance, cooking and presentation.

LE TRONCHET

35540 (Ĩ-et-V)
20 km SE of St-Malo

A very pleasant area with great walks through the Mesnil Forest, plenty of dolmens, several old manor houses and the ruins of the 17th-century Benedictine Abbey of Le Tronchet on the shore of a lake.

On summer evenings, in the grounds of the abbey, you can watch a re-enactment of the 14th-century joust in full armour and on horseback between Bertrand du Guesclin and the English knight, Sir John Chandos.

Hostellerie Abbatiale 🛏 ✕ M
tel: 02 99 58 93 21
fax: 02 99 58 11 08
closed: 6 Dec to end Jan

A lot of value here for a medium-priced hotel. The 72 rooms are very well furnished and have a bath or shower and TV. At 58–74€ they are reasonably priced, while the tennis court, the gardens and the swimming pool are extra luxuries.

It is an imposing building too. English and other languages are spoken and the cooking is well above average so that demi-pension at 44–52€ is worth consideration.

VANNES

56000 (Morbihan)
50 km SE of Lorient
market: Wed, Sat

Vannes was the capital of the Veneti, the Gallic tribe conquered by Julius Caesar after one of the most famous naval battles in early history. 'Gwened', it was called in Breton and its position as gateway to the Gulf of Morbihan has always assured that it has prominence.

Today, it is small enough to have an intimate feeling and old enough to have a medieval centre full of interest. You can see the old ramparts (which are still in good condition) by taking the stairway tucked behind the rue des Vierges. Fine views from the top of the ramparts and you can also see the black roofs of the Vieux Lavoirs, the old laundry houses.

You can go on to the 12th-century Cathedral St-Pierre on top of a hill and surrounded by old streets. The rue St-Gwénaël is one of the most attractive and on the other side of the cathedral, the Rue des Chanoines has a calvary, an old cloister and a porch with the 12 apostles, each in his own niche. The Treasury is resplendent with gold and jewels and is open in July and August every day from 10.30 am–6 pm except Sundays and holidays, June to September 1.30 pm–5.30 pm.

Opposite the cathedral is the Musée de la Cohue, named after the 14th-century building which used to house the Brittany parliament. Now it houses the Musée des Beaux-Arts, which is open from 10 am–12 pm and 2 pm–6 pm in July and August, and also the Musée du Golfe et de la Mer.

The Musée d'Archéologie is in the 15th-century Château Gaillard and has prehistoric stones as well as Greek and Roman artifacts. It is open from 9.30 am–12 pm and 2 pm–6 pm from April to September and all day in season.

In late July, the city hosts a four-day jazz festival and it overlaps with a classical music concert series while the *Grandes Fêtes d'Arvor* is on August 15th with processions, music and a carnival.

La Marebaudière 🛏 M
>4 rue Aristide-Briand
>**tel:** 02 97 47 34 29
>**fax:** 02 97 54 14 11
>**open:** all year

It's right in the centre of town but calm and peaceful. The fine service and the efficiency make the 41 rooms one of the best deals around at 56–72€ plus 8€ for breakfast.

Hôtel Aquarium 🛏 ✕ M
>Le Parc du Golfe
>**tel:** 02 97 40 44 52
>**fax:** 02 97 63 03 20
>**open:** all year

Right on the Gulf of Morbihan, the 48 rooms are more than modern – they're futuristic, but mellowed by all the greenery around. They are 72–96€ plus 9€ for breakfast, while demi-pension is 72–80€.

Régis Mahé ✕ M
>24 place de la Gare
>**tel:** 02 97 42 61 41
>**fax:** 02 97 54 99 01
>**closed:** two weeks in Nov, two weeks in Feb, last week in Jun; Sun eve and Mon

Régis Mahé has his own strongly personal viewpoints on cooking and does a masterly job of blending Breton and Mediterranean styles. Emphasis is on Atlantic fish and the dish named *Retour des Halles* at 46€ is a magnificent panorama of every kind of seafood. Other treats include the *galette de pigeon et homard* with a honey glaze and rare dishes such as the *ossobucco* of rabbit in orange sauce with saffron risotto. Menus are a very reasonable 27€, 33€ and 46€.

La Paella ✕ S
>7 rue Brizeux
>**tel:** 02 97 54 13 68
>**open:** all year but closed Sun and Mon

Very popular and built inside an old townhouse. Naturally, the specialty is paella and a heaping plate of it is delicious and only 7€. Most patrons accompany it with a jug of sangria at 5€.

VIGNOC

36530 (Î-et-V)
15 km N of Rennes

Château de la Villouyère (Cd'H) M
tel: 02 99 69 80 69
closed: 1 Oct to 30 Apr (except on demand)
no credit cards

Recently opened after extensive renovation by M. and Mme, Bruchet-Mery, you will love this delightful 18th-century château both outside and inside. The light stone exterior gives it a trim and smart appearance and its position, in the middle of a park planted with a large variety of unusual and exotic trees, is an invitation to pleasant strolls.

Inside, there is a real family atmosphere, lots of family touches and antique furniture. The two large bedrooms have antique furniture too but have modernized bathrooms. Both are 80€ including breakfast. No evening meal is served but there are plenty of restaurants.

The location is very convenient, being just near a sliproad off the N137 autoroute.

VITRÉ

35500 (Î-et-V)
37 km E of Rennes

The 15th-century castle is the big attraction here, especially as it is probably the best preserved in all of Brittany. Many come here during two weekends in June for a reconstruction of the Middle Ages. Then 350 people participate and there are seven tableaux with 28 riders and jousting tournaments.

The St-Nicolas Museum on rue Pasteur is a museum of sacred art and is housed in the 16th-century almshouse chapel. For a pictorial history of Vitre, the museum in the castle will give you a good outline and art exhibitions are held there too.

Just 10 km south of the town is the Château des Rochers-Sévigné where the famous Breton Mme. de Sévigné spent much of her time. It is a splendid subject for the photographer outside while inside it retains the traditional layout of a typical Brittany manorhouse of the 17th century. The chapel and the formal gardens are also in 17th-century style and the pathways in the surrounding woods are open to the public.

All three of these museums are open at the same times – July to September, every day 10 am–12.30 pm and 2 pm–6.15 pm, October to March 10 am–12 pm and 2 pm–5.30 pm but closed all day Tuesday and mornings Saturday to Monday, April to June every day 10 am–12 pm and 2 pm–5.30 pm.

La Grenouillère ⊨ ✗ S

route d'Ernée
tel: 02 99 75 34 52
fax: 02 99 75 38 15
open: all year

A smart, white, grey-roofed building with 34 rooms at a remarkable 28–48€, all well equipped including satellite TV. Breakfast is 5–6.5€. English is spoken and demi-pension is a good deal at 46–48€ for the cooking is honest and reliable and with a nice selection of Breton dishes.

☆ Hôtel du Château ⊨ S

5 rue Rallon
tel: 02 99 74 58 59
fax: 02 99 75 35 47
open: all year

The rest of the rue Rallon has had its fronts modernized but the Hôtel du Château still has its old stone frontage. It has 15 pleasant rooms, all with a bath or shower and cable TV, and, as there is no restaurant, the price is kept down to 37–42€ plus a mere 4.5€ for breakfast in the morning.

VITRÉ

Auberge Saint Louis ✗ S
31 rue Notre Dame
tel: 02 99 75 28 28
closed: Sun eve, Mon; two weeks in Sept, two weeks in Feb

The *auberge* dates from the 15th century and is now an inn, very well known to the locals. The wide variety of fish and meat dishes are served in a wood-panelled dining room and modestly priced at 12€, 15€, 20€ and 23€.

La Gourmandise ✗ S
26 rue d'En Bas
tel: 02 99 75 02 12
closed: Mon, Thurs eve

If you're looking for a light meal or a snack between visiting all the museums and castles, this is the place. You can have *crêpes*, salads, grills and there are specialities every day. The terrace is pleasant and there is a friendly, family atmosphere. Meals are 7–9€.

LE VIVIER-SUR-MER

35960 (Î-et-V)
20 km E of St.-Malo

The centre of mussel-breeding, Le Vivier is an important port in the bay of Mont St-Michel. The stakes in long lines across the sands cover a vast area. An amphibious vessel, *Sirène de la Baie*, leaves from the harbour here and takes you on a two-hour tour around the bay. The *Fête des Moules* is celebrated every July.

Hôtel de Bretagne ⇌ ✗ S-M
Rond Point du Centre
tel: 02 99 48 91 74
fax: 02 99 48 81 10
closed: Mon lunch in season, Sun eve and Mon

A popular place with locals and visitors. Naturally, its speciality is seafood. Oysters are high on the list but all the other products of the sea are here and there is a particularly good *agneau pré-salé* if you want something different. Menus are 16-52€.

Wines and Spirits by John Doxat

Bonne cuisine et bons vins, c'est le paradis sur terre.
(Good cooking and good wines, that is earthly paradise.)
King Henri IV

OUTLINE OF FRENCH WINE REGIONS

Bordeaux

Divided into a score of districts, and subdivided into very many *communes* (parishes). The big district names are Médoc, St-Émilion, Pomerol, Graves and Sauternes. Prices for the great reds (châteaux Pétrus, Mouton-Rothschild, etc.) or the finest sweet whites (especially the miraculous Yquem) have become stratospheric. Yet 'château' in itself means little and the classification of various rankings of châteaux is not easily understood. Some tiny vineyards are entitled to be called château, which has led to disputes about what have been dubbed 'phantom châteaux'. Visitors are advised, unless wine-wise, to stick to the simpler designations.

Bourgogne (Burgundy)

Topographically a large region, stretching from Chablis (on the east end of the Loire), noted for its steely dry whites, to Lyons. It is particularly associated with fairly powerful red wines and very dry whites, which tend to acidity except for the costlier styles. Almost to Bordeaux excesses, the prices for really top Burgundies have gone through the roof. For value, stick to simpler local wines.

Technically Burgundies, but often separately listed, are the Beaujolais wines. The young red Beaujolais (not necessarily the overpublicized *nouveau*) are delicious when mildly chilled. There are several rather neglected Beaujolais wines (Moulin-à-Vent, Morgon, St-Amour, for instance) that improve for several years: they represent good value as a rule. The Mâconnais and Chalonnais also produce sound Burgundies (red and white) that are usually priced within reason.

Rhône

Continuation south of Burgundy. The Rhône is particularly associated with very robust reds, notably Châteauneuf-du-Pape; also Tavel, to my mind the finest of all still rosé wines. Lirac rosé is nearly as good. Hermitage and Gigondas are names to respect for reds, whites and rosés. Rhône has well earned its modern reputation – no longer Burgundy's poorer relation. From the extreme south comes the newly 'smart' dessert wine, *vin doux naturel*, ultrasweet Muscat des Beaumes-de-Venise, once despised by British wine-drinkers. There are fashions in wine just like anything else.

Alsace

Producer of attractive, light white wines, mostly medium-dry, widely used as carafe wines in middle-range French restaurants. Alsace wines are not greatly appreciated overseas and thus remain comparatively inexpensive for their quality; they are well placed to compete with popular German varieties. Alsace wines are designated by grape – principally Sylvaner for lightest styles, the widespread and reliable Riesling for a large part of the total, and Gerwürtztraminer for slightly fruitier wines.

Loire

Prolific producer of very reliable, if rarely great, white wines, notably Muscadet, Sancerre, Anjou (its rosé is famous), Vouvray (sparkling and semi-sparkling), and Saumur (particularly its 'champagne styles'). Touraine makes excellent whites and also reds of some distinction – Bourgueil and Chinon. It used to be widely believed – a rumour put out by rivals? – that Loire wines 'did not travel': nonsense. They are a successful export.

Champagne

So important is Champagne that, alone of French wines, it carries no AC: its name is sufficient guarantee. (It shares this distinction with the brandies Cognac and Armagnac.) Vintage Champagnes from the *grandes marques* – a limited number of 'great brands' – tend to be as expensive in France as in Britain. You can find unknown brands of high quality (often off-shoots of *grandes marques*) at attractive prices, especially in the Champagne country itself. However, you need information to discover these, and there are true Champagnes for the home market that are *doux* (sweet) or *demi-sec* (medium sweet) that are pleasing to few non-French tastes. Champagne is very closely controlled as to region, quantities, grape types, and is made only by secondary fermentation in the bottle. From 1993, it has been prohibited (under EU law) to state that other wines are made by the 'champagne method' – even if they are.

Minor regions (very briefly)

Jura – Virtually unknown outside France. Try local speciality wines such as *vin jaune* if in the region.

Jurançon – Remote area; sound, unimportant white wines, sweet styles being the better.

Cahors – Noted for its powerful *vin de pays* 'black wine', which is the darkest red made.

Gaillac – Little known; once celebrated for dessert wines.

Savoy – Good enough table wines for local consumption. Best product of the region is delicious Chambéry vermouth: as an aperitif, do try the well distributed Chambéryzette, a unique vermouth with a hint of wild strawberries.

Bergerac – Attractive basic reds; also sweet Monbazillac, relished in France but not easily obtained outside: aged examples can be truly superb.

Provence – Large wine region of immense antiquity. Many and varied *vins de pays* of little distinction. Best known for rosé, usually on the sweet side; all inexpensive and totally drinkable.

Midi – Stretches from Marseilles to the Spanish border. Outstandingly prolific contributor to the 'EU wine lake' and producer of some 80 per cent of French *vins de table*, white and red. Sweet whites dominate, and there is major production of *vins doux naturels* (fortified sugary wines).

Corsica – Roughish wines of more antiquity than breeding, but by all means drink local reds – and try the wine-based aperitif Cap Corse – if visiting this remarkable island.

Paris – Yes, there is a vineyard – in Montmartre! Don't ask for a bottle: the tiny production is sold by auction, for charity, to rich collectors of curiosities.

HINTS ON SPIRITS

The great French spirit is brandy. Cognac, commercially the leader, must come from the closely controlled region of that name. Of various quality designations, the commonest is VSOP (very special old pale): it will be a cognac worth drinking neat. Remember, *champagne* in a cognac connotation has absolutely no connection with the wine. It is a topographical term, *grande champagne* being the most prestigious cognac area: fine champagne is a blend of brandy from the two top cognac subdivisions. Armagnac has become better known lately outside France, and rightly so. As a brandy it has a much longer history than cognac: some connoisseurs rate old armagnac (the quality designations are roughly similar) above cognac.

Be cautious of French brandy without a cognac or armagnac title, regardless of how many meaningless 'stars' the label carries or even the magic word 'Napoleon' (which has no legal significance).

Little appreciated in Britain is the splendid 'apple brandy', Calvados, mainly associated with Normandy but also made in Brittany and the Marne. The best is *Calvados du Pays d'Auge*. Do taste well-aged Calvados, but avoid any suspiciously cheap.

Contrary to popular belief, true Calvados is not distilled from cider – but an inferior imitation is: French cider (*cidre*) is excellent.

Though most French proprietary aperitifs, such as Dubonnet, are fairly low in alcohol, the extremely popular Pernod/Ricard pastis-style brands are highly spirituous. *Eau-de-vie* is the generic term for all spirits, but colloquially tends to refer to local, often rough, distillates. Exceptions are the better *alcools blancs* (white spirits), which are not inexpensive, made from fresh fruits and not sweetened as *crèmes* are.

Bringing Back Those Bottles

When thinking of what to bring back from France in the way of wines and spirits, apart from considerations of weight and bulk, there are a few other matters to bear in mind. Within the theoretically unlimited import for personal consumption of products which have paid any national taxes in the country of origin, there are manifest practical as well as some semi-official restrictions on your selections.

Wine: to choose sensibly is not inevitably to go for the least expensive. Unless you envisage having to entertain a lot of relatives, beware the very cheapest of French table wines! Though France produces many of the world's greatest, her prolific vineyards also make wines to which no British supermarket would allocate shelf-space. Quality does count along with value. Primarily what you are saving by purchasing in France is the comparatively high excise duties imposed in Britain against the minimal ones in France. However, the British tax is just the same on a bottle of the most ordinary *vin ordinaire* as on the rarest of vintage claret. When it comes to the latter, buying fine vintage wines in France does not automatically mean obtaining a bargain, unless you are an expert. There are not that many specialist wine merchants in France, a commerce in which Britain excels.

To summarize: it is undoubtedly sound, middle-range wines that are the most sensible buy.

If you like those famous liqueurs, such as Bénédictine, Chartreuse, the versatile Cointreau, which are so expensive in Britain, shop around for them: prices seem to vary markedly.

I have briefly dealt elsewhere with French spirits. If you are buying Scotch whisky, gin or vodka, you may find unfamiliar names and labels offering apparent bargains. None will harm you but some may have low, even unpleasant, taste characteristics. It is worth paying a trifle more for well-known brands, especially deluxe styles. Though they are little sold in Britain, former French colonies distill several excellent types of rum (rhum).

I deem it a good idea to make an outline list of intended purchases, after deciding what you can carry and how much you wish to spend. As to wines, do you want mainly red, or only white, or what proportion of both types? Can you afford champagne? Its best to buy when visiting the region where you should have the opportunity to taste and possibly find a bargain. What about other sparklers? What do you require in dessert wines, vermouths, liqueurs, spirits? Does your list work out at more cases (12 bottles) than you can easily transport? A conspicuously overloaded vehicle may be stopped by police as a traffic hazard. Now you have a list of sorts. What about cost? For essential comparisons, I would put against each item the maximum (per bottle) I would be prepared to pay in Britain.

Basic glossary of French wine terms

Alsace – See Outline of French Wine Regions (page 234)

Abricotine – Generic apricot liqueur: look for known brands.

Alcool blanc – Spirit distilled from various fruits (not wine); not fruit-flavoured cordials.

Aligoté – Light dry Burgundy.

Anis – Aniseed, much favoured in pastis (Ricard/Pernod) type aperitifs.

Anjou – See Loire, Outline of French Wine Regions (page 234)

Aperitif – Literally 'opener': any drink taken as an appetizer.

Appellation (d'origine) Contrôllée – or AC wine, whose label will give you a good deal of information, will usually be costlier – but not necessarily better – than one that is a VDQS 'designated (regional) wine of superior quality'. A newer, marginally lesser category is VQPRD: 'quality wine from a specified district'. Hundreds of wines bear AC descriptions: you require knowledge and/or a wine guide to find your way around. The intention of the AC laws was to protect consumers and ensure wine was not falsely labelled – and also to prevent overproduction. Only wines of reasonable standards should achieve AC status: new ones (some rather suspect) are being regularly admitted to the list.

Armagnac – See Hints on Spirits (page 235)

Barsac – Very sweet Sauternes of varying quality.

Basserau – A bit of an oddity: sparkling red Burgundy.

Beaumes-de-Venise – Well-known *vin doux naturel*; see Provence, Outline of French Wine Regions (page 235)

Beaune – Famed red Burgundy; costly.

Bergerac – Sound red wine from south-west France.

Blanc de Blancs – White wine from white grapes alone. Sometimes confers extra quality but by no means always. White wine made from black grapes (the skins removed before fermentation) is Blanc de Noirs – Carries no special quality connotation in itself.

Bordeaux – See Outline of French Wine Regions (page 233).

Bourgeuil – Reliable red Loire wine.

Bourgogne – Burgundy; see Outline of French Wine Regions (page 233).

Brut – Very dry; description particularly applicable to best sparkling wines.

Brut sauvage – Dry to the point of displeasing acidness to most palates; very rare though a few good wines carry the description.

Cabernet – Noble grape, especially the mix Cabernet-Sauvignon for excellent, if not absolutely top-grade, red wines.

Cacao – Cocoa; basis of a popular crème.

Calvados – See Hints on Spirits (page 235).

Cassis – Blackcurrant; notably in crème de cassis (see Kir).

Cave – Cellar.

Cépage – Indicates grape variety; e.g. cépage Cabernet-Sauvignon.

Chablis – See Bourgoyne (Burgundy), Outline of French Wine Regions (page 233). Fine Chablis is expensive.

Chai – Ground-level storehouse, wholly employed in Cognac and sometimes in Bordeaux and other districts.

Champagne – See Outline of French Wine Regions (page 234). Also *Méthode Traditionelle* below.

Château(x) – See Bordeaux,Outline of French Wine Regions (page 233).

Châteauneuf-du-Pape – Best known of powerful Rhône red wines.

Chenin-blanc – Grape variety associated with many fine Loire wines.

Clairet – Unimportant Bordeaux wine, its distinction being probable origin of English word claret.

Clos – Mainly a Burgundian term for a vineyard formerly (rarely now) enclosed by a wall.

Cognac – See Hints on Spirits (page 235).

Corbières – Usually a sound south of France red wine.

Côte – Indicates vineyard on a hillside; no quality connotation necessarily.

Côteau(x) – Much the same as above.

Crème – Many sweet, sometimes sickly, mildly alcoholic cordials with many local specialities. Nearer to true liqueurs are top makes of *crème de menthe* and *crème de* Grand Marnier (q.v.). *Crème de cassis* is mixed with white wine to produce *kir* or a sparkling white wine to produce *kir royale*.

Crémant – Sparkling wine with strong but rather brief effervescence.

Cru – Literally 'growth'; somewhat complicated and occasionally misleading term: e.g. *grand cru* may be only grower's estimation; *cru classé* just means the wine is officially recognised, but *grand cru classé* is most likely to be something special.

Cuve close – Literally 'sealed vat'. Describes production of sparkling wines by bulk as opposed to individual bottle fermentation. Can produce satisfactory wines and certainly much superior to cheap carbonated styles.

Cuvée – Should mean unblended wine from single vat, but *cuvée spéciale* may not be particularly special: only taste will tell.

Demi-sec – Linguistically misleading, as it does not mean 'half-dry' but

WINES AND SPIRITS

'medium sweet'.

Domaine – Broadly, Burgundian equivalent to Bordeaux château.

Doux – Very sweet.

Eau-de-vie – Generic term for all distilled spirits but usually only applied in practice to roughish *marc* (q.v.) and the like.

Entre-deux-Mers – Undistinguished but fairly popular white Bordeaux.

Frappé – Drink served with crushed ice; viz. *crème de menthe frappée*.

Fleurie – One of several superior Beaujolais wines.

Glacé – Drink chilled by immersion of bottle in ice or in refrigerator, as distinct from *frappé* above.

Goût – Taste; also colloquial term in some regions for local *eau-de-vie* (q.v.).

Grand Marnier – Distinguished orange-flavoured liqueur. See also *crème*.

Haut – 'High'. It indicates upper part of wine district, not necessarily the best, though Haut-Médoc produces much better wines than other areas.

Hermitage – Several excellent Rhône red wines carry this title.

Izarra – Ancient Armagnac-based liqueur much favoured by its Basque originators.

Juliénas – Notable Beaujolais wine.

Kir – Well-chilled dry white wine (should be Bourgogne Aligoté) plus a teaspoon of *crème de cassis* (q.v.). Made with champagne (or good dry sparkling wine) it is *kir royal*.

Liqueur – From old *liqueur de dessert*, denoting postprandial digestive. Always very sweet. 'Liqueur' has become misused as indication of superior quality: to speak of 'liqueur cognac' is contradictory – yet some very fine true liqueurs are based on cognac.

Loire – See Outline of French Wine Regions (page 234).

Marc – Mostly coarse distillations from wine residue with strong local popularity. A few *marcs* (pronounced 'mar') – de Champagne, de Bourgogne especially – have achieved a certain cult status.

Marque – Brand or company name.

Méthode traditionnelle – Most widely used description of superior sparkling wine made as is Champagne, by fermentation in bottle, now that any labelling association such as 'Champagne method' is banned.

Meursault – Splendid white Burgundy for those who can afford it.

Minervoise – Respectable southern red wine: can be good value as are many such.

Mise – As in *mise en bouteilles au château* ('château-bottled'), or ... *dans nos caves* ('in our cellars') and variations.

WINES AND SPIRITS

Montrachet – Very fine white Burgundy.

Moulin-à-Vent – One of the rather special Beaujolais wines.

Muscadet – Arguably the most popular light dry Loire white wine.

Muscat – Though used for some dry whites, this grape is mainly associated with succulent dessert-style wines.

Nouveau – New wine, for drinking fresh; particularly associated with now tiring vogue for Beaujolais Nouveau.

Pastis – General term for powerful *anis*/liquorice aperitifs originally evolved to replace banned absinthe and particularly associated with Marseilles area through the great firm of Ricard.

Pétillant – Gently, naturally effervescent.

Pineau – Unfermented grape juice lightly fortified with grape spirit; attractive aperitif widely made in France and under-appreciated abroad.

Pouilly-Fuissé – Dry white Burgundy; sometimes overvalued.

Pouilly-Fumé – Easily confused with above; a very dry fine Loire white.

Porto – Port wine: usually lighter in France than the type preferred in Britain and popular, chilled, as an aperitif.

Primeur – More or less the same as *nouveau*, but more often used for fine vintage wine sold *en primeur* for laying down to mature.

Rosé – 'Pink wine', best made by allowing temporary contact of juice and black grapes during fermentation; also by mixing red and white wine.

Sauvignon – Notable white grape; see also Cabernet.

Sec – 'Dry', but a wine so marked will be sweetish, even very sweet. *Extra Sec* may actually mean on the dry side.

Sirop – Syrup; e.g. sugar syrup used in mixed drinks, also some flavoured proprietary non-alcoholic cordials.

Supérieur(e) – Much the same as *haut* (q.v.) except in VDQS.

VQRPD. – See Appellation (d'origine) Contrôllée above.

Vin de Xeres – Sherry (pronounced 'vin de ereth').

Glossary of Cooking Terms and Dishes

This basic glossary provides an introduction to the terms you are most likely to encounter. For a more complete guide, see the companion pocket-sized book *French Entrée Companion to Food and Drink in France* (ISBN 1-904012-05-1) that provides a comprehensive bilingual menu dictionary together with all the useful phrases that will help you make the most of French food and restaurants.

Aigre-doux	bittersweet
Aiguillette	thin slice (*aiguille* is needle)
Aile	wing
Ailloli	garlic mayonnaise
Allemande (à l')	German-style, i.e. with sausages and sauerkraut
Amuse-gueules	appetizers
Andouille	large uncooked sausage, served cold after boiling
Andouillettes	(as per Andouille) but made from smaller intestines, usually served hot after grilling
Anglaise (à l')	plain boiled. *Crème Anglaise* – egg and cream custard sauce
Anis	aniseed
Argenteuil	with asparagus
Assiette Anglaise	plate of cold meats
Baba au rhum	yeast-based sponge macerated in rum
Baguette	long, thin loaf
Ballotine	boned, stuffed and rolled meat or poultry, usually cold
Béarnaise	sauce made from egg yolks, butter, tarragon, wine, shallots
Béchamel	white sauce flavoured with infusion of herbs
Beignets	fritters
Bercy	sauce with white wine and shallots
Beurre blanc	sauce from Nantes, with butter, reduction of shallot-flavoured vinegar or wine
Beurre noir	browned butter
Bigarade	with Seville oranges
Billy By	mussel soup
Bisque	creamy shellfish soup
Blanquette	stew with thick, white creamy sauce, usually veal
Boeuf à la mode	braised beef
Bombe	ice-cream mould
Bonne femme	with root vegetables
Bordelais	Bordeaux-style, with red or white wine, marrowbone fat
Bouchée	mouthful, e.g. *vol-au-vent*
Boudin	sausage, white or black
Bourride	thick fish soup
Braisé	braised
Brandade (de morue)	dried salt-cod pounded into mousse
Broche	spit
Brochette	skewer
Brouillade	stew, using oil
Brouillé	scrambled
Brûlé	burnt, e.g. *crème brûlée*
Campagne	country-style
Cannelle	cinnamon
Carbonnade	braised in beer
Cardinal	red-coloured sauce, e.g. with lobster, or in *pâtisserie* with redcurrants

GLOSSARY OF COOKING TERMS AND DISHES

Cassolette or **cassoulette**	small pan	**Crécy**	with carrots
Cassoulet	rich stew with goose, pork and haricot beans	**Crème pâtissière**	thick custardy filling
		Crêpe	pancake
		Crépinette	little flat sausage, encased in caul
Cervelas	pork garlic sausage	**Croque-monsieur**	toasted cheese-and-ham sandwich
Cervelles	brains		
Chantilly	whipped sweetened cream	**Croustade**	pastry or baked bread shell
Charcuterie	cold pork-butcher's meats	**Croûte**	pastry crust
		Croûton	cube of fried or toasted bread
Charlotte	mould, as dessert lined with sponge fingers, as savoury lined with vegetables	**Cru**	raw
		Crudités	raw vegetables
		Demi-glâce	basic brown sauce
		Doria	with cucumber
Chasseur	with mushrooms, shallots, wine	**Émincé**	thinly sliced
		Entremets	sweets
Chausson	pastry turnover	**Étuvé**	stewed, e.g. vegetables in butter
Chemise	covering, i.e. pastry		
Chiffonnade	thinly cut, e.g. lettuce	**Farci**	stuffed
		Feuilleté	leaves of flaky pastry
Choron	tomato Béarnaise		
Choucroute	Alsatian stew with sauerkraut and sausages	**Fines herbes**	parsley, chervil, bay leaf
		Flamande	Flemish style, with beer
Civet	stew		
Clafoutis	batter dessert, usually with cherries	**Flambé**	flamed in spirit
		Flamiche	flan
Clamart	with peas	**Florentine**	with spinach
Cocotte	covered casserole	**Flûte**	thinnest bread loaf
Compôte	cooked fruit	**Foie gras**	goose liver
Concassé	e.g. *tomates concassées* – skinned, chopped and juice extracted	**Fond (d'artichaut)**	heart (of artichoke)
		Fondu	melted
		Forestière	with mushrooms, bacon and potatoes
Confit	preserved		
Confiture	jam	**Four (au)**	baked in the oven
Consommé	clear soup	**Fourré**	stuffed, usually sweets
Coque (à la)	e.g. *oeufs* – boiled eggs		
		Frais, fraîche	fresh and cool
Cou	neck	**Frangipane**	almond-cream *pâtisserie*
Coulis	juice, purée (of vegetables or fruit)		
		Fricadelle	Swedish meatball
Court-bouillon	aromatic liquor for cooking meat, fish, vegetables	**Fricandeau**	veal, usually topside
		Fricassée	stew (usually of veal) in creamy sauce
Couscous	N. African dish with boiled grains of millet, served with chicken or vegetables	**Frit**	fried
		Frites	chips
		Friture	assorted small fish, fried in batter
Crapaudine	involving fowl, particularly pigeon, trussed	**Froid**	cold

243

GLOSSARY OF COOKING TERMS AND DISHES

Fumé	smoked		with vegetables
Galantine	loaf-shaped chopped meat, fish or vegetable, set in natural jelly	Jarret	shin, e.g. *jarret de veau*
		Julienne	matchstick vegetables
Galette	Breton pancake, flat cake	Jus	natural juice
Garbure	thick country soup	Lait	milk
Garni	garnished, usually with vegetables	Langue	tongue
		Lard	bacon
Gaufre	waffle	Longe	loin
Gelée	aspic		
Gésier	gizzard	Macédoine	diced fruits or vegetables
Gibier	game		
Gigot	leg	Madeleine	small sponge cake
Glacé	iced	Magret	breast (of duck)
Gougère	choux pastry, large base	Maïs	sweetcorn
		Maître d'hôtel	sauce with butter, lemon, parsley
Goujons	fried strips, usually of fish	Marchand de vin	sauce with red wine, shallots
Graine	seed		
Gratin	baked dish of vegetables cooked in cream and eggs	Marengo	sauce with tomatoes, olive oil, white wine
Gratinée	browned under grill	Marinière	fisherman-style e.g. *moules marinière* (mussels in white wine)
Grecque (à la)	cold vegetables served in oil		
Grenadin	nugget of meat, usually of veal	Marmite	deep casserole
		Matelote	fish stew, e.g. of eel
Grenouilles	frogs: *cuisses de grenouille* – frogs' legs	Médaillon	round slice
		Mélange	mixture
Grillé	grilled	Meunière	sauce with butter, lemon
Gros sel	coarse salt		
Hachis	minced or chopped	Miel	honey
Haricot	slow-cooked stew	Mille-feuille	flaky pastry, (literally 1,000 leaves)
Haricots	beans		
Hochepot	hotpot	Mirepoix	finely diced carrot, onion etc. used for sauces
Hollandaise	sauce with egg, butter, lemon		
Hongroise	Hungarian, i.e. spiced with paprika	Moëlle	beef marrow
		Mornay	cheese sauce
Hors-d'oeuvre	assorted starters	Mouclade	mussel stew
Huile	oil	Mousseline	Hollandaise sauce, lightened with egg whites
Île flottante	floating island - soft meringue on egg-custard sauce		
		Moutarde	mustard
Indienne	Indian, i.e. with hot spices	Nage (à la)	poached in flavoured liquor (fish)
		Nature	plain
Jambon	ham	Navarin	stew of lamb with spring vegetables
Jardinière	from the garden, i.e.	(d'agneau)	

GLOSSARY OF COOKING TERMS AND DISHES

Noisette	nut-brown, burned butter
Noix de veau	'nut' (leg) of veal
Normande	Normandy-style, i.e. with cream, apple, cider, Calvados
Nouilles	noodles
Onglet	beef cut from flank
Os	bone
Paillettes	'straws' (of pastry)
Panaché	mixed
Panade	flour crust
Papillote (en)	cooked in paper case
Parmentier	with potatoes
Pâté	paste, of meat or fish
Pâte	pastry
Pâte brisée	rich shortcrust pastry
Pâtisserie	pastries
Paupiettes	paper-thin slices
Pavé	thick slice
Paysan	country-style
Périgueux	with truffles
Persillade	chopped parsley and garlic topping
Petit pain	bread roll
Petits fours	tiny cakes, sweetmeats
Piperade	peppers, onions, tomatoes in scrambled egg
Poché	poached
Poêlé	fried
Poitrine	breast
Poivre	pepper
Pommade	paste
Potage	thick soup
Pot-au-four	broth with meat and vegetables
Potée	country soup with cabbage
Pralines	caramelized almonds
Primeurs	young vegetables
Printanier (printanière)	garnished with young vegetables
Profiteroles	choux pastry balls
Provençale	with garlic, tomatoes, olive oil, peppers
Pureé	mashed and sieved
Quenelle	pounded fish or meat bound with egg, poached
Queue	tail
Quiche	pastry flan, e.g. *quiche Lorraine* – egg, bacon, cream
Râble	saddle, e.g. *râble de lièvre*
Ragoût	stew
Ramequin	little pot, ramekin
Râpé	grated
Ratatouille	Provençale stew of onions, garlic, peppers, tomatoes
Ravigote	highly seasoned white sauce
Rémoulade	mayonnaise with gherkins, capers, herbs and shallots
Rillettes	potted shredded meat, usually with pork or goose fat
Riz	rice
Robert	sauce with mustard, vinegar, onion
Roquefort	ewe's milk blue cheese
Rossini	garnished with *foie gras* and truffle
Rôti	roast
Rouelle	nugget
Rouille	hot garlicky sauce for *soupe de poisson*
Roulade	roll
Roux	sauce base – flour and butter
Sabayon	sweet fluffy sauce, with eggs and wine
Safran	saffron
Sagou	sago
Salade niçoise	salad with tuna, eggs, anchovies, tomatoes, beans, black olives
Salé	salted
Salmis	dish of game or fowl, with red wine
Salpicon	meat, fowl, vegetables, chopped finely, bound with sauce and used as fillings
Sang	blood

GLOSSARY OF COOKING TERMS AND DISHES

Santé	literally healthy, i.e. with spinach and potato
Saucisse	fresh sausage
Saucisson	dried sausage
Sauté	cooked in fat in open pan
Sauvage	wild
Savarin	ring of yeast-sponge, soaked in syrup and liquor
Sel	salt
Selle	saddle
Selon	according to, e.g. *selon grosseur* (according to size)
Smitane	with sour cream, white wine, onion
Soissons	with dried white beans
Sorbet	water ice
Soubise	with creamed onions
Soufflé	puffed, i.e. mixed with egg white and baked
St-Germain	with peas
Sucre	sugar (*sucré* is sugared)
Suprême	fillet of poultry breast or fish
Tartare (sauce)	mayonnaise with capers, herbs, onions
Tartare	raw minced beef, flavoured with onions, etc. and bound with raw egg
Tarte Tatin	upside-down (apple) pie
Terrine	pottery dish/baked minced, chopped meat, vegetables, chicken, fish or fruit
Thé	tea
Tiède	lukewarm
Timbale	steamed mould
Tisane	infusion
Tourte	pie
Tranche	thick slice
Truffes	truffles
Tuile	tile, i.e. thin biscuit
Vacherin	meringue confection
Vallée d'Auge	with cream, apple, Calvados
Vapeur (au)	steamed
Velouté	white sauce, bouillon-flavoured
Véronique	with grapes
Vert(e)	green, e.g. *sauce verte*, with herbs
Vessie	pig's bladder
Vichysoisse	chilled creamy leek and potato soup
Vierge	prime (virgin) olive oil
Vinaigre	vinegar (literally bitter wine)
Vinaigrette	wine vinegar and oil dressing
Volaille	poultry
Vol-au-vent	puff-pastry case
Xérès	sherry
Yaourt	yogurt

FISH – Les Poissons, SHELLFISH – Les Coquillages

Alose	shad
Anchois	anchovy
Anguille	eel
Araignée de mer	spider crab
Bar	sea bass
Barbue	brill
Baudroie	monkfish, anglerfish
Belon	flat-shelled oyster
Bigomeau	winkle
Blanchaille	whitebait
Brochet	pike
Cabillaud	cod
Calamar	squid
Carpe	carp
Carrelet	plaice
Chapon de mer	scorpion fish
Claire	oyster
Coquille St-Jacques	scallop

GLOSSARY OF COOKING TERMS AND DISHES

Crabe	crab	Seiche	squid
Crevette grise	shrimp	Sole	sole
Crevette rose	prawn	Soupion	inkfish
Daurade	sea bream	St-Pierre	John Dory
Écrevisse	crayfish	Thon	tuna/tunny
Éperlan	smelt	Tourteau	large crab
Espadon	swordfish	Tortue	turtle
Étrille	baby crab	Truite	trout
		Turbot	turbot
Favouille	spider crab	Turbotin	chicken turbot
Flétan	halibut		
Fruits de mer	seafood		
Grondin	red gurnet		

Hareng	herring
Homard	lobster
Huître	oyster

FRUITS – Les Fruits
VEGETABLES – Les Légumes
NUTS – Les Noix
HERBS – Les Herbes
SPICES – Les Épices

Julienne	ling		
Laitance	soft herring-roe	Abricot	apricot
Lamproie	lamprey	Ail	garlic
Langoustine	Dublin Bay prawn	Algue	seaweed
Lieu	ling	Amande	almond
Limande	lemon sole	Ananas	pineapple
Lotte de mer	monkfish	Aneth	dill
Loup de mer	sea bass	Arachide	peanut
		Artichaut	globe artichoke
Maquereau	mackerel	Asperge	asparagus
Merlan	whiting	Avocat	avocado
Morue	salt cod		
Moule	mussel	Banane	banana
Mulet	grey mullet	Basilic	basil
		Betterave	beetroot
Ombre	grayling	Blette	Swiss chard
Oursin	sea urchin	Brugnon	nectarine
Palourde	clam	Cassis	blackcurrant
Pétoncle	small scallop	Céleri	celery
Plie	plaice	Céleri-rave	celeriac
Portugaise	oyster	Cèpe	edible fungus
Poulpe	octopus	Cerfeuil	chervil
Praire	large clam	Cerise	cherry
		Champignon	mushroom
Raie	skate	Chanterelle	edible fungus
Rascasse	scorpion-fish	Châtaigne	chestnut
Rouget	red mullet	Chicorée	endive
		Chou	cabbage
Sandre	zander	Chou-fleur	cauliflower
Saumon	salmon	Choux de	
Saumonette	rock salmon	Bruxelles	Brussels sprouts

GLOSSARY OF COOKING TERMS AND DISHES

Ciboulette	chive	Navet	turnip
Citron	lemon	Noisette	hazelnut
Citron vert	lime		
Coing	quince	Oignon	onion
Concombre	cucumber	Oseille	sorrel
Coriandre	coriander		
Cornichon	gherkin	Palmier	palm
Courge	pumpkin	Pamplemousse	grapefruit
Courgette	courgette	Panais	parsnip
Cresson	watercress	Passe-Pierre	seaweed
		Pastèque	water melon
Échalote	shallot	Pêche	peach
Endive	chicory	Persil	parsley
Épinard	spinach	Petit pois	pea
Escarole	frillysalad leaves	Piment doux	sweet pepper
Estragon	tarragon	Pissenlit	dandelion
		Pistache	pistachio
Fenouil	fennel	Pleurote	edible fungi
Fève	broad bean	Poire	pear
Flageolet	dried bean	Poireau	leek
Fraise	strawberry	Poivre	pepper
Framboise	raspberry	Poivron	green, red and yellow peppers
Genièvre	juniper	Pomme	apple
Gingembre	ginger	Pomme de terre	potato
Girofle	clove	Prune	plum
Girolle	edible fungus	Pruneau	prune
Grenade	pomegranate		
Griotte	bitter red cherry	Quetsch	small dark plum
Groseille	gooseberry		
Groseille noire	blackcurrant	Radis	radish
Groseille rouge	redcurrant	Raifort	horseradish
		Raisin	grape
Haricot	dried white bean	Reine Claude	greengage
Haricot vert	French bean	Romarin	rosemary
		Safran	saffron
Laitue	lettuce	Salsifis	salsify
Mandarine	tangerine, mandarin	Thym	thyme
		Tilleul	lime blossom
Mangetout	sugar pea	Tomate	tomato
Marron	chestnut	Topinambour	Jerusalem artichoke
Menthe	mint		
Mirabelle	tiny golden plum	Truffe	truffle
Morille	dark brown crinkly edible fungus		
Mûre	blackberry		
Muscade	nutmeg		
Myrtille	bilberry, blueberry		

MEAT – Les Viandes

GLOSSARY OF COOKING TERMS AND DISHES

Le boeuf	beef	Chevreuil	roe deer
Charolais	the best		
Chateaubriand	double fillet steak	Dinde	young hen turkey
Contrefilet	sirloin	Dindon	turkey
Entrecôte	rib steak	Dindonneau	young turkey
Faux Filet	sirloin steak		
Filet	fillet	Faisan	pheasant
L'agneau	lamb	Grive	thrush
Pré-salé	the best		
Carré	neck cutlets	Lièvre	hare
Côte	chump chop		
Epaule	shoulder	Oie	goose
Gigot	leg		
		Perdreau	partridge
Le porc	pork	Pigeon	pigeon
Jambon	ham	Pintade	guineafowl
Jambon cru	raw smoked ham	Pluvier	plover
Porcelet	suckling pig	Poularde	chicken (boiling)
		Poulet	chicken (roasting)
Le veau	veal	Poussin	spring chicken
Escalope	thin slice cut from fillet		
		Sanglier	wild boar
		Sarcelle	teal
Les abats	offal		
Foie	liver	Venaison	venison
Foie gras	goose liver		
Cervelles	brains		
Langue	tongue		
Ris	sweetbreads		
Rognons	kidneys		
Tripes	tripe		

POULTRY – Volaille, GAME – Gibier

Abatis	giblets
Bécasse	woodcock
Bécassine	snipe
Caille	quail
Canard	duck
Caneton	duckling
Chapon	capon